CRY
from the
Highest Mountain

TESS BURROWS

Foreword by His Holiness the Dalai Lama
Introduction by Joanna Lumley, O.B.E.

Published by

eye books
Challenging the way we see things

Cry From The Highest Mountain
Sixth Edition

Published by Eye Books Ltd 2005
8 Peacock Yard
Iliffe Street
London
SE17 3LH

Tel. +44 (0) 845 450 8870
www.eye-books.com
Set in Times New Roman

ISBN-10: 1903070570
ISBN-13: 9781903070574

Printed and bound in Great Britain by Creative Print and Design

*I offer this book with love,
that Tibet and the Earth may be free from oppression
and find peace*

Acknowledgements

I would like to send warm and heartfelt thanks to all of my family and friends who have given me their help, support and encouragement and have stood by my need to give the writing top priority during the growth of this book.

With special thanks to:
His Holiness the Dalai Lama for His inspiration and Universal Love.
The other patrons – Joanna Lumley, Uri Geller and Doug Scott for their belief in the spirit of 'Climb For Tibet'.

All those who gave of themselves by sending peace messages and sponsorship to 'Climb For Tibet'.

All whose names walk across these pages in the unfolding of the story, especially Mig, GT and Pete – a team forged in caring.

Lawley and my three sons for their unending love and support and all that they teach me – not least the arduous task of how to press the right buttons on the computer without panicking. Paul for sharing his higher truth and for feeding me, Scott for translations and dependable priority assistance even when under university pressures, and Mark for the continuous use of his room which houses the computer and his technical know-how – aided by two little black and white cats whose job it was to sit on all the papers with love.

My soul partner Pete, for all things – including painstakingly transcribing all the tapes and peace messages, and always being there for me with love and strength at every twist and turn and every tired-out writing moment… and for not giving up on me.

Dan at Eye Books for the glorious vision of how to share heart journeys, and for believing in me and giving me guidance.

The illustrators Robert Beer, Mig, Paul and Scott whose combined beautiful efforts had no definite edges as to which picture belonged to whom – sketching for the greater good of the whole.

The Duffy family, especially Yannick's Godmother Filly, for literary advice.

Those in spirit who held my hand.

Chris at Samye Ling for reminding me to write with love.

eye**Opener**

Eye Books publishes books that 'challenge the way we see things.' Never, in all the publishing we have done have I been more challenged, to the better, than by Tess Burrows. Tess is the embodiment of love, peace and care. Some six years and six editions of this wonderful book later I am still unsure how she is able to be as she is. Her trust and willingness to believe in the good is admiral and infectious.

In fairness it is my parents to whom I must give credit for finding Tess. They had met her at a friend's Druid wedding and said that I must publish her book. After meeting Tess myself I was in no doubt. Her energy and focus for the cause of the Tibetan people is relentless – I had to help.

Tess is a wonderful example of someone who never lets go of a dream. She told me that as a child she had dreamed of writing books and climbing mountains. Books eluded her until now, but she realized on her first climb – that climbing was a good way to raise awareness about important issues. Her banner waving from atop Sugarloaf mountain during the World Peace Conference in 1980 created front page headlines and highlighted problems in the flavela's of Rio.

Cry From the Highest Mountain is the story of climbing and campaigning for peace. Tess encouraged schools, friends, family and strangers to provide her with peace messages that she would take with her on an expedition to the point furthest from the centre of the Earth. And from the summit of Mt Chimborazo shout them down to the world below. Eye Books is proud to be a messenger in spreading her call for peace and helping Tess fulfill a life-long dream of writing a book.

Tune in with us on page 255 to see how you too can work for Earth Peace every month.

Dan Hiscocks
Founder and Publisher

eye books
Challenging the way we see things

Contents

Foreword by HH the Dalai Lama 7
Maps 8
Introduction by Joanna Lumley 9
Diagrams 10
Prologue 11

1   Born of a dream 13
2   'Climb For Tibet' 19
3   Messages of Peace 26
4   Tibet the Light 33
5   Tibet heart pain 38
6   Gift from the Universe 47
7   Star to follow 61
8   Fit for Ecuador 71
9   Getting high 79
10 The way to Chimborazo 86
11 Watchtower magic 95
12 The Snow Lion-Heart 103
13 Condor brother 112
14 Wisdom in the unseen 122
15 Wondrousity 133
16 Nitty-grittiness 137
17 Jaws of the volcano 148
18 No strings attached 154
19 Currency of the Spirit 161
20 One for the road 166
21 Gathering strength 175
22 Tell the world 183
23 Independence 188
24 Blessing 193
25 Penguin readiness 196
26 Between tomorrow and eternity 203
27 Heaven's gateway 212
28 Crystal heart 221
29 A Light for Peace 227

Special Acknowledgement 237
Peace Messages 238
eyeSight 249
eyeCommunity 250
eyeBookshelves 252
Tune In – Climb for Tibet 255
eyeAuthor 256

Foreword

THE DALAI LAMA

When the Communist Chinese first invaded Tibet more than forty years ago, they talked about peaceful liberation. Instead, we Tibetans have experienced the greatest period of loss and destruction in our history. Hundreds of thousands of people have died and thousands, who had committed no crime other than patriotism, have suffered long years of imprisonment. Our monasteries and nunneries, the repositories of our rich and ancient culture, our source of education, have been demolished. Our institutions of government have been set aside, so that the destiny of Tibet and its people is no longer in the hands of Tibetans. Our natural resources, which we used carefully and treated with respect, have been wantonly plundered and the environment spoiled. Even the wild animals who once lived without fear of human beings have been ruthlessly eliminated.

A climate of oppression currently prevails in Tibet. Virtually everything of significance to Tibetans is under attack. At the same time, the people of Tibet are almost powerless to respond. The Chinese authorities brook no opposition to their rule. Protest provokes an invariably harsh reaction. This is where we Tibetans who live in exile have a special responsibility, for we have the freedom to speak up for our brothers and sisters in Tibet. We can make known the reality of life in our homeland. We can help increase awareness of the value of Tibetan culture and the loss to humanity if it should be allowed to disappear.

This book written by Tess Burrows tells the story of 'Climb For Tibet' and seeks to make readers aware of Tibet's indomitable spirit and our undiminished determination so admirably shown by one young man, Migmar Tsering. It embraces the spirit of compassion, which we Tibetans value so highly, that is to be proclaimed from the mountain in thousands of messages of peace. We Tibetans live in a distant and remote land, but like everyone else, we want to live in peace and happiness and like everyone else we have a right to do so. I hope readers whose interest is stirred by this book may also be inspired to give their support and see their own way forward in love and respect for all beings. Let us all, brothers and sisters of the single human family, live together in peace.

His Holiness the Dalai Lama, December 1999
Winner of the 1989 Nobel Peace Prize

Map of The World

TIBET

ECUADOR

Map of Ecuador

100 KM
50 MILES

COLOMBIA

EQUATOR

PICHINCHA   Quito

PASOCHOA

ILINIZA   COTOPAXI

Latacunga

CHIMBORAZO   Ambato

ECUADOR

Riobamba

Guayaquil

PAN AMERICAN HIGHWAY

PACIFIC
OCEAN

PERU

Introduction

Of course it seemed crazy, impossible and over-ambitious: but at the same time Tess Burrows' 'Climb For Tibet' project sounded thrilling, engaging and daring. Could they do it? Or more importantly, could she do it? The expedition would be extremely tough by any standard. And would anyone actually send any prayers? Would the tiny team even reach the summit?

I became a patron on the spot with great pride and anxiety. There were so many aspects of the trip that intrigued me – a woman of nearly fifty attempting something so dangerous: a unique idea which sounded mad but was to be presented at the Royal Geographical Society; a passionate belief that prayers can change the world; the extraordinary fundraising efforts, all for charity; and the support of the Tibetan community headed by His Holiness the Dalai Lama, who had readily agreed to become the chief patron.

It had everything to make a good story, lecture, book or film – the planning, the ascent, setbacks and triumphs, illustrated by photographs and so forth. But gleaming brightly above all this was the inspiration – if you want something enough, go for it.

This is an enthralling journey of courage and endurance. Now the peaceful crystal shines from Chimborazo. Below it, mankind stands yet again at the crossroads of war and peace, still wondering which path to take...

Joanna Lumley O.B.E, May 1999

Diagram of the Earth as an Oblate Spheroid

Chimborazo

Everest

CENTER
* OF THE EARTH

Diagram of Heights Above Sea Level

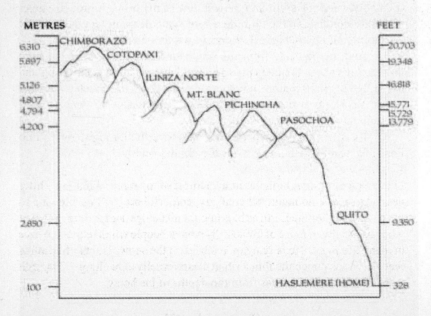

METRES		FEET
6,310	CHIMBORAZO	20,703
5,897	COTOPAXI	19,348
5,126	ILINIZA NORTE	16,818
4,807	MT. BLANC	15,771
4,794	PICHINCHA	15,729
4,200	PASOCHOA	13,779
2,850	QUITO	9,350
100	HASLEMERE (HOME)	328

Prologue

If you wanted to express a really important message that would affect the future of humanity, then you could do worse than shout it from the highest mountain.

First look at the shape of the Earth and see that the point furthest from the centre is in fact not Everest, but a little-known extinct volcano in Ecuador called Chimborazo. Although this mountain is only 6,310 metres (20,703 feet) above sea level, it is 2,150 metres (7,059 feet) further from the centre of the Earth than Everest is. Ah! It is the bit that sticks out into space more than any other bit.

Then see that the ancient Inca name for Chimborazo was 'Watchtower of the Universe' – Aha! This could be the place to express the highest ideals.

But first you would have to get there.

This book is about just that. Seen through the eyes of the journey of my body and my spirit and the window of my heart, it brought me to the realisation that, in the ultimate act of symbolism, in fact the struggle was also to climb my highest mountain within – myself.

And the message from the mountain? Well, this book is about that too. It's about the deep pain that the Tibetan nation is suffering and has suffered for 50 years. It's about the words of the Tibetan spiritual leader, His Holiness the Dalai Lama who offers humanity a way forward in brotherhood – if only we could listen…

It's about the sheer dedication and love that brought the 'Climb For Tibet' team together and made the climb a reality…

I have a picture carved forever in the temple of my mind: Floating whiteness on a sacred mountain; ethereal joy; colourful prayer flags blowing in the wind; a gift for the Earth as blessing for all beings; and a young Tibetan who has just given more of himself than most people would expect to give in many lifetimes. He is lying on his back in the snow, Tibetan flag at his feet. His arms punch the thin air that clasps cruelly at his lungs. Through tears of exhaustion he cries from the depths of his being:

'Peace on Earth'

1 - BORN OF A DREAM

6th July 1998 (The Dalai Lama's birthday) – Diary Extract

I knew I was going to die… even before we reached 6,000 metres. The summit of Chimborazo waited, elusive, shrouded in bright cloud.

… White out… where is the Earth? There's only this cold white existence… so little above me, and yet so much… a couple of dots on a map… but it's to be my final resting-place. The summit must be so close now… so close… but still all that oxygen away.

Four times I've made the decision not to turn back, when all reason and sense were shouting at me, 'Return alive, go down, now. You're in the final stage of altitude sickness… it's Cerebral Oedema… the brain is starved of oxygen… swelling and expanding.' Surely my brain is going to explode… too big for my head… trying to get out… like it's on fire. Bits of time are going missing. I must go down quickly… go down.

But the stakes are too high… How can I turn away now? My life is not my own to save… Cry, cry, Heart… tears of pain for Tibet and for the violence of humanity… we must reach the summit, that the light may shine for peace… we must reach the summit. We must go on. Heart, carry this body… beat strong… courage born of a dream.

For what is death… here in this white, white world? Is the snow real at my feet? Is the brittle ice of my hair any different from the moving snowflakes that dance around my still warm body? They're all molecules of coldness, though the blood courses through my veins as it has all these earthly years. How strange that it's to stop now. How easy it's going to be to take off all my clothes and lie down on this carpet. I can't be cold because my body isn't aware. It isn't really mine anymore… cold is not… beauty is … yes, it's beautiful and, yes, there's joy… supreme utter wonderful joy at being so close to the angel of death who holds me by the hand and in blissful golden light. There is perfection, more than I have ever known… even beyond total beauty. All is forever well… there are no other moments of time or existence… touch me, Divineness… I am one with all things.

I'm drifting in and out of rationalism. Am I already in a different world? My body is another entity… remote, borrowed. I'm being drawn towards an unseen force… magnetic, like a swarm of insects to a light. My reality is dropping off either side of me… touch the snow… bitter sweet… do not let the body stop… too much pain to stop… but I want to lie down and die...

Please, help me… I need help… I can go no further… this is the end of the road... Previously you gave me help. Was it evoked from pity? Or was it that I was your messenger and the wages of duty bear wings? 'Not so', you reply, 'we will help you no more. You must give every ounce of your life… everything… so that there is nothing left of your self, no individuality… no longer child, mother, sister, lover... In the knowledge of the giving of your life, there is a letting go… a humility. Only in this way can there be an arrival at the summit on your knees, giving out the vibrational energy that is needed… the energy of unconditional love.'

Rambling hallucinations are my friends. Where is my brain? Where is my mind? Ah… the focus… peace… peace within our hearts. The goal is so important… so big. I'm just a tiny pawn in a huge game of survival for the Earth. I can only move forwards. I'm being placed and taken by an unseen hand like a speck of dust in the wind… irrelevant… yet vital, for I'm part of the whole… I'm the runner who carries the torch that so many have borne and blessed... I will not let them down.

But my children… what thoughts of my children? That's another lifetime. I'm here now. There is only now… there is no other. Is this detachment? Or maybe just that I'm not properly connected to my body which is attached to my mind and so normally holds together my past and my future… Yet, I know that I must be grateful to my mind for bringing me this far. It's strong. It's worked and struggled for this day. It's carried me through half a century of effort gaining strength for this moment. This has been the purpose of its existence…

The sun was shining so brilliantly through the small oval window of the aeroplane that I had to shield my eyes to see the curvature of the cotton-wool horizon.

'It's not a commonly known fact that the Earth's not round.' I remarked.

The Dutch businessman in the aisle seat on the KLM flight 1028 from Heathrow to Amsterdam turned to look at me. There was just a hint of disdain on his knitted brow. Dressed conventionally with immaculately combed hair, he gave the impression of being a regular commuter accustomed to level-headed conversations. He was stuck next to me for the journey.

'Did you say you were going on to Quito?' he enquired politely as though he was trying to change the subject to something normal that would fit in to a well-structured day. If sensitive, he would have had an impending sense of doom that he was about to be the next victim of a sponsor collecting attack.

'Yes, we're going to climb the highest mountain in the world.'

'Oh.' Then followed a thinking sort of silence. What more could he say, apart from 'Aren't you on the wrong plane?'

'It's in Ecuador, you know,' I went on.

The stocks and shares section of the newspaper he was reading wavered a little.

'Everyone always thinks it's Everest,' I threw in, trying to pull the carpet from under a nice safe view of the world.

He finally put his newspaper down, glancing round a little nervously at the other suited businessmen who filled the rest of the Boeing 737, all happily studying the daily papers… *Kosovo awaits Nato jets – the world's main military powers seek authority to launch assaults. Fox hunting – the people will decide. Eritrean air raid kills four at aid centre – scene of bitter fighting. Radioactivity tests go on – indications of five times the accepted level. French perfume maker shot by armed raiders. Pensioner dies after attack by street gang.*

'Isn't it Everest?'

'Well,' with familiar enthusiasm and the sense of fun at the intrigue it always caused, I started out 'Everest is of course the highest from sea level, at 8,848 metres or 29,028 feet, but if you measure it from the centre of the Earth then the highest is a mountain near the equator in the Andes of South America.' I could see from the widening of his steely grey eyes that I had his interest now.

'So why…?'

15

'The Earth's not round. It's an oblate spheroid.'

'Ah.'

'In other words, it's bulgy at the equator, and flattened at the poles.'

'Oh.'

'A learned geographical friend of mine says this is due to what he calls 'the pizza effect'. Have you ever seen an authentic pizza being made with the dough spun around? The outer edges of the pizza push out into a yummy bulgy bit. Well, it's the same with the Earth. The spinning on her axis causes a sort of lesser holding onto gravity at the equator than there is at the poles. It's the thing that scientists used to call centrifugal force.'

'So why don't we all learn about that at school?' he asked, his interest building.

'I don't know, maybe it's because people tend not to stand back and look at the Earth as a whole, or maybe because it's only a small difference we're talking about. If you had a metre and a half globe, then the yummy bulgy bit would only be sticking out about three millimetres.'

I thought about how I had explained it in this way at one of the school assemblies I had spoken to about our project. The youngsters seemed to have understood it well, as I had demonstrated spinning a huge old illuminated globe. This did, however, have holes in it where the light shone through, and parts of countries had been hanging off. 'Our Earth's falling to bits,' I had said, 'she needs help to be put back together.'

My Dutch friend persisted, 'So what's the difference on the world scale?'

'Well, the oblate-spheroidness,' I replied, enjoying getting my tongue around such a wonderful word, 'can be seen by measuring the diameter of the Earth at the equator, which is roughly 42½ kilometres longer than it is at the poles.'

The puzzled look seemed to imply that this fact had somehow upset his sense of order, that we were spinning through space on a less than perfect planet.

'And the oblate-spheroidness,' I continued, 'in fact means that the summit of the mountain we're going to climb is 2,150 metres, that's more than 7,000 feet, further from the centre of the Earth than the summit of Everest is. It's the bit that sticks out the most.'

'Does this mean that your mountain is the point on the world that's nearest the sun?' he asked.

'No, that honour goes to different places between the tropics everyday due to the tilt of the Earth and the moving position in her orbit. But in fact our mountain is the point nearest the sun on about March 15th and September 27th, near the spring and autumn equinoxes.' Again I mentally thanked my learned geographical friend for his research.

The conversation was interrupted by a predominantly plastic snack arriving off the trolley of a glamorous airhostess. 'Long-life sandwiches and tea or coffee, with special pretend chemical milk?' she may as well have said.

'Any chance of hot water?' I asked, not sure if there was anything that my body on a good training programme could absorb, but enjoying the feeling of being fed and looked after as though I was a child.

Distracted, my mind wandered back to my childhood spent in Surrey and then Hampshire. I was a tomboy of sorts and never happier than when I was playing with my older brother, Graham, whom I adored (even though he had tried to discover electricity by plugging me, his baby sister, into the mains). I had a peaceful, loving relationship with my younger sisters, but the expected pastimes of girls were not to be entered into. I was so cross that I wasn't a boy that I'd even crept out of bed one night and cut half my hair off. When morning came my long-suffering mother, in her inimitably gentle way with a lovely rock-like demeanour, couldn't understand what had happened, though she was never angry. Graham and I used to always play for hours creating model towns and animating the lives of little characters, lives relating to the safe everyday suburban world around us.

One day he returned from school excited at a book he had found... *The New Believe It or Not*, by Ripley, published in 1930.

'Look Tess, see this page. It says that Mount Everest is not the highest mountain in the world, but that it's a mountain in Ecuador.'

A seed had been sown.

A while later he came home with another significant book, a prize... *Banner in the Sky*, by James Ramsay Ullman, a fictitious account of the first climbing of the Matterhorn. It became my favourite reading. When I reached the part when the young hero Rudi was unable to climb to the very top of the mountain, I would cry bitter tears until the end of the story and then immediately start again at the beginning. Whilst Graham was dreaming of inventing a rocket to go to the moon, I was dreaming of climbing the highest mountain.

But childish dreams get lost in growing up, in pleasing parents and society, and in searching for one's own fulfilment. It was to be more than thirty years before I remembered.

2 - 'Climb For Tibet'

The plane shifted in its temporary orbit and I felt the release of gravity as we started our descent into Schipol airport.

'Come on then, which mountain is it that you're talking about, the one which is the furthest from the centre of the Earth?' pressed the Dutchman amicably.

'It's called Chimborazo.'

'Nice name.'

'And it's actually 6,310 metres above sea level. That's nearly 21,000 feet.'

'Still a hell of a climb then?'

'Yeah, should test us,' I replied, not knowing then quite how true those words were to be.

We were now dropping fast away from the sun towards the cloud cover which blanketed the Earth and my sense of being on a planet diminished. Protection or pollution, I wondered as we banked slightly to enter the greyness and headed towards modern industrialised Europe.

'Er, I just happen to have a sponsorship form with me. I was wondering if you would, er, like to sponsor us. It's actually quite an important peace climb and we're raising money to help Tibet and Tibetan refugees.' With a smile I handed my new friend a 'Climb For Tibet' form. It was a thing of beauty with our logo in the corner, in full colour in honour of the stunning Tibetan flag.

The flag like so many Tibetan things is full of meaning. It expresses more than stirring national pride, more even than the hopes of a people whom history dictates should be a lost people, but for the spirit from its heartland which burns with an unquenchable flame.

The white mountain represents the land of snows. The two snow lions embody strength in the duality of the Tibetan government, political and spiritual. The wheel denotes harmony. The jewel portrays wisdom. The yellow sun depicts Tibetan Buddhism radiating out, and the red stripes stand for the six original tribes of Tibet. But the yellow border of Buddhism which encases the spirit of the nation on three sides is left empty to the right, representing the openness of the land, that all are welcome to enter in peace. It is very poignant that it was from the east that the invasion came to this once free and beautiful country.

'Do you know what happened in Tibet?' I asked

'I have the feeling you're about to tell me,' he answered not unkindly, so I piled in quickly while he was attentive 'Well, in 1950 the newly formed Chinese communist regime marched in and declared Tibet to be part of China. The peace-loving Tibetans were no match for the Chinese red army. They tried for the next few years to work with their invading neighbours, but by 1959 it was clear that negotiations were of no use and Tibet's young spiritual and temporal leader, His Holiness the fourteenth Dalai Lama, was forced to flee across the Himalayas just escaping with his life. The Indian administration generously gave Him refuge to establish a government in exile at Dharamsala in the foothills of Northern India.'

'Is that where He lives now?'

'Yes, from there He's tried for forty years to peacefully regain freedom from oppression for His people. He has had to watch the rape of His homeland, cultural and religious genocide, murder, torture and other horrendous human rights abuses, all in the attempted annihilation of the identity of the Tibetan nation that He represents.'

'But surely He's had help – from the international community I mean.'

'No, to this day, the governments of the rest of the world have done very little. After all, how did it affect other countries? There was no oil dependency like in Kuwait, it was not on the periphery of the Western world like in Kosovo, there was no direct threat... and trade with China is so important.'

Few who had time to absorb what we were doing could resist supporting the cause, particularly to spread the knowledge of this injustice.

'Well, of course. I'd be delighted to sponsor you,' the Dutchman responded, reaching for his wallet, and went on, 'very sad, yes, the situation is very sad. I'm sure many people in my country too must be aware, but what is to be done?' He shrugged. A shrug is a small act, just a little raising of the shoulders. It implies a kind of indifference, an attitude of 'well, what can I do about it? I have my own life to lead and I can't help everyone'. But when you multiply that shrug by millions and even billions around the world, then you have a major shrug problem – a huge lump of indifference towards the inhumanities that are going on in Tibet. We were trying to eat away at that lump.

An Englishman on the other side of the aisle leaned across in front of the obstructing legs of the airhostess who was trying to enclose belongings in the overhead compartments and check that all her passengers were captives and safely tied to their seats. There was an air of efficiency that all was secure and that our everyday lives were not at risk.

'I say, what are you raising money for?' he said, 'I couldn't help overhearing what you were talking about. I saw the film *Seven Years In Tibet* recently – a superb film. Have you seen it? It portrayed the tragic end to a way of life, maybe the last of its kind, tucked away there in the Himalayas, not hurting anyone. It must have been such a beautiful country. You know, the thought of it stirred all my yearnings to be an explorer in the days when an ancient civilisation existed that was unaffected by modern pollution and greed for material things.'

Our project seemed to have a habit of drawing people who had an interest in the legendary land of Shangri-La.

'I really think that Tibetan Buddhism could do so much to help the 'dog eat dog' problems of the world today,' he went on, as I smiled and nodded in agreement. 'It was a culture where the religion was more a way of life, where kindness was more important than money.'

It was the moment to pass him a sponsorship form before he got too carried away with the irrelevance of money.

'Yeah, even though the film's in Hollywood style, it does do a lot to raise awareness of the Tibetan situation and strike a chord with this sort of thinking,' I responded, my mind drifting a little.

The great teacher Sogyal Rinpoche speaks of the Tibetan word for 'body' which is '*lü*', meaning 'something you leave behind,' like baggage, reminding us that we are only travellers, taking temporary refuge in this life and this body. He says that in Tibet, people did not distract themselves by spending all their time trying to make their external circumstances more comfortable. They were satisfied if they had enough to eat, clothes on their backs, and a roof over their heads. So, as we obsessively try to improve our conditions, an end in itself and a pointless distraction, he asks 'Would people in their right mind think of fastidiously redecorating their hotel room every time they checked into one?'

I wondered if this belief of reincarnation and also that of karma, the natural law of cause and effect, made it easier to put kindness first, knowing that what you give out always comes back to you at some point.

I remembered something that my father, Ken, had said. We had been very close and during the last ten years or so of his life had the wonderful gift of sharing spiritual discoveries and learning together. He had always delighted in the fun and the skill of financial schemes, but one day he had said to his grandchildren whilst looking at their school reports 'It's not being the cleverest in the class that counts. It's being the kindest.' Great sentiments, although they were always so hard to live up to, especially when tired and grumpy and stressed out. Undoubtedly, catching this plane had been about my worst example. There had been weeks of build-up of 'Climb For Tibet' before our departure, reaching a frantic and frenetic state, trying to get two more months work into the last couple of days with virtually no sleep. It's the most stressed out I've ever been and being kind to those nearest to me had gone out of the window, especially to Pete, who now sat beside me. I turned to him with an eye contact smile born of the closeness of having worked so hard together to create our baby 'Climb For Tibet'. He was my partner, my boyfriend and my gift from the Universe.

'Tell them where the money's going,' he urged with a squeeze of my knee. As always he was the one with his feet on the ground.

I had a captive audience so I began to explain 'We're splitting the funds we raise two ways. Fifty per cent is going directly to help refugees who have just escaped across the mountains. They're teenagers and young people in their twenties. Most of them arrive in a pretty bad state with severe frostbite, malnutrition and clothes in tatters after weeks of footslogging by night and hiding out in the daytime from the Chinese patrols.'

'Sounds tough.'

'Yeah, and even when they do cross the border, most commonly into Nepal, there's no guarantee that the Nepalese authorities won't send them back. Our refugee camp is in India. It's one of the projects of the Tibet Relief Fund, the charitable arm of the Tibet Society. I asked their director last year what the most needy situation was and he told me that the Khanyara Transit School, about 11 kilometres from Dharamsala, was desperate for help. At the moment it's just tin sheds in mud, but they find a haven there, somewhere to sleep, education, clothes and badly needed food.'

The smartly dressed airhostess rushed by with a heap of wasted meals as the plane circled preparing to land.

I continued 'More than that, it's spiritual nourishment, as every refugee has a chance to see His Holiness the Dalai Lama, the most revered 'star' in their lives. You probably know, He's frequently described as a 'God-King'. I once heard a lovely Tibetan singer dedicate a song to Him, declaring 'Without Him there is no light.' That says it all. It's amazing really that, even after all this time in exile, His life still gives such strength to the Tibetan people... keeps their flame of hope alive.'

'A truly great leader.'

'Definitely. The escapees, though, must find it hard. So often they leave their families in Tibet and many are still only children who are sent out by their parents to get an education with Tibetan culture and to have freedom.

You know, we take so much for granted the freedom in our country, the freedom to say what we believe, to support who we want.

Imagine not being able to have a photograph of the Queen, or the Pope, or Elvis, or whoever your star or most revered person is.

Imagine being found with the picture on your person or in your house and because of it you're tortured or forced to renounce your support for this person... tortured perhaps in a way that doesn't show, like sticks and electric battons being shoved up personal parts of your body. Then if you still don't renounce this person you're taken off to gaol with no fair trial.

Imagine you get angry and shout 'long live the Queen', or whoever, and you're then tied with your hands behind your back and strung by them from the ceiling... and left to hang for days, with no clothes on.'

Can we imagine?

'Here, let me give you all the cash I've got in stirling,' interjected the Englishman.

'Great, thanks so much,' I smiled, hoping he'd just been to the bank, and carried on, 'The second half of the money we raise actually works for that freedom. It goes to the Free Tibet Campaign. It's an independent British organisation, which operates to change the situation and apply pressure at a political level. They do a huge amount to raise awareness through public education and direct action.'

I rummaged around in the heap of stuff at my feet that went by the name of hand baggage - a bottle of filtered water, inspiring books to read, contact lens kit, wash bag, precious notes from my children, camera, unmentionables, nuts and seeds, stuffed penguin, diary, homeopathic remedies, peace messages, half-eaten apple, vital package of things for the summit, flag, sponsorship forms...

'Ah, here's one of their leaflets. Look, Free Tibet Campaign stands for the

Tibetans' right to decide their own future, an end to the Chinese occupation of Tibet and the Tibetans' fundamental human rights to be respected.'

The Englishman leaning across to take the leaflet looked perplexed, 'So, you're doing what you can to help Tibet at a practical level, but there's something I don't understand. Why are you carrying out a sponsored climb for Tibet in South America, on the other side of the globe?'

'Because that's where the highest mountain is… the point furthest from the centre of the Earth.'

'Ah, yes,' he responded with a twinkly sort of a smile.

'Anyway, we can't go waving flags around and supporting Tibetans actually in Tibet, even in the unlikely event of the Chinese giving us permission. It'd bring reprisals on any local Tibetans who'd even vaguely 'collaborated' with us. They'd be called 'splittists' from the motherland, part of the 'Dalai clique.' In all likelihood they'd become political prisoners, be tortured and possibly worse.'

By now I was beginning to feel a bit woozy with the bending forward to talk and the bumpy motion of the plane coming in to land. But it was always so important to tell people what we were doing, not only to raise awareness for Tibet and to collect funds but also to put across the wider picture.

'I feel that the problems in Tibet are a microcosm of those of the Earth. Yes, as you said, there is a state of imbalance due to the values of greed and power being more important than those of caring for other people and the environment on which we all depend. The Earth is crying out in need. Humanity has pushed her beyond what her natural systems can recover from without huge pain to our species. Many people are aware that unless we stop taking now and start giving back, then the planet as we know it will not survive.'

'Certainly, and we all hide from this fact, don't we?' agreed the Englishman.

'Yeah, but already there're grumblings and rumblings with the shifts necessary to try and rebalance. Look at all the unusual stuff like droughts, floods, hurricanes and avalanches… Yes, there are areas of hope, but the more individuals who take on responsibility, even in a small way in their lives, and work with the Earth and not against her, then the more chance there is of survival. This is the only way it'll happen.' I looked him straight in the eye and saw kindred understanding 'We're talking about our own tomorrows.'

One of my yesterdays that had influenced my way of thinking was as a student at Edinburgh University. I had been lucky. They were fun carefree days, filled with friends. I have a picture of reminiscence - piling heaps of people onto an open car (I think the record was sixteen) so we could drive around waving and putting smiles on glum faces.

I also have an enduring academic memory. I was studying ecological science, the first course of its kind in Britain. In the late 1960s no one had ever heard of ecology – plants and animals in relation to their environment? Interdependence? What's that? I remember drawing population 'S' curves for animals (plotting changes in numbers against time). The population always intrinsically controls itself and peters out at the top of the 'S'. I felt sure then that the human population would be controlled by the levels of pollutants which would rise to a critical point, leaving people without the ultimate control.

They were the days of Rachel Carson's *Silent Spring*, a ground-breaking book describing the effects of poisons and disrespect for our environment, creating for the first time a general awareness that we were messing up the world around us.

We hit the Earth with a thud, as if to confirm that we were all in this same 'life boat' together, sailing through space – rocks, minerals, soil, water, atmosphere, plants, animals and humans of every race and creed.

'Would you like to sign the pledge on our sponsor form?' I asked both men, not at all sorry that I had been getting stirred up. 'It's like making a commitment to be part of the solution, rather than part of the problem.'

As a citizen of the Earth I pledge to take personal action to help the healing of the world, expressing the Tibetan spirit of compassion for all life, non-violence and universal responsibility, for we are all inexorably bound together in a physical, mental and spiritual ecology.

They signed, with not a hint of Oh-help-I-can't-get-out-of-this-now.
'Thanks very much.'

I knew that every signature was an important part of our mission, for the pledge always rang an urgent bell in my mind that sent it racing back to one day in 1993.

3 - Messages of Peace

At this point I would like to have a little aside with my reader. If you're someone who doesn't accept that there is anything beyond the physical, then that's OK. You can skip the next few paragraphs, or you could read them and think 'that's a weird bit, she needs burning at the stake' and get on with enjoying the rest of the story.

Most people who haven't had this experience are rightly sceptical. Those who have, do not doubt its authenticity, but of course like many things in life it sounds weird until you've actually been there and done that – like a coconut might appear to an Eskimo. For sometimes truth is stranger than fiction.

We were a small group gathered in a house for a meeting. Outwardly the building was no different from the rest in the street. The plants looked cared for, the cat fluffy and content. We waited in a darkened room filled with atmosphere and anticipation. Candles were lit and flickered, whilst a prayer for protection was spoken. My nervousness was calmed by the knowledge that the Tibetans have always consulted the Oracle spirit on important matters, such as the confirmation of the reincarnation of the Dalai Lama or His flight out of Tibet. For in the same energy of universal purpose, spirits from the world of the non-physical were to speak to us through the body of a trained medium. I sat barely two metres away. We were to meet two of the greatest world leaders of this century. If they had not lived, the freedom of mankind would have been the poorer.

On this occasion we were lucky enough to experience the words of Winston Churchill and Mahatma Gandhi. They told us about life in the spirit world where they were trying to help the Earth today and of the urgency in finding inner peace.

Their characteristic personalities had remained as they were known. Their perceptions and wisdom had expanded to the extent that each of their words was like a jewel to marvel at and to hold.

Churchill came through with:

'...Climb for peace, not only peace in the human condition, but also what is most important, peace in the human spirit... There is one power far greater than the atom bomb, far greater than guns, tanks, whatever armaments you have. It is the power of love and the projection of that love, the essence of which creates throughout the whole of this planet a movement of conscious light. How is it expressed? From the highest mountain, the vision is for the eyes, the energy is from the heart... But we must express it in groups so that they and us united together project an immense power and counteract that of the demons, which live in so many hearts and cause so much devastation in this world now...'

The palpable sense of presence changed and I felt greatly honoured that the body arose and shook hands with me. The touch was gentle and firm.

Gandhi then spoke, and it was as though he was bestowing gifts on us:

'...What I would say to those who are listening and to those who will read your book in the future is... we do not own anything... we only share it for the duration of our lives and therefore our responsibility is to return it in good condition for others to enjoy. We must now see ourselves as part of the great global family... we must share in the restoration of all that we have damaged... in the end if there is no Nature, then we must also die. There is a time lapse left of seven years. If our thinking about caring for the Earth has not changed by then, we will have passed the point of no return. The planet will start to become barren and will die.'

This warning of Gandhi's above all else I have not been able to forget.

I hope and believe that at this critical time now, swaying in the balance, there is powerful enough love and compassion.

There was one more vital thing to do before we were all disgorged into the busy international terminal. Perhaps it was the most valuable of all, for it was an incentive to open to love and compassion.

'Would you like to fill in the 'message from the mountain' box on the form?' I persisted. 'It's giving us your personal message in support of Tibet and 'Earth Peace'. By using the words 'Earth Peace' we are including the harmony of the natural systems of the Earth as well as that of humanity, rather than 'world peace' which tends to mean only the peace of people.

We ask too that the messages be in the Tibetan spirit, that is an expression of the ideals of His Holiness the Dalai Lama – compassion for all life, non-violence and universal responsibility.

We'll read them all out from the mountain. It's a bit like the age-old Tibetan tradition of flying prayer flags from the highest place possible. You know, you would have seen them in the film. Their bright colours represent the elemental make-up of all things. There's blue for sky, white for cloud, red for fire, green for pure life-stream and yellow for earth. They're imbued with mantras and messages of peace and then the wind-horse carries them far and wide to invoke blessings and well-being to all. That's what our messages will do too. So far we've collected nearly a thousand.'

'What a super idea,' came the English reply. 'It's as though all those people supporting you are actually being part of the climb, and making its effect much more powerful.'

Yes, and it was more than that. As with my understanding behind the signing of the pledge, the changing of an individual changes the whole. An individual finding of peace changes the peace of the Earth. It's an expression of the law of interdependence. Furthermore, if a person produces a thought and turns it into something 'concrete' by writing it down, then it will help manifest the physical actuality of that thought. For the path of creation leads from intention, through the mind, into matter – from the intangible to the physical. The focus of many peace messages coming together will help create the reality on a larger scale… like many little sparks coming together to generate a light.

The Englishman considered briefly and with a flourish of his gold pen gave us:

"May the Tibetan light shine across the world in peace for all nations and for all beings."

With happy compliance the Dutchman carefully wrote:

"Earth get Love Energy."

'Thank you,' I beamed, 'They're really beautiful messages.'

I was sure that working at mind level they had far reaching effects, particularly those that came from children, as then they were shaping the future and helping expand the awareness of the importance of caring for the Earth. Happily, many of this generation of youngsters do seem to know that we are each responsible.

One of my favourite messages was from a pretty eleven year old girl, Siobhan. One day I had been talking with her mother who confided in me 'I can't understand it. She and her brother have always ended up fighting when they've been left alone. It's been a real problem. Now suddenly they're getting on so well together.'

I had looked up Siobhan's peace message. It announced:

"I will be loads and loads less annoying to my brother."

Her mother and I had been stunned by the simplicity and expanding beautiful effect of one little girl's personal change.

Another message that I particularly liked had been from a young Tibetan, Dugdak, who declared with great courage:

"Peace to the young people of Tibet and peace to the young people of China."

Here was a touching of the spiritual power of His Holiness' teachings. There can be little more humbling than the example He sets. After having to stand by for nearly fifty years watching China brutally invade His country, destroy the unique culture and ruthlessly carry out the genocide of His people, He still says 'We must love and respect our Chinese brothers and sisters.'

29

Sometimes in my life when things upset me, relatively tiny things even though they may seem huge at the time, I think of these words and the great strength of them helps me try and convert anger into compassion.

He also says 'Maybe sometimes your children teach you patience, but always your enemy will teach you tolerance. So your enemy is really your teacher. If you have respect for your enemy instead of anger, your compassion will develop. That type of compassion is real compassion, which is based upon sound beliefs.'

I felt that we were honoured to be setting out to express these highest of ideals from the highest of mountains, as it gave a sense of sacredness to the whole event and an opening up to higher aspiration. Indeed, as the ancient Inca name for Chimborazo was 'Watchtower of the Universe' it seemed entirely fitting that there should now be a Tibetan sentinel.

I was moved to read the precious peace message that His Holiness had sent us:

"I am pleased to offer my prayers to 'Climb For Tibet' and all that it touches. The determination of the climbers to undertake a difficult task to highlight a humanitarian problem is indeed inspiring.

The non-violent Tibetan struggle for freedom has gained us the sympathy and admiration of the international community. Through our non-violent freedom struggle we are also setting an example and thus contributing to the promotion of a global political culture of non-violence, compassion and dialogue."

'C'mon, Tess. Let's go.'

Pete was trying to get me stirred into action. We were last off the plane. As always I was daydreaming and slow at finding all my bits and pieces and getting myself together. I like to be distracted by thoughts of the moment and read words that seem to compel me to them, but it must be so annoying to continually have to wait. I would always tell Pete that our souls had been drawn to each other to learn the things that they needed to learn, and that he was learning patience and I was a very good teacher.

There had been milling around, 'good lucks' and shaking hands with those whose lives we had touched in with, and a rush for everyone to leave the plane and hurry on with their seemingly agitated existence.

The face of Amsterdam's international terminal Schipol was efficient, organised and shiny clean with all the state-of-the-art technology having computers behind everything that moved, although the ladies rooms couldn't compare with the ones in the French Alps where the light goes on when you shut the door and the loo flushes on opening it again, nor the ones which gift wrap what you've done in plastic bags. It took us about half an hour to walk from one end of the airport to the other even with the 'people-whooshers'. Smart shops abounded and were filled with goodies to tempt currency away from the myriad of humankind who came and went, mingling their 'energies'. Some gave out happiness, some sadness, excitement, annoyance, frustration, tiredness, scheming, anticipation, loving thoughts that brushed against resentment, joy against fear. There were all colours, languages, ways of life and different ideologies. There were those who liked bread without butter, those who had had to fight for their bread and those who knew what it was like with no bread at all. I wondered how many ever thought 'Ah, we're all one species, citizens of one world, part of one life force, and with what currency are we paying the Earth for all this fantastic convenience? How are 'Earth Peace' shares doing on the stockmarket?'

There was no denying it, we were inextricably part of the detrimental problem, as once again we defied gravity and took to the skies. Just for a moment I imagined that we were flying in the belly of a huge white garuda, the mythical half-bird of ancient Tibetan teachings who symbolises the perfection of our primordial nature. His essence would help for it was his job to devour disease and pollution in our world...

31

By now the sun's rays were diffused through the Earth's atmosphere creating a pretty salmon pink glow. This changed man's grimy, smoke-filled habitat into a thing of gentle beauty, finally to be hidden completely leaving twinkly lights of civilisation reflecting the distant stars. The larger MD11 retraced our flight path back to London but this time we followed the sun south-west across the Atlantic. I settled back into the comfy seat and took Pete's hand, always steadying for me even though he had been through great trauma in his life to be here. I tried to relax, the first time for days and days and days. We could do no more frenzied preparation for 'Climb For Tibet'. The adventure had begun. For now at least there was time to get myself together and time to reflect.

I felt positive and happy about gathering sponsorship, pledges and messages, but I had questions. There was a mountain to climb. My climbing ability was not particularly good. How would I manage over 6,000 metres? The highest I had ever been before was about 4,600 metres - a failed attempt on Mt Blanc where I had been forced to turn back close to the summit when my companion became hypothermic. How would the rest of the team cope? What could I do about my own inner peace that I was struggling with and which eluded me so often? I had read many times that inner peace produces world peace. I so wanted to get it right. Could something on this trip help me find it? And why indeed had my soul been drawn towards this pilgrimage?

4 - Tibet the Light

How easy it was to be at 10,000 metres in the pressurised cabin. There was nothing to it. We had just walked in and sat down. The space allotted to me in the middle of the ten-strong row was soft and cocoon-like and my body, good at curling legs up underneath when room is restricted, was happy to be still. There was no longer any need to be stressed out. This was the gap in time whilst turning the page from preparation to enactment chapter. Turn slowly, I thought, we need these gaps in life. Too often it's rush through the book of existence with no time to take stock, to work out why things happen, what we have learnt, where we are going and, to check we are on the right path. Perhaps even more important is to take time just to 'be'. I thought lovingly of my eldest son, Paul, who is a master at this. The world tries to push him into physical achievements, you must do this, you must do that, whilst he just floats serenely with a peaceful smile. Sometimes I find strength in just standing next to him and bathing in his aura, sometimes I like to think myself with him in a 'what do you say about this problem?' way, a sort of tuning into his energy and it helps me find answers and calmness. The levels where we help each other don't always have to be physical, or even conscious, although intention is a powerful part of the mind force.

The engines droned, producing a soporific effect on all the passengers, similarly suspended in time, to be broken only by the next tummy-filler happening. The dry air had that typical airline cologne smell that suggests a recycling entity that goes on and on. The hidden almost pale green lighting was dimmed, inviting sleep, but my mind was in turmoil. It was far too excited and over-tired to switch off.

Pete and I were the advance party. Our job was to establish a base in Quito, sort out communications, research some training peaks, reconnoitre the mountain and generally find out how things work in Ecuador, a remote South American country of which little seemed to be known in Britain. We did not even know if there would be much English spoken. Our Spanish was non-existent, although I had spent a little time in Mexico City in my student days hitch-hiking about and had ended up at the Olympic Games. Then it had been a smile, rather than my language skills, which had enabled me to enter the Olympic Village posing as a wrestler. Now, opening a book on how to speak Spanish was yet another job that had not happened before leaving. I would clutch a dictionary for the next month, but maybe being armed with a smile was still the best way to travel. I opened my little phrase book… *Have you got these shoes in black? That's a funny noise. Where is the bullring?* Ah well, I thought, I guess we'll muddle through somehow. No doubt GT will charm everyone with his Italian, though Migmar's Tibetan and Hindi may not be that useful and Pete's French seems to only work on girls.

I looked forward to GT and Mig completing the team by arriving a few days later. This delay meant that they were risking being less well acclimatized than us by not being able to spend so much time preparing their bodies at altitude, but their life commitments demanded it.

Graham Treacher, known as GT, was a busy musician from Bristol and as an eminent conductor and composer had performances to be there for. Warm and lovely, with a great sense of humour, everyone adored him. He had found our 'Climb For Tibet' advertisement in the Alpine Club newsletter and, with strong Buddhist and climbing interests going back to his teens, had known at once that he must try and be part of our outlandish way of helping the Earth. It had felt right for us to welcome him. He had had considerable mountaineering experience in many of the world's principal ranges, notably putting up first ascents high in the Tien Shan and in Arctic Norway. However he had expressed doubts on his fitness, which was cause for concern because of his age. At sixty-five he was the 'old boy' of the team. How would he now go at altitude?

Migmar was twenty-one years old and Tibetan. As a student at the London School of Fashion and a staunch and active member of the Tibetan community in Britain, battling to help his country and his people, he was attending a huge Freedom for Tibet charity concert in Washington USA and promoting T-shirts which he had designed. Also he would have been visiting members of his family lucky enough to have been given refugee residence in New York. He was thrilled at the impending arrival there of a new Tibetan baby - his sister's.

I had met Mig in 1991 whilst working for the charity organisation Climb For The World – on behalf of the United Nations. We had had an international event wherein representatives of all continents carried parts of the UN 'flags of all nations' flag to come together symbolically on the summit of the Eiger in Switzerland portraying 'One World'. We needed to choose two young teenagers to take part. They were to be a Tibetan and a Nepalese from the Pestalozzi International Children's Village near Battle, West Sussex in Britain. This was where Mig had been living since he had been brought over from his Tibetan settlement in southern India at the age of nine. He was disappointed not to have been chosen, but his day was to come. He had always taken seriously the responsibility that came with the chance he had been given of a good Western education and the opportunities it opened up to help his people. He was a young man fired up with determination and energy and frustrated at the lack of progress towards freeing his country.

'I want some action!' he had declared to Pete and me one day, whilst lunching on soup and momos at the Tibetan restaurant in London.

'OK,' we had responded, 'we'll give you some action. Come and climb our highest mountain with us.'

He had simply replied, 'All right, I will.'

It was this character trait of actually going ahead and doing things that he talked about, grabbing life with both hands and driving himself with great purpose that endeared him to so many people. Handsome, friendly and outgoing, he had what it takes. However there was one big worry. He had never climbed before.

Can the belief that you are able do something outweigh all the drawbacks? The intention of the mind helps manifest at a physical level, but what percentage of the total picture is this? Does it depend on the strength of the belief?

Certainly, the belief in a cause and the fact that one is helping others or the Earth makes a difference. When I carried out a parachute jump for charity in 1989 I had been in a state of complete and utter terror. My face had gone grey. Everything in me was shouting 'Don't move!' It was only the thought of others depending on me that had propelled me to that open door to throw myself out.

Also I knew that visualising an end result contributes to the commitment to overcome physical limitations. In 1994 my youngest son, Mark, and I had undertaken to bicycle from John O'Groats to Land's End, raising charity funds and collecting pledges from people to 'not use their cars'. We had barely ridden on roads before. I was actually frightened of traffic especially at roundabouts and we were heavily laden with all our camping gear. The first day we had managed all of 8 kilometres. For the next month we struggled, cursed and cried along the 1,600 kilometres, but every day Mark would call 'Mum, have you seen us there?' Then we would picture ourselves safely arriving at Land's End. When we did arrive, without even having had to change a tyre, it was largely due to the determination and mindfulness of my amazing thirteen year old son who had hung onto the fact that we had seen ourselves there. At some level we knew that we had already arrived.

Curled up on the plane high over the Atlantic, I had gut pangs of missing him and my other two sons. I felt that they still needed me even though they were now virtually grown up. The mother-child bond was so intense that I always found it hard to break. I hated leaving them. I could relate well to the Tibetan Buddhist word for the most compassionate love, which translates as that of 'mother sentient beings'. This refers to the fact that over lifetimes we have each been in a mother role and thus understand the extreme lengths we would go to in the caring for our offspring. I was comforted by knowing how wonderful my children always are in accepting my need to do rather wild and dangerous things. At least, I reflected happily, we are all very good at 'tuning in' over a distance to each other's presence and protecting each other with 'white light' – call it love, prayer, healing energy or what you will. It always gives a safe feeling that there is a protective force and that by directing it to surround a loved one something positive is being done to help, rather than creating negative energy by sending fear or worry. This is merely another aspect of the power of thought, creating our own reality - quantum physics at its best perhaps.

I sighed at the thought of some of the events in my life, which were like signposts along the silver chord of purpose. It was as though an unseen force was asserting 'You will help the Earth. We have to get it right.' Yet it was also part of me that was saying 'Listen to what you most love to do. Find your passion. Reach for that moment that cries loudly from the heart 'this is what I was born for'. Sense for the direction of purpose. Search for where you feel most alive. Listen to that voice. If you get the path right, then it will flow easily and all the hard work will not be in vain. If you don't bother, then it's snarl-ups or worse still – boredom.'

So why was I now giving so much for Tibet? Where was this stirring coming from? What were the signposts that I had followed to bring me along this path?

Curiously, I can remember very little Tibetan influence. It was something that was always just there, something that I was drawn to. At the age of twelve, I can recollect a school exhibition. There were long tables laid with a feast for the eyes – strange pictures and brocades of the brightest colours, exotic statues, unfamiliar musical instruments, shining jewellery and mementoes of a culture completely foreign to my experience. The exciting scene was mingled with tales of sadness, and something there moved me. There was a feeling of empathy. It was the first time that I remember feeling a surprisingly physical reaction, an inexplicable pain in my heart.

Why did it hurt me? For some reason it always did whenever I heard about the torture, the murder and the other atrocities. There are so many causes that need help at every corner of life, but some touch much deeper than others, and I had always reacted to the story of Tibet with a pain in the heart area as though it was happening to me.

Then one night there was a revelation. I was sitting quietly reading just before going to sleep, when I saw a crystal clear mind picture, combined with the way I tend to see things by sensing energy. I saw Tibet. It was gently cradled by the Himalayan Mountains. Out of the mists rose the Potala Palace, ancient fortress of light, representing all that is Tibet – wisdom, knowledge and high spirituality, radiating out like a sun to all corners of the globe. In that moment I understood why all the terrible things had happened to Tibet. I was being shown the overall picture. High in the mountains a level of spirituality had been reached that needed to be shared with the world. Truly, it was being forced out like ripe seeds from a seed capsule.

I knew then that someday, somehow, I would work for Tibet.

It was a poignant wake-up call to my psyche when I discovered that a Tibetan couple, Pala and Amala, were actually living in my hometown. I remembered well the day that they told me their story.

Migmar was with me and we took the car to pick them up from their small but fairly new council flat. It had pretty flowers outside contributing to the gentle and happy nature of the neighbourhood. With typical Tibetan hospitality they pressed us to come in and have a cup of tea. They always offered any food they could, although they had little money. I knew from previous visits that they sat in their one main room, bright and colourful with Tibetan carpets, thangkas and pictures of the Dalai Lama, with rugs over their knees to keep warm as they quietly meditated or read through loose-leaf Tibetan prayers.

Pala was sixty-two and Amala sixty-one, but they seemed older. Four decades as refugees had taken their toll and life had been hard. Pala had trouble with his back and suffered ill health, but although his round brown face often looked troubled and lost, it lit up with a devastating smile when he enjoyed simple pleasures like watching a child or talking to a cat and his eyes portrayed the cheekiest sparkle. Amala was more earnest. The name she went by means 'mother' in Tibetan, and it was maternal energy that she oozed, always caring and making sure that everyone was all right. She was small in stature and still pretty, but her sweetness and warmth seemed to give her great strength. They did not use their real names. Maybe this was part of the cloak of protection that covered their heart pain.

We arrived at my semi-detached redbrick cottage on the outskirts of Haslemere. It is leafy, commuter-to-London country, typically risk-free and British. They were coming for an evening meal.

'Very good house, very good house,' enthused Pala, smiling in his broken English, which was charming but sometimes hard to understand.

'Just like a Tibeti house', was Amala's immediate impression. For some reason I really liked that comment. It was something about the synchronicity of different cultures thousands of kilometres apart and in a different time frame. Had I been in a similar environment lifetimes away somewhere on the four winds?

'Why is it like a Tibetan house?' I asked.

She pointed at all the wood and rocks, and Mig interpreted the word 'natural'. At least they'll feel at home, I thought to myself happily. We ate supper and their initial reticence gradually turned into a torrent of Tibetan tales as they both simultaneously poured out their lives.

'I'll try and translate,' said Mig manfully.

Their early years in Tibet had been spent around Gyantse, about four days travel by horse south-west from the capital, Lhasa. It was here that in 1904 the adventurer Younghusband, having decided to invade Tibet on behalf of the British Empire, had met with Tibetan resistance leading to considerable loss of life. He subsequently became great friends with the thirteenth Dalai Lama and there have been good relations between the two countries ever since.

Pala and Amala were married at the young ages of seventeen and sixteen, as was the custom. A year later they produced a beautiful little girl, Chime. They lived with Pala's parents until he took up a job as a civil servant and they moved to Shekar, a small village about ten days by horse from Lhasa. Life was content for them. Pala was twenty-two, a young man just starting out.

I watched him glance tenderly at Amala. It was clear that they had been very much in love.

The invasion of 1949/50 had not affected them in their rural area to any large extent. The Chinese 'reforms' had been concentrated in the east. Then in 1959 Tibet would never be the same again. On fearsome wings the Chinese military 'machine' moved west, faster than a horse could travel. No news system went before them. Into Shekar came the soldiers. They forced the monks and nuns out of their monasteries at machine-gun point, tied their hands behind their backs and put them on trucks. They ordered everyone to get out of the government building where Pala was working and took control. The first load of workers had their hands tied behind their backs and was pushed onto trucks. Amala and Chime were with Pala. They clung to him and cried so much that a sympathetic Chinese soldier said 'OK, you can go on the next load, but you really have to go then.'

Pala's tone of voice became very definite as he directed his Tibetan words to Mig. He remembers very clearly making his decision. He had no way of knowing that Lhasa had been taken over by the Chinese army and that the Dalai Lama had fled. He did not know about the desecration of all the monasteries, nor about the murders, the torture, the rape, and the impending starvation. He just saw all his friends being forced into trucks with their hands tied. He did know, however, that they were to be driven to Shigatse, the second biggest city in Tibet, famous not only for the Tashilumpo monastery, seat of the Panchen Lama, but also for the large high security gaol. The Chinese soldiers told him 'The Dalai Lama has been taken by thieves. The Potala Palace has been crushed.'

Pala knew that his future looked very bleak and decided that he was going to escape. There were soldiers everywhere, but he had been lucky enough to have arranged a meeting place with Amala before they were separated. He was locked in under house arrest. While the Chinese slept he opened the window and with his heart in his mouth slid out into the waiting night. The landing was soft but smelly.

His eyes danced with mirth in the telling, for he had fallen into a ditch full of yak dung.

At the appointed meeting place there were Amala and Chime and very fortuitously Thupten, a friend of theirs who had also decided to escape. He was a trader and therefore accustomed to travelling through the mountains and to finding the route to India, albeit normally by horse or yak.

As the crow flies, the border with Nepal and Chomolungma, the mighty Everest, is only 180 kilometres away, but their route was to take them round mountains, over passes and across steep and difficult terrain to Sikkim, the Indian 'arm' sandwiched between Bhutan and Nepal. They walked and scrambled at night and hid up behind rocks in the day. At least it was March and spring was on the way, but the nights were icy cold.

After ten days and nights they reached Khambazong and then a further five nights found them approaching the village of Lachen just as the sun was coming up. This was a mistake. There was a patrol of fifteen Chinese soldiers who were on the look-out for escapees, in particular a high nun, head of the Sakya nunnery. The little group were spotted and were caught.

Amala leant forward speaking intently to stress how completely terrified she had been.

She had been shaking all over. She had never been so scared. They were taken back to Khambazong by truck and interrogated. What were they doing? Why were they near the border? They told the soldiers that they must have taken the wrong road, that they were trying to get to Shigatse. The soldiers seemed convinced, gave them tea and tsampa, and said that they would be taken to Shigatse by truck. Chime was crying and distressed, upset at the machine-guns, the harshness of the Chinese men of war and the atmosphere of fear. So Amala begged the soldiers 'Please let us go by ourselves', Pala pleaded too, saying 'I'll sign you a letter stating that we are definitely going to Shigatse', and in the end the Chinese let them go. The following morning in full view of all the soldiers they were shown the road to Shigatse. They felt that, looking like a group of peasants, little importance had been attached to them, but they hid in the mountains for two days and nights fearful for their lives.

At this point Amala recalls a heart-breaking dilemma. All her family were living in Shigatse – her father, mother, brothers and sisters. She really wanted to go to Shigatse. In the disagreement that ensued, Pala feeling that perhaps His Holiness had escaped, remembers saying 'Well, I'm going to India and I'm taking Chime with me'. Their fate today would have in all likelihood been miserable and tragic had they changed their resolve here. Pala knew that he would have been killed.

So they turned south again even more stealthily. Moving at night helped them against the bitter temperature, but little Chime was exhausted and carrying her was not easy. Local people, a mixture of Tibetans and Sikkims, assisted from time to time with food and water and once, for a little way, the loan of a donkey.

Eventually they reached Lachen again, and with great alarm again at sunrise. Fear seeped through them - fear born of the uncertainty of their own fate coupled with the brutal certainty that their country was in the cruel grip of a foreign power. As they neared a little stupa in sight of Sikkim, they stopped at its colourful fluttering prayer flags to offer blessings on the wind-horse, but they had one over-riding memory of a less compassionate moment. Thupten, answering a call of nature, sneered with loud disdain 'Well, you Chinese, eat this!'

Mig caught up in the relating of the story relaxed into a heap of giggles at Pala's recollection. He did not know then that many Tibetans had had to search for food in their gaolers excrement.

So they crossed the border to safety, and to a refugee life of exile and further uncertainty. For the self-reliant Tibetan having to accept aid was particularly hard. Helping travellers and those around them was natural, but there had never before been poverty in Tibet. Now, as thousands followed His Holiness into exile, the tide of homelessness was beginning.

Pala and Amala settled into the job of breaking stones for road-works on behalf of the Indian government, until after ten years Amala became too ill to go on, and they moved to Simla where they worked for Save The Children. From there they were chosen to look after Tibetan refugee children and were sent to Wales in Britain as house-parents. Chime, to their dismay, had to stay in India.

I sensed deep sadness as Pala said that he believed they were the lucky ones. No one else had escaped from their village. They had had to leave everything and Amala said she was particular upset at leaving all her beautiful jewellery, important to a Tibetan girl, but more than anything they were troubled at leaving their families whom they would never see again. There was no way of contacting them and finding out how they were until more Tibetans escaped bringing the news that gradually filtered through to them over the years. They had never even said goodbye...

Mig and I were keen for them to talk about their families, but even after all this time they found it distressing. They looked down and spoke quietly. There was much that they did not know. Pala learned that his brother had been shot in the uprising in Lhasa about the time of his own escape. Amala discovered that her brother had been imprisoned without charge for fifteen years and that her father had died in gaol. It seemed that, crazed by starvation, he had eaten the flesh of a long-dead dog and was poisoned. She believes the rest of her family to be living in Lhasa sweeping the streets in desperately poor conditions, second class citizens in their own country. Those who did what the Chinese wanted had suffered less. The extent of the courage of those who, with typical Tibetan loyalty, did not, may never be known.

Many with longer and more arduous and winter journeys out of the country did not make it. I can recall one such refugee telling me of her escape at the age of fifteen and of how her younger sister had died in her arms.

We drove Pala and Amala home. Their soft smiles said 'we accept the cards that life deals us, but thank you for listening to our story'. It was late, long past their bedtime, for, in spite of their poor health, they would rise at 4.30 am to meditate and to travel early to work cleaning houses.

They were the lucky ones.

My heart was touched by the experiences of Pala and Amala. It had been brought home to me not only that it was real people's lives that were being shattered, but also that the Chinese are of course real people too. Twice in Pala and Amala's story the Chinese soldiers showed sympathy and compassion. In spite of all the atrocities, can we see life from the Chinese soldier's point of view? Can we put ourselves in their shoes? They thought that they were liberating Tibet from serfdom and an antiquated way of life. They had been brainwashed to inflict suffering. The state was telling them what to do and how to think. Killing was their job. They were used to the cruelty and low regard for human and animal life.

His Holiness says that we must love and respect our Chinese brothers and sisters, and that ultimately all people want happiness. At an individual level, in spite of the unbelievable horrors of the tales of brutality, can we somehow reach for that level of compassion to be able to move forward?

I pondered on compassion. How lovely it was to have some time to let my thoughts roam the skies. Given the Tibetan Buddhist belief of reincarnation, how would it have been if in their last life one of the Chinese soldiers had been a Tibetan and Pala had been a Chinese soldier? Maybe he owed him one. What if the roles were to be reversed in the next life? Is it not a good idea, holding a wider view of many lifetimes, to err on the side of compassion? The taking-it-in-turns aspect is analogous to climbing with someone on a rope. First one holds the other climber's life in one's hands, by belaying the rope safely, then it is the other climber's turn to hold one's own. It is definitely in one's own interest to be compassionate and hold the other's fall, indeed there is a natural tendency, for being tied together there is a need to act as one entity for survival.

What if I chose to come back next time as a tortured and unjustly imprisoned Tibetan so that my soul could learn the lessons that it entailed? What if my karma dictated that this should be so? Oh help, I thought, worse still, what if I came back as a torturer? My case for compassion was growing. If I were able to stand back and view events over many lifetimes, then the things that I had thought to be bad would not seem so, for they would have purpose. I would have drawn them so that my soul could grow towards enlightenment (or whatever terminology one wanted to use for the highest energy state.) In the process, as His Holiness says, my enemies would be teaching me and giving me opportunities to progress. What if there was a great queue of souls waiting to incarnate into human bodies because of this staggering scope for advancement? Should I not make the most of my chances? As that saying goes 'Every trouble is a gift from God'.

So if I choose to give out compassion in the middle of a troubled situation, then my soul is likely to grow and my karma is likely to come back at me with better things. Surely, though, this will only work if it is genuine compassion, the real desire for others to be free from suffering and the intention in my mind is of unconditional love. OK, I thought, good ideals, but when in a situation that is a typical emotion-ridden problem on a day-to-day basis, I forget totally about compassion, and wallow in my anger, hurt, frustration or whatever emotion seems to be taking an airing. Then my inner peace goes out the window. As an unenlightened being, how can I stand back and rise above emotions at these times?

Maybe the knowledge that we are all part of one energy helps. Scientists say that many studies are complicated by the energy of the observer affecting that of the observed, making it impossible to look at anything completely separately. We are all interdependent. But whilst my intellectual understanding is that nothing is in isolation, I find it hard to actually feel this at a deep level as the bit that identifies as me doesn't always like to think that it is part of somebody or something else.

I like the picture of everything in the universe as 'energy soup'. This may not relate well to school physics, but I appreciate that the building blocks of all things are dynamic energy particles, which are vibrating at different frequencies, with the dense stuff such as rock appearing to be more stable than the ethereal substance like thought. My way of understanding the soup best is by seeing all these building blocks emitting 'energy waves' which intermingle and act on everything else that they come into contact with. I see anything that happens, therefore, as the result of the sum total of these different forces acting on it. So bumping into someone who you actually want to meet anyway may not be the random coincidence that it appears. Or thinking unkind thoughts about your neighbour could lead to his dog being sick on your sitting room carpet.

Given that we are all irrevocably interconnected as part of the same universal energy system, and thus every single happening makes a difference to some extent to everything else, it would seem very negative to give out uncompassionate thoughts or actions to another part of the universe. It would at some point come back to the giver in a sort of knock-on effect, like ripples in a circular pond. Equally, imagine how powerful really genuine loving compassionate thoughts and actions can be. My belief is that these, giving out a higher vibration, are imbued with Divine Energy, thus magnifying their effect manifold.

I find it helpful to equate this universal energy system to the human body. Suppose you have a big toe that has gone septic and is giving you a lot of pain. Do you become angry and try and get rid of the toe? No, you won't want to (well, you probably won't want to). In the long run you need to be able to stay on your feet and every part of your body is necessary. Therefore the only answer is to heal it. In these terms, thinking of the body of humanity, I can understand better His Holiness' wonderful humbling response to the pain of the Chinese situation – To heal with love and compassion.

My thought processes, like the aircraft, purred on and on into the night. The hours came and went. There were to be thirteen in flight. I was beginning to feel cramped and longed for some space, somewhere to run, greenery and a place where my spirits could soar and I could feel free. I stirred restlessly and tried to stretch. Pete dozed to my right. He was always able to sleep anywhere. My neighbour on the left turned to me, away from the book she was reading, illuminated by the little circle of overhead light which reminded me of the excitement of a head-torch lighting the way into the unknown on a night climb. I noted that she was reading in English though she looked South American with typical olive skin, dark hair and brown eyes. Perhaps she would like to chat?

'It shouldn't be too long before we land to refuel in Aruba.' She smiled, mother-like, with only the slightest hint of an accent. She had an air of being a regular traveller on this route. 'Will this be your first time in Ecuador?'

'Mm,' I nodded

'Holiday?'

'No, we're going to climb a mountain.'

'Ah, lovely. There are many beautiful ones there.' She glanced at my bare feet and I chuckled to myself with the distinct impression that she felt that climbers should always be prepared and have their boots on. 'You're going to need some good boots,' she advised.

Some people are really funny, I thought, though if KLM hadn't generously given us twice the weight allowance I may well have had them on.

'It's a sponsored climb,' I went on, 'to raise funds and awareness for Tibet...'

'Why do you want to help the Tibetans?' She interrupted.

'Probably because I was a Tibetan in my previous life,' I replied, watching her face carefully.

She laughed condescendingly. 'How quaint.'

Help, I thought, remembering that some religions believe that more than one incarnation is an anathema and stops you getting to Heaven. 'The Dalai Lama says that religions are like the spokes on the wheel of life, all vital, but just different.'

She looked at me rather blankly.

How can I get out of this, I wondered, without offending the first South American that I had met...? 'Different ways of thinking are just like different paths up a mountain. We're all aiming for the same high spot.'

The look she gave me still said it's a question of right and wrong.

'Truth's a funny thing isn't it? We all have to work out our own.' I mumbled, as she had a sudden need to leave her seat and head for the toilet sign.

Oh dear, I thought, you win some, you lose some, and resolved to be more sensitive. I'll ask her about the weather later. I bet she thinks I'm funny. Wooh! I could have shocked her a lot more. There were all my experiences with conscious dreaming, going back into previous lives and the theories on Atlantis - how my incarnations there meant that I was now part of a group who, having blown technology then, was determined to help the Earth and get it right this time. I remembered some of the stages on the path of my learning – scepticism, fun, disbelief, excitement. I smiled to myself – maybe my neighbour had once been my mother. Far out!

I reminded myself that just because reincarnation fits into my set of beliefs, and those of the authors of countless books I had read and digested over the years, it doesn't mean that it does with other peoples', in fact with those of over half the world. I wondered though, why all the references to reincarnation were taken out of the Bible at the Fifth Ecumenical Council meeting in 553 AD at Constantinople. At least every religion goes for the continuation of the human spirit.

Perhaps if I had known then that I was on the way to test out my own expectations in this regard I would have been less critical.

6 - Gift from the Universe

Like a dream that came and went, we touched down at Aruba, the Caribbean island off Venezuela. There was little reality to it. A wall of heat met us at the aircraft door, the sticky atmosphere across the tarmac was thick with the sweet scent of frangipani and hibiscus, while palm trees rustled and waved in the ocean breeze. I breathed deeply. Dark smiley island people herded us in and out of the terminal building. My mind gently absorbed the contrast thrust upon it. We had left a now alien grey Western world rushing about with high technology where money is king and achievement his consort, whilst here, a mere hallucination away, I guessed that daily lives were governed by the sun, the sea, tourism and debt. The difference in cultures only serves to highlight the strength in diversity of the human species, but would we, of the family of the Earth, in the end, understand that each member of every nation has the same desire for happiness, the same need for inner peace?

Back on the plane I continued my search for some inner peace of my own, a little stilling of the mind. I really wanted to relax. I knew good meditative methods to try to achieve this, though I usually tend to not bother enough with the mechanics and rush through all the preliminary stages. I start off by tensing up every part of my body bit by bit, holding it for a few seconds and then letting it go in an exaggerated way. It helps to have a lead-in thought like 'I now let go of all my tension' and then see or sense it going out of my body with my mind's eye. I find that to create an actual shape or colour representation helps as a rubbish-removal vehicle. So if I wanted to get rid of tension, fear, anger or whatever, I could see it as a red blob in part of my body and visualise it blowing up or dissolving. These are mind games, but none-the-less useful.

Breathing is my next stage. I try to slow everything down by concentrating on the breath. The focus fields wandering thoughts. I count to ten breathing in, hold it for a count of four, count to ten breathing out, hold it for a count of four and then start the cycle again. Gradually elongating the counts helps the process. Then more mind play - on every in-breath I imagine bringing in love, white light, healing energy and all manner of positive good stuff, and on every out-breath I let go everything negative that the body doesn't want.

Sometimes I utilise a cleansing routine working with the body's seven main energy centres, the chakras, each with its representative colour of the rainbow. I do this by simply imagining the body swimming through water of red, then orange... yellow... green... blue... indigo... violet and then into white light, whilst holding the intention of releasing blockages and renewing harmony.

Then I like to rest in a special healing place deep in my mind. Usually it is a rock cave full of crystals, luminescent, magical. It could be a clear mountain pool, a forest glade or anywhere that expresses beauty and peace.

Normally at this stage I can meet with my personal healing guides. I know that they have been with me at least since my awareness started to open up a few years ago, about the time I started devouring spiritual books in a search for the knowledge of how to guide my children. I sense them always to the right side of my body. I know them only as 'Large' and 'Small' and they are always there for me. They give me advice particularly on my health or they zap me with necessary energy for needy spots. However, they only come if I ask for help, and very often I do not ask.

Spatially around my body I know that there are other forms of assistance offering answers to problems, understanding, love and access to the Divine Energy. I know where the doors are, so why do I so rarely find the time to sit quietly and open them?

Often I find more motivation in trying to help others rather than continuing to get lost in the mists of the hard work of my own problems. So, once in a deeply relaxed and cleansed state, it is a good moment to offer myself up as a channel. The method I like to use is to picture white light becoming available to me from the Divine Energy. I am then acting as a transformer, converting energy to a vibration usable at a physical level by directing the stream of light to where there is healing needed, near or far, loved one or stranger, animal or human, illness or sadness. However I can only send healing energy and love, which is then one of the forces

48

acting on any situation. I cannot decide how anything should be, such as whether a sick person should live or die. That is up to each individual soul's game-of-life plan. Purposeful prayer is a fine line between the state of ignoring and interference. The power is there, call it God, Divineness, Love, the Universe, the Highest Energy, Life or whatever terminology is the least baffling or touches the aspect of the moment. It can be directed by the loving intention of the mind for the greater good. It just has to be asked for.

Assisting others in this way also helps oneself in a sort of Divine viscosity, but today, although my state of mind was calming, I did not seem to want to concentrate on any of the wonderful ways of self help. I was still carrying the tension in my back. If all else fails, I thought, resort to the other excellent method of bringing about relaxation and stress release - a neck and shoulder massage from the boyfriend.

'Pete… you know you're so good at massaging…'

'Flight massage parlour at your service… short back and shoulders, Madam?'

I smiled with pleasure. He was always there for me. How lucky I was to have someone who had taken on not only me and my way of thinking which had been so different from his own, but also so completely my dream.

The love of Pete's life had always been climbing and all its aspects, from rock climbing throughout Britain to all the major mountains of the European Alps. He was a highly experienced mountaineer. He had been employed by an insurance company for thirty-four years, a workaholic, exceptionally full of drive and energy, and had done very well. Instigating the opportunity for early retirement at the age of fifty, he had taken on a few charity events and was busy becoming a ski instructor whilst waiting for life to come at him with ideas on what to do with the next fifty.

Well, life 'came at him' when we were introduced at the Argentière campsite in the French Alps on an Alpine Club meet. I had heard about six events that he was doing for charity in this one year to celebrate the big five 'O'. There was nothing easy, just… skiing 130 kilometres across the Haute Route of Europe… running the London Marathon… windsurfing 42 kilometres across Lake Coniston… a triathlon of a 160 kilometre cycle, 3 kilometre swim and 42 kilometre run… the 130 kilometre South Downs Way run… and the climbing of Switzerland's tallest mountain. Here be Superman. Also he too had recently cycled Land's End to John O'Groats.

I admired his energy and commitment and, knowing how hard it is to raise interest and sponsorship and actually collect in the money, I wanted to offer him a contribution.

My first impressions were of a tall, fit, fine-looking, rather hairy Viking, wearing sunny colourful gear and with an intensity of the joys of life. He gave an air of someone with confidence, who loved people, running things, achievements and being busy doing things for others. He oozed strength and dependability. It was not until later that I was to discover the unerringly kind and gentle nature of his heart.

'Hi, pleased to meet you.'

The handshake was warm and eminently friendly.

'How would you like to come and climb the highest mountain in the world with me?' I had given no thought to the words. They had just come out, so I went on 'It's Chimborazo in Ecuador.'

He gave me a quizzical look, 'That's ridiculous. It's definitely Everest.'

'No it's Chimborazo. It's the point furthest from the centre of the Earth. The world's not round, it's an oblate spheroid, so everything on the equator sticks out more. That makes Chimborazo the highest mountain.'

'What height above sea level?'

'It's not much more than 6,000 metres, that's less than 21,000 feet. Compared to Everest it's meant to be quite an easy climb.'

'Well, I was just going to have one of these beers actually. Do you want to join me?' He continued being charming as though it was the most normal everyday discussion, and then in typical response, 'Fill me in on the details.'

Of course I had no details beyond the sense that this was the right thing to do. It was an illustration of the balance of our future partnership; he, left-brain dominated, logical and practical; me, right-brain dominated, intuitive and motivated by inspiration.

'Our lives do seem to have similarities, don't they?' I chatted 'like raising charity funds by doing tough and interesting events.'

'Yeah, people think that you're mad, but you can do some useful stuff.' His eyes sparkled at the fun of his challenges.

'I hear, though, that you did Land's End to John O'Groats with a back-up vehicle,' I taunted. 'That's taking the soft option a bit isn't it? Fancy having all your gear carried, and cups of tea made for you.' Was this really the man of steel that was at first portrayed? 'I mean, it's a bit off-putting.'

'Well, I bet we did it quicker than you. We were limited by time. We only had nine days.'

'Speed isn't everything, you know.'

I was struck by the fraternal energy of our easy relationship. It transpired that he was almost an astral twin with my brother Graham. Their births were only a couple of days apart.

We became part of the same team setting off with the aim of climbing Mt Blanc, sneaking into the ladies loo at 3,800 metres at the top of the Aiguille de Midi téléphérique to 'sleep' there before the start at midnight - all part of the ambience of mountaineering.

There was to be a gestation period of nine months, before we got together on a ski-mountaineering trip, and finally organised a meeting about Chimborazo. The dream was starting to turn into a reality.

Then came that fateful day when he felt that he had to make the choice. On one side were his wife and his four children whom he loved dearly, a fine home, cars, a life's work and all that went with it, strongly weighted with the desire not to hurt his family. On the other side was setting out into the unknown, risking everything, a new woman whom he loved and who loved him, and a new challenge that was beginning to tug at him. The decision tore him in two. He could not be true to himself and be faithful to both. There was no easy way out. There would be heartbreak and anguish whichever way he went.

He chose the open door. The sacrifices were enormous and the pain intense for all concerned... I believe that only his own inner self with its life perspective knew if he had chosen the right path for his greatest soul growth. For each soul, in co-operation with those around it, organises its own challenges to overcome, for the purpose of gathering the strengths that it needs along the way.

I glanced at him lovingly. 'Thanks for the massage, my Viking warrior, fighting for peace.' I wondered if this was a contradiction in terms, after all peace is a state of being, fighting a state of action.

'Come on then, let's go into battle and collect some more sponsorship money and messages. People look a bit more responsive now. You take that aisle, I'll take this one.'

'You're such a slave driver.'

The plane was coming alive again and the oh-help-how-can-I-eat-at-this-time-of-day breakfast had just been cleared away. There was the faint magenta stirring of a dawn of light somewhere over the South American continent.

'Did you know that it was considered right for Vikings to have more than one wife, and right for Tibetans to have more than one husband?' I asked, unsuccessfully trying to draw him into conversation rather than action. Maybe, I mused, the words 'right' and 'wrong' should really be replaced by 'feels right for me in my present situation' or 'is morally wrong for me as dictated by the society in which I now live'.

I was reminded of the time we had been having a meal at a Chinese restaurant and Pete had bravely produced our form, bright with the Tibetan flag and asked the Chinese proprietor for sponsorship. He, not surprisingly, had not given us any money, but rather than throw us out, had engaged us in deep conversation as to why Tibet was part of China. He stressed that Tibetans had been living in the dark ages, under a cruel feudal system, that the Chinese had done them a great service by bringing liberation and modernisation. China had therefore been right to invade.

Had the Chinese soldiers been told that it was the right thing to do when on countless occasions they forced Tibetan children to shoot their own parents? Were they wrong to allow the basic compassion of human nature to surface as in the helping of Pala and Amala?

The question of the morality of right or wrong was here something totally dictated by the point of view of the evaluator. However I felt that this should not stop us, or anyone, fighting for what we believe to be an important issue to effect changes on. Yet if people passionately believe this and are on opposing sides then war will result. Is that a reason for keeping quiet and doing nothing? Maybe it works if one holds in one's mind the intention of doing things for the greater good of all. The flip side of this is the many examples in history of the passion of religious beliefs leading to crusades of death and destruction. The answer that is often cited is that the world would come together with a united government and sort out its problems if we were aggressively threatened from outside - perhaps overrun by little green Martians. However this could bring an added risk of expanding the use of violence and war as a way of solving a crisis, created again by differing values of what is right and wrong, and allow it to adversely touch other parts of the universe.

Surely the answer is to implode, to come back down to the individual who says no I cannot judge others but, yes, this is what I myself believe to be right or wrong. If I live by this code I shall have my own inner peace, therefore I cannot be at war with anyone around me. In fact I shall be giving off inner peace energy which will affect all those around me in a powerful beneficial way. As an individual I can make a difference.

This is reiterated by the Dalai Lama's definition of non-violence that refers not only to the physical level, but also to our thoughts and to our essential inner beingness, which are tools for giving off this energy of peace and harmony.

It is of course one thing to say and quite another to do when confronted by the battles of life, but we could set out aiming for the highest ideals. And if enough people tried...

I set to work with the forms. The girls in the next row looked English.

'Excuse me, we're collecting messages for a peace climb in Ecuador. Would you like to contribute? We're asking that they be in the Tibetan spirit of non-violence, compassion for all life and universal responsibility...'

'Oh lovely, that sounds interesting. Let's have a look.'

They thought long and hard and then wrote:

"Peace for all mankind."

"Let the violence of the past give way to understanding in the present, that peace be of the future."

"I pray that we may all expand our love for one another, for our Mother Earth and for God, and that our voices may be heard."

The Indian guy behind returned his form with:

"The peace in our hearts is the essence of our souls."

The Scottish businessman said:

"Let us look after the Tibetans and all people of the world. Everyone is precious."

The Ecuadorian student scribbled:

"Love our beautiful Earth."

I thought I'd try again with my South American neighbour who was smiling at me nervously. I handed her a form.

'So, what do you think the weather will be like in Quito?'

She looked relieved. 'Ah, now, I can tell you all about that. There is a wonderfully happy climate there. The dry season has just started so it should be sunny all the time.'

Surely, I thought, she must work for the tourist board. The only bit out of the travel guidebook that I could remember was that the predictable thing about the weather was its unpredictability... but I kept quiet.

'It should be about 15° centigrade when we get there at about 9 o'clock in the morning.' She continued 'The temperature is always pleasant. It rarely gets above 21° or below 7°; but you must remember that it's over 2,850 metres, that's 9,000 feet, above sea level and the radiation is very intense. Now, you must use sun cream all the time and wear a hat. Do you have one?'

'Um... I'm not sure that I do.'

'Most Ecuadorians wear one, though not so much in the city as in the rural areas. You can buy them on most of the street stalls and there are markets everywhere.'

I looked forward to sampling some of the local wares, though had a strong suspicion that I would be getting whisked off up a training mountain before I had time to catch my breath. There was a lot of work to do – maybe after the climb...

'And another thing, the altitude will make you feel very bad. For at least two days you will be nauseous, breathing will be harder and you will probably have headaches. You must take it easy for a bit until your body begins to adapt. Oh, and drink lots of water. It helps, as does coca tea.'

'Thank you, yes, that reminds me...' I searched in my bag for my little case of homeopathic remedies and pulled out the coca phial, taking one of the little white pills. The body needs all the help it can get, I thought, offering one to Pete too, but he refused. He was taking Diamox, the standard climbers' altitude remedy.

Also it was time to take my homeopathic 'vaccinations'. There was one that covered tetanus, typhoid, polio, hepatitis and yellow fever and there was the malaria one - time too for cocculus, which helps with jetlag. I felt that these treatments work with the body rather than giving it more foreign substances to fight against. I had, in the last month, searched out a handful of doctors to discuss the homeopathic protection method. Points of view differed widely, but the majority opinion had been that, although they felt obliged to recommend the standard injections, they themselves would prefer to use this holistic approach.

Back in my bag I came across Yannick, brought him out and played peek-a-boo with the little child with big brown eyes who was peering over the seat in front of me. People think that Yannick is a teddy bear, I suppose because he's round and cuddly; others rudely think that he's a duck, I never have discovered why; and some dismiss him altogether, probably because he's pink and purple.

This colouring incidentally matches my rucksack on which he always travels, tied on behind carrying a spare karabiner. Yannick is a particularly smart and well-ordered penguin. In fact he's had a lot more adventures than most penguins. He's bounded out of a plane at 600 metres, floated down a river in a climbing helmet, jumped from a helicopter to a mountain top skiing wildly down virgin snow, posed on many a hard-won summit, rock climbed, ice climbed, ski-mountaineered, flown from tall pinnacles, spent the night on a sea-stack, on major summits and in a snow-cave. The greatest indignity is repeated swimming lessons in the washing machine and I can barely mention the times he's had to double up as a rugby ball.

I gave him a cuddle. He makes a wonderful pillow.

'You're too attached to Yannick.' Was the comment from Pete.

'I am not!'

'You should have left him behind. There were more important things to bring than ducks.' He taunted.

'You're just jealous.' I retorted. I nearly had left him behind in the panic to pack and get to the airport. That would have been awful, like leaving part of me behind. Hmm, I thought, maybe I am too attached. We cannot be happy with anything or anyone if we are attached because then we have fear that we might lose it or them, and that produces a need and then we start manoeuvring to keep that need satisfied. It's possessive love, not unconditional love. *If you really love something set it free. If it really loves you it will come back to you.*

So often we deny others that freedom, that space where they need to be, in which to discover their true self, to learn and to grow their soul. The love and respect that His Holiness says we should have for our enemies is maybe what we should be cultivating for those close to us too. To respect another's soul by giving it freedom from attachment is hard for the fear for oneself sneaks in, but perhaps it is as important as love. Maybe that's part of what converts possessive love to unconditional love. How we love is so important.

Wooh! I thought, it's complicated loving penguins.

'Loving kindness to all beings is good Tibetan Buddhism as well as non-attachment,' I continued to Pete.

'Yannick's not a being.'

'Maybe he is if I think he is.'

'Don't be silly!'

I laughed and carried on stirring, 'Well, thoughts are powerful. They create reality, and love is the most powerful force of all, 'cept sometimes it seems to act like a sort of glue and messes up non-attachment.'

'Surely, though, love is more important than non-attachment?'

'Well, I guess it needs to be seen in the context of putting your soul in a position of greatest growth potential.'

'Huh.' Pete wasn't convinced.

I always enjoy trying to work at some of the Buddhist principles even though I am not a Buddhist per se. However it usually serves to highlight the long way I have to go before reaching enlightenment, which always seems so unobtainable. I find it easier to think in terms of baby blobs of enlightenment that will gradually strengthen, expand and grow up. These could be sparked by moments of love such as a flash of understanding towards an upsetting neighbour with different beliefs. I glanced warmly to my left...

The cabin was suddenly flooded with sunlight as the promise of a new day hit the plane.

'Good Morning, South America,' I said eagerly.

Smiles in anticipation of landing and the end of a long journey appeared on tired faces all around. I dug out my sunglasses, and longed to be sitting next to the window to see my first glimpse of Ecuador, though as we veered left and started our descent through bumpy thick cloud, the brightness left us and visibility was dramatically reduced.

'What's the name of this place?' I asked my neighbour, who happily still seemed keen to talk.

'This is Guayaquil. We won't be allowed off the plane here, though, as it's a very brief stop. It's the largest city in Ecuador, right at sea level, a very busy port. This is where most of the trade happens.'

'Bananas?' I enquired hopefully. My body was already in withdrawal missing its usual dose of breakfast fruit.

'Yes, though oil is now a far more important export.'

'Where does it all go to?'

'The USA is the biggest trading partner, but I believe much of the income earned goes to pay off the interest on the national debt rather than alleviate the massive poverty of the country.'

'World imbalances.' I had the feeling that there would be many moments of Western guilt as one of the 'haves' in a country of 'have-nots'.

'Mm, and also imbalances within Ecuador. There are a few very rich…'

'Is inflation still very bad?'

'Yes, about fifty per cent per annum, though it had been up to a hundred per cent. You must be sure to keep your money in US dollars and just change into sucres when needed.'

'Thank you, OK.'

'And you shouldn't carry much cash, there are bandidos everywhere.'

'Do you mean bandits? Oh help!' But she couldn't dampen my enthusiasm.

The wheels touched down on Ecuadorian soil. Wow! We were here… in a far country of mystery, gold, rainforest, mountains and strange animals… of panpipes and ponchos. By dint of the position of the equator through its heart and the reaching up of the Andean volcanoes to the sky, we were to be the latter-day explorers of the treasures it held. The adrenaline stirred in excitement at the adventure, the unknown and the new experiences to come. It was just another international airport through the open doors of the plane but this was the legendary Ecuador tantalising us with dreams of Incas and Spanish Conquistadors…

Then, like a sidewinder snake briefly touching down on hot sand, our flight path retraced its steps again. We were on the last leg with only thirty minutes to go until Quito… flying obliquely into the early morning sun.

The energy on the plane was restless. There was much moving about and chatting and ladies queuing for the put-yourself-back-together-again loo. At last we were so nearly there.

Something in the far reaches of my tired befuddled head was calling. What was it? There was something I was not doing. And then it dawned on me … Chimborazo… we must be flying near to Chimborazo… Quick the map… where is it? Things all over the place… Yannick… wash-kit… papers… chaos… there… open up… yes, of course, it should be coming up to our south-east on the right hand side of the plane. It must be there, but I'm stuck in the middle of the seats away from the window…

Pete, video camera at the ready, chatted up the airhostess with affable charm.

'Tess it's brilliant. The flight crew are going to let me film from the cockpit. Isn't that fantastic?'

'Wow! Great.'

'But apparently it's very rarely visible and they think that there's too much cloud cover. We might be lucky. C'mon, get with it. Get your camera out.'

I scrumbled through my gear to find it, my loyal friend, my little Leica CL which had never let me down. Grabbing it I staggered into the aisle. I had to find somewhere I could get close to a window. Peering across the three deep seats I could just see the shape of an isolated peak rising from the swirling clouds. Could it be Chimborazo? no…but it has to be…no it can't be…but the map…

Pete dashed back down the aisle. 'That's it. It's really it. I'm going to the cockpit.'

My heart was racing. Wow! I wasn't prepared for this encounter… I had to find a window. I started rushing up and down, headless chicken style. The right hand seats all seemed to be occupied, at the back by the galley the window was thick with people looking out, the window in the middle was taken also and the wing was masking the view from the only other one. Oh no... to come this far and not be able to see it properly… I darted up to the front through the curtains into the first class area. Here was a chance. One of the large double seats had only one person sitting there, next to the window. He was a smartly dressed rather swarthy looking businessman, quietly reading a magazine - at least it was quietly until he was startled to find himself with a peculiar agitated woman lying across his knees.

'Excuse me, excuse me… I just have to photograph.' I had my camera up against the window and was snapping away a reel of film. I wished desperately that I had brought my long lens and promised never to go anywhere again without it.

'That's our mountain. We're going to climb it. It's the highest mountain in the world.'

The astonished businessman was wriggling uncomfortably beneath me, but I couldn't tell from his grunts whether he spoke English or not.

'I'm so sorry to disturb you. It's so important.'

I placed my hand on the thick translucent plastic 'glass'. It was hard to the touch. It was real. It held, as though invented by my own personal mind screen, the most exciting panorama I had ever seen.

The KLM insignia on the wing strut and the gaping circular hole of one engine with its silver halo dramatically gave the scene perspective. In the foreground, not cold enough to warrant the far blanket of cloud, was a tumble of steep ridges, valleys and round volcanic craters playing with the dark shadows. The colour was as indigo as the sixth chakra. They were the bastions of the Andes, running north-south for the length of South America. They served merely as moats for the fortress that arose majestically out of the sea of white cloud just tinged with the last pink of low dawn light. Then, as I watched, its personal cover moved and a dazzling snow summit revealed itself to me. Everything else was dwarfed to insignificance. Even the horizon seemed to fall away in supplication.

Far out!

Chimborazo – Oh mighty Chimborazo, Watchtower of the Universe, are you really there? I felt deeply humbled at the silence of the reply as my mind sensed rays of light from the magnificent peak spreading out around the world. I knew then of the enormity of the job that we had been asked to do, and of the required focus of energy and love for the Earth. Please give us the strength to help us achieve our goal, I prayed, and let us follow our pilgrim path with joy. I determined that we would not fail.

I had seen my mountain. We had met. It was no longer a dream. I wanted to talk excitedly to Pete about it, but my eyes were so heavy. As though all the tension, all the woundupness had been waiting for this moment, it was now safe to let go. For the first time since leaving home, just minutes before touching down in Quito, I finally slept.

I woke with a start as landing rubber met runway. However, instead of the expected usual roar of braking, we floated back up into the air and came crashing down very heavily in a jarring bounce effect. There was a flash of fear from passengers around, but all I could sleepily manage was 'Aha, we've made it over the equator!'

It was with genuine warmth that my neighbour and I said goodbye. We had survived the initial misunderstanding by tiptoeing around issues of differing beliefs. She set off down the plane and turned back.

'Good luck with the mountain, and by the way do be careful not to drink tap water, and only eat fruit and vegetables that have been washed with bottled or boiled water.'

I smiled at her concern. 'Bless you for your help… Bye.' I never did discover what job she did.

'Here, you've got to fill in your immigration card,' urged Pete. It was not as easy as it sounded.

'What do you think the purpose of our visit is? It's not a holiday or business.' I wrote *'Peace business'*.

'I've got to put down what relationship you are to me. What do you reckon?'

'Well we're in Latin America now.'

'OK.' I wrote down *'Lover.'*

'And this bit - What articles are you carrying…?' I wrote *'Personal effects, climbing equipment and messages to the Earth'*.

I decided not to put *'A spoon bent with the strength of world peace coming down'*, nor *'A magic ring to bring back snow from the summit to ensure our safe return'*, nor did I write *'An unbelievably powerful crystal programmed by masters from the other side to help lighten shadows on the Earth'*.

7 - STAR TO FOLLOW

Quito, at 2,850 metres, stands in the ranks of the world's highest capital cities, alongside Lhasa and La Paz at around 3,650 metres. The sense of altitude was elating and was enhanced by a warm and friendly feeling of informality. We had the tarmac to ourselves as we wandered away from the plane, not quite sure which of the airport doors to head for. I sighed in contentment and breathed in deeply the rarefied air that was bright and surprisingly clear. It almost tasted good.

We appeared to be in a wide, densely populated valley with enticing, chocolate coloured mountains to the east and west. I had read that one could actually see snow-topped volcanoes from the city, but today, like most days, distant cloud covered the anticipated vistas along the high valley which runs north-south with the Andean range for the length of Ecuador. Quito nestles naturally into this, the famous 'Avenue of the Volcanoes', so named by Humboldt the German explorer in 1802. The conurbation sprawls for nearly 17 kilometres and is 4 kilometres wide, with a fast growing population of some 1.2 million. Most of the 11 million Ecuadorians live either here in the Sierra or in the sizzling heat of the coastal plain. To the east is the sparsely populated Amazon region of tropical rainforest, the Oriente, and far to the west is that jewel of ecotourism, the Galapagos Islands. I longed to explore all of the wonderful diversity of the country.

No one seemed to mind whether we queued to have our passports stamped or not. In the event we did.

'Buenos dias,' I smiled, with a very English accent, giving my passport to the immigration official who was attempting to look stern by peering down at me through his glasses. It wasn't until later when we were trying to leave Ecuador that I realised that mine had not been stamped anyway. This was about the time when the emigration official did not believe that I had actually come into the country.

Paying US$1 each for baggage carts we wheeled our luggage to the front of the building to be set upon by the reception committee of locals out to get money from unsuspecting new arrivals 'Dinero!', 'Dollars!', 'Taxi', 'Dinero!' There was one scruffy sad-faced lady in a long grubby skirt with a tiny baby and an outstretched hand. I gave her a $1 note. It upset me that not a flicker of warmth entered her expression as though she thought that I was being mean – more likely it showed the harshness of her existence. Further open hands appeared.

'C'mon, let's get in this taxi before we get mobbed,' pressed Pete, chucking our mountain of bags bulging with ropes, ice axes and other climbing equipment into the boot and back seat of the nearest bright yellow vehicle, fending off the bewildering demands, and requests for employment. Diving into the front seat beside the driver I thrust him the address of the hotel. 'Café Cultura, por favor'. Ah well, I thought, as we sped off, that's the sum total of my Spanish. From here on in I'll be making it up – but I didn't work out what to say next, nor did I notice the new world passing by, I just saw the face of the mother with her outstretched hand.

I had been unprepared for the begging. I would have taken it as a matter of course in Asian countries, but why had I not realised that so many South Americans are poor? I had not known then that eighty per cent of Ecuadorians live below the poverty line, whatever that is, and that there is fifty per cent unemployment. Maybe it's only in the Western world that we don't confront real need in such an obvious way. However, being removed from it, in our comfortable lives of 'havingness', only brings with it the responsibility of helping the world balance out – of helping bring harmony. Perhaps so many of humanity's problems are caused by this imbalance. Perhaps, I pondered, China would not have invaded Tibet if it had had enough of what it needed – enough mineral resources, enough timber, enough space for its people. Tibet has such a harsh environment, but China still gives it the name 'Western Treasure House'.

I was still shocked, though, when the taxi driver charged us double the price that the guidebook said was the going rate.

The Café Cultura hotel danced with the energy of bygone colonial days. There were Spanish archways and whitewashed walls reflecting the sun's intensity, cool stone slabs underfoot, grand well-used fireplaces, hanging dried flowers intermingled with tropical plants of intriguing colours, textures and sizes and a welcoming smell of coffee. Our room was dark, slightly musty and washed in a warm rust-brown stencilled with voluptuous bodies in action, ghosts of the character and enticement of gracious living. The doors through to the bathroom were of the slatted high-noon swing variety, as if expecting a lazy cowboy. In our dazed state it felt like we were playing out a part in a film. Happily, we stepped into a cocoon of gentle comfort in which to try and get our bodies and minds into a state of recovery for the work ahead and from which to absorb the exciting new environment.

I sat on the large wooden groaning bed amongst our half-unpacked bags, trying not to fall asleep. My eyes rested on the old rickety carved chest alongside. It displayed a single glass ashtray in the shape of a star.

'Wow! Look Pete,' my befuddled mind sprang to life, 'A six-pointed star.'

Until a few days ago a star had just been a star. Now it mattered how many points it had. This had all come about when a parcel had dropped through my letterbox amongst all the sponsorship forms, cheques, enquiries and cards of good wishes. It was just a normal brown padded post-office bag, but it had held something extraordinary. Well-wrapped in popping plastic protection was a quartz crystal, only about 5 centimetres long but perfectly balanced. A clear masculine pointy end reflected light via the precise symmetry of its sides. The smoky female end was milky and mysterious. Unwrapping it I had held it in the palm of my hand and stared at it, mesmerised. It had felt almost sacrilege to touch it for it carried a sense of unfamiliar and awesome power.

Written on a card were these words:

Channelled by Ivy Smith
Dear Tess,
Souls have been chosen within your earthly world, to carry the light into many remote places. To the mountains that groan for the pain of humanity. You will carry this light, the Divine presence will fill the crystal heart and the pureness of this love will be received by those who live in shadow. Blessed are the souls who by the effort and the purpose of their lives bring the light to others. Your purpose and your dedication will expand throughout the world. The crystal will become a signal, constant in its flow, for many masters have gathered in the spiritual world including myself, Advarr, forming the energy of a star vehicle of pure light. Your imagery as you hold the crystal should be the star. Blessings to you as you journey with heart full, mind open to receive and each step becomes a prayer.

Master Advarr

My body had gone cold, as though an unseen force was walking up and down it. I had been stunned by the implications. We had to undertake to put this crystal on the summit of Chimborazo. Wooh!

Then, two days after, during the frantic preparations to leave, I'd had a phone call from Beverley. He is a mysterious friend who always appears when there is a need, helps and then disappears, like a celestial messenger.

'Hey, Tess. Good luck with the climb. This is my message from the mountain. It's in two parts:

"We hold in the healing light of the Christ star (in the Universal sense)
His Holiness the Dalai Lama - Tenzin Gyatso - Ocean of Wisdom -
and the true leaders and people of Tibet.

We hold in the clear light of love and forgiving compassion the leaders
and people of China."

I had copied his message down over the phone, and then he had said in soft words that imparted loving wisdom 'I have taken council. Mountains have guardian angels. You should recognise and respect this. Ask to be shown the gateways to the approach. Prepare the way sensing the light from the heart of the angel. Feel the loving presence. Know also that your head rests on the heart of your own angel who is in the same light. An angel is a thought of God. Go in willingness, humility and gratitude. And always aim for the highest in your own heart.'

Whilst I was trying to absorb this sagacity, he continued... 'Oh, and you should visualise a six-pointed star.'

Why, I had wondered, further astounded into silence, was he asking me to visualise a six-pointed star? He did, I knew, assist with the healing work at the White Eagle Lodge which was symbolically represented by a six-pointed star.

'It manifests harmony. It cannot be off balance whichever way up it is.'

What deep synchronicity, I had marvelled, was producing the need to tell me to visualise a six-pointed star after the directive from Advarr? There had been no question in my mind that the two requests were connected. It was all very intriguing and strange. It was also beautiful. Maybe there were six spiritual masters working on this.

64

It had been the beginning of a feeling that I was a pawn in a huge game. There was so much going on out there that I just didn't know about, so much that I didn't understand; and yet I had absorbed the sense that it was very important and that my job was a vital part of a mission that was affecting everyone and everything.

Now, here in Quito, to see the ashtray was a jolt for me saying 'Don't forget your quest. You're on the right path.'

I delved into the things-for-the-summit bag and laid the objects out on the bed. It was an extraordinary and precious collection.

I had protected the crystal in a tiny velvety drawstring bag, maroon in colour. Taking it out I placed it on top and stroked it gingerly, as though making friends with a once wild animal. It seemed to glow gently in the dimness of the hotel room. I resolved to carry it in the spirit of love and harmony.

Next to it lay the ring, designed to be worn on the climb. It held a 2 centimetres long rectangular box, fashioned carefully and exquisitely in copper. The lid opened to reveal a small cavity. I read the letter that accompanied it:

…I also enclose a ring I have made with a Tibetan 'OM' on the front. I hope it will bring you good luck. Inside the ring is a message for you, Pete, Migmar and GT. If possible you should open the ring at the top of the mountain. Also if possible you should fill the box on the ring with a grain of rock, snow or air from the top of Chimborazo and bring it back to me. This way you are obliged to come back safely.

Know that our thoughts are with you on the way down the mountain as well as up.

Love Bill

The beautiful words produced a lump in my throat, as the poignancy of our mission lay heavy on me. Bill was the close friend of my son Paul. He cared deeply about the Earth and about what we were doing. To me he was a representative of my children's generation. We were working that there should be an Earth in harmony for their future…

This was Bill's message from the mountain:

"Them can chain me – them can beat me
Them can take me thing – them can stop me sing
Them can mute me – them can shoot me
Them can steal me friend – them can send me dividend
Them can rape me - them can reshape me
Them can bar me light – them can delay me flight
Them can tax me - them can ajax me
Them can kill me body – them can screw me mind
But
Them can't kill I
And – them can't stop me loving them."

Then there was the birdseed – a little cellophane package bulging with yummy-looking, different coloured seeds. It had been sent by Lawley, my children's father. Though we were not married any more, we were still very close and supported each other. During one long telephone conversation I had told him about Vanya Kewley's book *Tibet, Behind the Ice Curtain*, in which she, as a brave journalist, investigates eyewitness accounts of the Tibetan holocaust. She had written of how, on inquiring as to why she had neither seen nor heard any birds during her extensive journeys through Tibet, she had discovered that Chairman Mao of China had ordered all birds, being parasitic to society, to be exterminated. To add to this grave injustice to the Earth, one of the methods by which this perverted deed was carried out was to force the Tibetan children to do it, using fear as a tool to achieve things however abhorrent.

Lawley, as a forester who has worked with nature all his life, very sensitive to its design and handsomeness and with a great love of the wilderness, had been deeply touched by this account. He had asked that the birdseed be distributed on the winds from the highest place in honour and memory of all the birds that had been killed - along with his lovely message from the mountain:

"Tsinghai Plateau
Kisses the sky
Feathered lovers
No longer fly

Nestlings cuddled
Their forest lair
Once nature's belfry
No longer there

Ghosts soar now
Above the peaks
Ghosts of birds that
Never speak

A vision, veiled with
Tears, an old heart weeps   For the whole world
And weeps, prepared on   Remains silent
Borrowed wings to fly   As brave birds die."

The next item was a tiny parcel from Candy, my friend from up the lane. She had been keen to join us on the venture but had not wanted to leave her lifelong pal, an old retriever, Tarka. She had thoughtfully offered to stay behind and assist in the manning of the 'Climb For Tibet' home base along with my kind neighbour, Mary. Then, two weeks before our leaving, Tarka had become sick and had died. In the letting go of this dear and special bond, Candy had written on our form, *'I enclose a small amount of Tarka's fur as the essence of pure love to be scattered across the planet from the Watchtower...so love may blossom...'* with the message:

"Oh, Great Mother Earth, we salute you!
From this the Watchtower of the Universe, may a small seed of understanding sprout and grow so that we may truly realize that we are one and that we may transcend our fears and judgements, pain and separation and all that cripples the world... and know the perfection around us.

Loads of love to Tess, Pete, GT and Migmar. Well done! Now get down safely! xxxx"

Alongside was the small tape-recorder that she had lent us, with which to play a very special tape. It had been made by a talented friend, Gandiva Lorcan, a sacred sound percussionist, using Tibetan singing bowls, gongs and conch horns. I gazed at the case wonderfully decorated with pictures of stars and planets and a magical Buddha hologram that reflected light in all colours. He had given us the tape to play these amazing stirring sounds from the mountain, for the healing of the Earth. It had been lovingly written on with his message and expressions to share:

"Much strength – bravo! Yes! – Harmony – courage – love and peace – respect – beauty – love – joy – brill! – OM MANI PADME HUM."

And then there were Uri's gifts. Again, there had been a phone call out of the blue in that busy week before we had left home.

'Are you going to make it?' came a distinctive and positive voice down the line.

'Er…yes.' I replied cautiously.

'You know that you are going to make it without any shadow of a doubt?'

'Yes, definitely… Who is this?'

'It's Uri Geller here.'

It had been exciting to have his interest. I have long been a fan of his and the unprecedented paranormal powers that he displays. A couple of years previously I had attended one of his talks. He had spoken of holding seeds in the palm of his hand and using mind power to cause them to germinate, of using his psychic powers to aid police work and of coaching footballers in the art of using the mind. He had demonstrated by holding up a key and asking the 300 people in the audience to concentrate on bending it. It had bent double. But most clearly I had remembered his eagerness at the potential of using many minds to bring about world peace.

His trademark that he is renowned for is bending spoons with his mind. I have watched carefully as his fingers, barely touching, stroke the neck of a spoon, which bends mysteriously and carries on bending when he is no longer close to it. It has that 'wow-effect' to draw people's attention so that he can then come in with his important work, that of promoting peace.

It had been arranged that Uri should come on board as one of the patrons of 'Climb For Tibet'. He sent us all copies of his *Little Book of Mind-Power*, one of which he asked could we take to the summit along with a spoon which was to be bent for us. Wooh! I thought, is it the right thing to go littering a mountaintop with so much stuff? It wasn't until much later that I was to be shown the vital significance.

I felt the cold normality of the crazy-shaped spoon and augured with the little orange book, full of inspiring quotes. It opened at the page with one from Shakti Gawain…

'In order to cause a shadow to disappear you must shine light on it.'

This is the quote that we use on all our 'Climb For Tibet' papers. Yeah, that figures, I thought… synchronicity with Uri… just tiny signals that all was flowing well along the path.

I smiled at all the items that I was guarding, thinking no necromancer ever had such opportunity to cast so many good spells. In the spinning of time the different colours and structure of matter, sent in the intention of love and healing, would blend into a blaze of white light…

'Hey Gorgeous,' Pete always had a way of making me feel special. 'If you've finished dreaming, it would be good to have your company to go out and explore the city.'

We wandered out through the little iron gate of Café Cultura. Being Sunday there were few people about giving an unnatural hollow feeling to the streets. There was an empty-looking Chinese restaurant across the narrow road, other hotels and private houses on either side, all with tough lockable gates and impenetrable walls barring access from the street. They were all softened with masses of beautiful flowers, large-leafed tropical plants, palm trees and even the lovely tumbling jacaranda, so that the harshness of mistrust was soon forgotten. There was a random spaciousness that lacked the order of a European city. Half-finished buildings mingled with all types of shops, cafés, banks, hotels, residential dwellings, tourist agencies, empty street trader stalls and welcome green parks. Rubbish was a frequent decoration, but one of the main differences from our own townie existence was the holes and lumps in the pavements and the roads and their ubiquitous state of disrepair.

We were in what is known as the 'new' area of Quito, sprawling north from the 'old' part, which is more colonial, cobbled, churched, crowded and impoverished. The city is a melding of ancient cultures. The Incas had overrun the original Native American Indians in the early 1400s. They were craftsmen of gold, silver and fine cloth, and skilled engineers, creating roads, bridges and remarkable constructions using large blocks of stone. Quito had been the Inca capital in the region until 1553 when the Spanish Conquistadors and their horses had moved in, claiming vast tracks of South America for their European king. Ecuador had finally gained full independence in 1830. Today, the 'new' area is heavily coloured by world trade, especially with the USA, so burger bars and specialist restaurants abound and smart shops aimed at the tourist nestle alongside tiny stalls cooking sweetcorn or sellers offering only chewing-gum and matches.

We managed to find one shop that was open close to our hotel, a little emporium packed with enticing tourist goodies of wonderful colours and textures. It was run by a warm friendly Ecuadorian, with whom we had fun trying to communicate in half English, half Spanish. He showed us hats, ponchos, rugs and pretty woollen clothes, jewellery, trinkets and silver items, bags, pots and ornaments, wonderfully carved and brightly painted wooden figures and plates, and all manner of Andean goods. I was tempted to start buying my presents-to-take-home immediately, but settled for a lovely chess set for Pete's impending birthday. The pieces were carved from plant ivory, tagua, which is a kind of coconut shell. Buying products made from the tagua palm nut is an excellent way of supporting a harvest in a sustainable way that leaves the tree standing, thus helping preserve the threatened but vital 'lungs of our planet', the rainforest.

It was not until we were saying 'Adiós' to our smiley salesman and walking out the door that I noticed a glass jewellery cabinet and glanced in at the display. There, gazing back at me was a necklace. It was the deep blue of lapis lazuli flecked with unique swirl markings and encased in a superbly crafted silver six-pointed star. I was riveted. I knew that this was the star that I was meant to be visualising and that I had been guided to it. Ten minutes without it was enough. Back at the Café Cultura, we immediately turned around and went back. Pete bought it for me as an early birthday present. I have worn it ever since.

Things felt good… and the path led enticingly over the horizon…

8 - Fit for Ecuador

A new day in South America was trying to coax us out of our much-needed fourteen-hour sleep. We breakfasted on plane leftovers and smuggled-in English fare. Tea was made on our little gas canister stove. No irate Ecuadorian maid came charging in with hands held high in horror at the smoke and bubbling steam coming forth from our room, so we figured it was all right to do so.

Making friends with our water filter was quite another matter. We had to devise the best method of operation. It was a two-person job. One had to hold the going-in end of the lively hosepipe underwater, in this case in the basin. The other had to man the pure water coming-out end with bottles, avoiding the inevitable flood. In the middle at least three hands were needed to hold the main filter and move the pump up and down. With the use of knees, towels and co-operation we did eventually get water production.

We knew however that we had to be careful to use only filtered water for everything even the brushing of teeth. Our fitness programme was too important to jeopardise with a dose of the 'runs'. We had to keep our bodies going with the right fuel and exercise. Mine was only reasonably fit. I had not been able to live up to the superman training programme that Pete had devised. I had managed fairly well to fit into each week two jogging sessions of thirty minutes, two or three swims of forty minutes, a ski on the plastic slope, two climbing sessions on the wall, five yoga sessions, a sauna and even to sneak in two games of tennis which was not really considered aerobic enough... but I had found that I was not able to increase my work output by running faster or swimming more lengths. Pete had told me 'You'll never get up Chimborazo if you don't do more.' However, if I pushed myself further I tended to get injuries and strains and I had not wanted to cause a serious setback by having to rest and do no exercise at all. That would have been worse, especially as I have the sort of body that objects if it has a day without some sort of movement, either by seizing up or by letting the mind go

71

soggy. So my fitness training had always been a bit like Buddhism, trying to find the middle way, doing enough but not too much.

Pete's own build-up training had always been impressive. I would get asked out on a date, 'Fancy a nice day out? Let's do a twenty-mile run.' I suppose I could have teamed up with a weakling.

Food knowledge had been much more my cup of tea. After many years of studying the best nutrition for my children, I find myself very sensitive to what my body feels good on. It likes bananas, lots of bananas. Eating twelve in a morning is not unusual. Maybe there was some sort of karmic debt payback in finding myself in a country that is the world's biggest banana exporter and where one can buy a bunch of fifty bananas for less than the price of an English nail.

Ideally, I like as much fruit as possible early in the day. Then I go for salads, steamed vegetables, eggs, some dairy protein, nuts, seeds, pulses, and wholemeal rice, bread and pasta. I try to stick with simple organic wholefoods wherever possible, no fat, no sugar, no chemicals, no tea, no coffee, no alcohol… at least that was until Pete and I met up and we made an agreement. He would become vegetarian and I would become alcoholic. He kept his part of the bargain and gave up meat. I immediately took up having two small beers per year and little sips of wine – but it's not always easy to keep to.

I know that I feel better on not mixing carbohydrates and protein in one meal as it simplifies the digestion making more energy available. I also know that I feel more alive without wheat and dairy products, although I don't often stick to that one. If I want to feel great I have a day on only fruit. It's a tough discipline, but it helps detoxify. Strictly it should be without bananas, but bananas keep me going.

If I want to get the best out of my middle-aged body machine, I find I have to work hard caring for it. I have to keep out the ubiquitous rubbish, I have to not overfeed it or everything slows down and goes soggy, and I have to put in the most real and live foods and supplements I can find. Everyone is different. By contrast to mine, Pete's body seems to be fit whatever he puts in it, even Mars Bars and custard.

What to eat seems to be a battle between putting into one's system that which will give the body optimum aliveness and energy, and that which 'civilisation' throws at one in a convenient form made to look and taste yummy. Sadly, these two aspects are usually conflicting. So diets strict at home are much harder to maintain when one is out and about. It needs foresight. Stemming from my mothering principal of always carrying healthy snacks to keep children happy, I tend to always have with me supplies of apples, dates, seeds, nuts, oatcakes and of course bananas. We had been able to bring with us useful quantities of these (even dried bananas). This gave us the opportunity to keep up a reasonably similar diet to the lead-up training programme. Our goal was important. We were going to ask our bodies to push to their limits of fitness. Therefore, we had had to raise that level. Now, muscles had to be maintained with protein, fuelled with carbohydrates and kept in good working order with vegetables. The latter, I knew from experience, was the hardest to find in a safe edible form. Friends of mine were used to me pacing up and down restaurants growling with salad-withdrawal symptoms. I wondered how it would be now in Ecuador.

'Right! Let's go!' Pete as always was ready to go out long before me. 'We've got a long list of things to do today.'

My body groaned quietly. Why was he always so efficient and full of energy? I was feeling very lethargic in spite of the long sleep and would have happily spent the day curled up reading a book. I was not thinking very clearly and had a bit of a headache.

'Everyone says that you should spend the first day here resting and getting used to being at nearly 3,000 metres,' I tried, knowing full well what the response would be.

'Well, I feel quite normal and anyway it's absolutely essential that we climb something tomorrow. We've got to start the acclimatization programme. I think we should head in the direction of the volcano Pichincha, with two summits at 4,700 and 4,794 metres. It would be great to go high, but let's see how far we can get. It's really close by, right on the western outskirts of the city, but we've got to find out how to get there.'

I had to admit that, so far, I had not been feeling breathless at all. The books said we probably would do at this altitude. The reduced oxygen here from the lower pressure meant that we should be breathing nearly fifty per cent more often to obtain the same amount of oxygen that we had been used to at home, close to sea level. We had to give our bodies time to increase the red corpuscle count and make biochemical changes in the blood to be able to absorb the oxygen necessary to function at normal capacity. It would take months for complete acclimatization, but generally it seemed to be accepted that over a period of at least two weeks, with gradual increase in altitude exposure, it was safe for climbers to be at 6,000 metres. The maxim is 'ascend at 300-500 metres per day'. In practice many people overdo this for they lead lives too busy, and have too many mountaineering ambitions to fit in the optimum rate. Pete and I had three weeks to acclimatize, Mig and GT rather less, but we thought that this would be fine. The plan was to spend time at the Quito altitude, and progressively go up higher and higher mountains. This would work the body walking and climbing, whilst carrying out the physiological changes necessary, ready for the 6,310 metres push on Chimborazo.

I wondered if Mig would carry any genetic adaptations to altitude. Although he had never lived at any height other than near sea level, his parents had escaped out of Tibet and all their previous generations had lived there above 3,500 metres. Certainly the descendants of the high-living Inca Indians have enlarged lung capacities. Time would tell.

It was not possible to know for sure how well or how badly any of us would cope. The acclimatization process is something unique to the individual and to each occasion. Fitness, surprisingly, does not seem to be relevant. GT had climbed previously at 6,000 metres in the Tien Shan with no altitude problems. Similarly Pete had scaled all the major European Alps to 4,800 metres. I had experienced no adverse effects at 3,500 metres whilst men around me were on their knees, vomiting and with excruciating headaches. I had suggested at the time that I was not suffering because of being female, a theory that had not gone down at all well.

I did know that, if we got the preparations wrong, it would not be much fun. People die. Climbing too high, too fast leads to Acute Mountain Sickness or 'soroche' as it is known in the Andes. It manifests as dizziness, headaches, shortness of breath, nausea, vomiting, fatigue, insomnia, dehydration, loss of appetite and periods of not breathing during sleep. This progresses to High Altitude Pulmonary Oedema which is fluid collecting in the lungs, and High Altitude Cerebral Oedema which is fluid accumulating in the brain. Both of these conditions demand an immediate descent to lower altitude for survival.

We could help keep altitude sickness at bay by taking things gently - some hope! We could drink a lot of water - but I did not yet know the word for 'loo' in Spanish. We could take Diamox, which acidifies the blood thus increasing respiration

74

- although side effects include tingling extremities and even more trips to the loo, and we could also take coca. The coca plant has been widely cultivated in the Andes for 4,000 years. The leaves are chewed and coca tea, or maté, is drunk. This wards off the effects of altitude, hunger and fatigue. It also relieves pain. By its use in sacred ritual it has long been an important part of the spiritual life of the Andean peoples, who now find their livelihood threatened by the plan to eradicate its growth – the civilised Western world derived cocaine from it and put it to 'good abuse'.

I decided not to take any Diamox, but took my homeopathic coca pill and dragged my complaining body out. To have the best chance of getting up Chimborazo we had to take every opportunity to adapt to the rarefied air, so I reluctantly agreed that we should plan to go up something the next day. Anyway it was Pete's birthday tomorrow so what better way to celebrate it than to climb a mountain.

We headed into the hustle and bustle of the now busy Monday morning streets. The exhaust pollution in the air was noticeably bad, and on the main arteries every other vehicle seemed to be a bus belching huge black smoke signals. The clamour of the engines and the frequent horns of the rattling old taxis added to the furore of trying to find our way around, but everyone we communicated with in trial Spanish words, gesticulations and smiles was friendly and helpful. Surprisingly, a few people even understood English and we would occasionally hear American pop songs wafting out from some of the cafés. The sun shone down with a perfect T-shirt temperature and I very soon felt at ease.

We found the South American Explorers Club on Jorge Washington Street. The whitewashed colonial façade displayed the colourful Ecuadorian flag, blowing proudly in the breeze. At its heart was the national crest. It depicted Mount Chimborazo. Standing guard was the Andean condor, wings outstretched. The striped background was of yellow for sunshine, corn and wealth; blue for rivers, sea and air; and red for the blood of patriots who fought for freedom and justice. Just for a moment my hand went to the Tibetan flag on the 'Climb For Tibet' T-shirt that I was wearing. The colours were similar, but the Tibetan blood that had been spilt had not brought about freedom and justice. I prayed that it would not have been spilt in vain. I prayed that the courage of the Tibetans and their long patient battle in the spirit of non-violence would result in a wider lasting freedom and justice for the world.

The South American Explorers Club is a wonderful haven for travellers. It offers all sorts of advice and local information, books, tea, mail, message collection, email and fax facilities, although we never did coincide with an occasion when the latter was actually working. We fired copious questions at Roger and Sheila, the warm multilingual North Americans who ran the club… places to stay?… how to travel around?… mountains to climb?… money to change?… where to find food?… what are the best type of bananas to buy?… where to see condors?… when will it rain?… what to do about taxi rip-off syndrome?… do the Indian men here really drink kerosene to kill the germs inside?… what is the significance of the Incas eating guinea pigs?… is Chimborazo in good condition?

… Yes, Pichincha would be an excellent mountain to climb for early acclimatization… thought to be the first major peak in the world to be climbed by a European (the Spaniard, Ortiguera, in 1582)… The summits are Rucu Pichincha, meaning 'old boiling mountain', and Guagua Pichincha, meaning 'baby boiling mountain'… Opinions vary as to their actual heights… Nice and close to Quito, only 10 kilometres or so… Yes, fine for a day trip… Ask a taxi to drop you off at Cruz Loma… no problemo… Have a nice day… and whatever you do don't go on foot up the first bit, it's far too dangerous… Our thoughts went to rock-fall and other climbing hazards… but no… it was rape, bandidos and rabid dogs…

We walked the streets of the city a little taken aback by the rawness of the Ecuadorian way of life, and the feeling that we were in a Wild West movie that underlay the smart tourist façade. The guide book said watch out for strangers offering you biscuits that have been injected with horse tranquillisers and be wary of robbers who like to give rucksacks the slit-open-with-razor-blade treatment. I felt that if it was possible to keep a high vibration by holding love and not fear in our hearts, then no harm would be attracted to us. So I did not worry. After all we were giving out the energy of the intention of a peace climb to help the Earth, and we were carrying many loving messages, so surely all would be well.

I thought of the beautiful understanding that my father had given to me a few weeks after he had passed out of his body. I had felt that we were communicating at a mind to mind level. You could say that it was my imagination, but I had sensed and seen him as he had been in the prime of his life, with dark hair at about twenty-five years of age. He had been with his mother, my grandmother. They had been laughing and joyous. He had explained that he could now be involved in our world, and in guiding loved ones, not so much by seeing what we are doing but by seeing the energy that we are giving off. Thus it is not what we do or say that matters, so much as what we feel about it, what thoughts we have and what we hold in our hearts. These determine the vibration of the energy we give off. He could see the emanations from the trees and the animals and especially from us all. So he knew if we were feeling love in our hearts and thinking loving thoughts. This view from a different reality had been scary in that it took away the apparent privacy of individuality, but its perception had been a precious gift for me. I knew that I forgot it all too easily. Now, in its remembering, it gave me comfort and strength.

Outside the money exchange agency there was a security policeman with a huge rifle. He looked barely sixteen years old. Inside we changed travellers cheques in US dollars into hundreds of thousands of sucres. It would be easy to become a millionaire, but we were careful not to have too much inflation-loving local currency. Anyway it seemed possible to pay all large bills in US dollars.

Our new-found wealth seemed to draw those in need. On the busy Avenida Amazonas lined with enticing shops and extravagantly displayed market stalls, Pete suddenly found himself with a hitchhiker. A tiny girl in a baggy pink top and a long skirt above dirty bare feet had grabbed one of his hands with both of hers and would not let go. She looked about three years old. Her mother, who was sitting on the pavement training her little one to attract attention and beg for money, was encouraging her 'Vas! Vas!' It took much dinero for Pete to be able to extract his hand.

A long walk through parks lined with palms and araucarias and a circular road up a hill made us catch our breath just a little and slow down. At the top was the only place in the country to buy large-scale maps, *Instituto Geographico Militar – Unidos por la ciencia y el espiritu para el progreso del Ecuador*. We reluctantly left our passports at the gate with armed soldiers and emerged nearly two hours later with a 1:50,000 map of Chimborazo and a 1:25,000 of the Quito area. Neither of these ended up being detailed or accurate enough for the kind of let's-not-get-lost use that we had in mind - but there was a good view of the city from the hill.

On the way down we stopped at the smallest of shops, about half a metre wide, decorated with cheerful bunting. It was selling bright yellow homemade-type confectionery and apples and plums. The sweets might have worked as unusual paperweights to take home, but we decided to go for bags of the fruit, which we longingly carried back to be washed in our water filter production line.

Visiting eco-tour operators, finding butane camping-gaz cylinders, unsuccessful attempts at finding fax machines and telephones, and being postman for friends in England, finally left even Pete tired and hungry. We managed to track down 'el Magic Bean', the renowned hangout eating house which advertises 'all vegetables washed in boiled water', and enjoyed to my great delight a huge salad, sitting under a lovely hanging vine. We would have also enjoyed the soup if my linguistic abilities had ordered pea and beans instead of pea and ham. I never did discover how to say the word for vegetarian.

Ecuador, you have welcomed us with colour and a smile, I thought, as I crawled wearily into bed that night. Our friend Avril, from Amora International who were planning to produce a documentary on the climb, had advised us on what to shoot with the video camera. She had said 'Always look for things that are beautiful'. Yes, no problemo, there will be plenty of stuff to film here.

9 - GETTING HIGH

It had to be a pre-dawn start, to organise morning tea in bed for the birthday boy. The chess set, well received, was artistically wrapped up in the Ecuadorian equivalent of 'The Daily Mail', and tied with deep pink ribbons. These I had borrowed from three special scrolls on their way to Chimborazo. They had been sent with us by our friend Delphine who had given 'Climb For Tibet' enormous support. In her wise sensitivity to the Tibetan cause and understanding of the spiritual implications, she had asked that we gather rocks and build three 'stupas' at the gateway to the mountain. These were to be little cairns or monuments, which in the Buddhist tradition are a focus of prayer and pilgrimage. They work as symbols of peace and harmony in the embodiment of the limitless compassion of a pure heart, which is said to be free of the ignorance, attachment and aversion that cause personal and global suffering. They transmit positive energy. Stupas hold great importance.

In each of these was to be buried a scroll, inscribed with a prayer by Kuan Yin, the Chinese Goddess of Ultimate Compassion, and they were then to be activated by speaking peace messages. In this way we would be helping to create the energy of compassion necessary for the climb and its long-term effects. The job of the pink ribbons was to tie up with grace the representations of birth.

'Happy Birthday, old boy. Now you're so ancient, maybe it'll slow you down a bit,' I suggested hopefully.

'C'mon, you cheeky thing, get ready. We've got a long climb ahead. I'll organise the taxi to Cruz Loma.'

I gobbled my favourite action breakfast of organic oats, dates, sunflower seeds, soya protein powder, vitamin C and guarana, which is the legendary ground-up seed long used by the Amazon Indians for endurance and clarity of mind. I then threw into a rucksack the essentials – Spanish dictionary, water-proofs, fleece, hat, gloves, water bottles, carbohydrate foods and dried fruit, compass, ski sticks, camera, flag and Yannick penguin – grabbed my boots and headed out into the waiting day. It did not seem much preparation for a mountain with a summit the height of Mont Blanc but then, I figured, things work differently in South America.

The old yellow taxi seemed particularly rickety as we bounced happily along the Quito streets with the smiley driver chatting away to us. I was enjoying the conversation, but seemed only to understand every tenth word or so. I discovered that if one took a French, Latin or English word and added an 'o' to it then it was possible to get along quite nicely in a friendly sort of a way. Every now and then I would say 'Por favor, bamus a Cruz Loma, si? Bamus a monto escalo a Pichincha'. Roughly translated, I noticed later, this means something like 'We are going to ride the ladder at Pichincha', but the driver always nodded and smiled assuredly 'Si, si. No problemo.'

It took us a while to become orientated being in the southern hemisphere with the sun in the north-east, but after about an hour of driving around we realised that we were going generally south. We had thought that the journey should be about twenty minutes to the west. Enquiries still produced 'Si, si. No problemo,' so there was nothing for it but to sit back, enjoy the view and wait to see where the driver thought that we should be going. This was a technique that we became quite good at during our stay in Ecuador.

We left the old part of the city, with its narrow crowded cobbled streets, and red tiled colonial buildings, passing through poverty stricken residential areas and took a dirt road uphill. Huge gravel trucks passed us in clouds of dust as the little taxi struggled onwards, reaching a pass and then wound its way down to a small village. Suddenly we had stepped into an agricultural area that looked as though it had remained unchanged for hundreds of years. There were chickens and dogs and small children playing, but scarcely a suggestion of the modern world.

Our driver, whose name we learned was Fernando, drove back and forth with much wrong turning and asking of directions from the villagers. This was obviously not a regular taxi route, but he eventually found a rough track going north-west that he seemed to be happy with. Not so the little car which spluttered and coughed as the gradient became steeper and steeper, crunching its undercarriage on the rocks that had been piled into the ditches and holes, and skidded on the soft dry sand. Pete's concern over where we were was shifting to the battering the car was taking.

'He's very brave, but it's getting wrecked.'

It was a Lada. Somehow I managed to communicate to Fernando that back home in England I had a Skoda, a near relation. He beamed and responded with a tirade of expletives.

'We're OK now,' I turned to Pete. 'I think we're life-long buddies. He's so impressed that I drive a Skoda.'

'He's just being polite,' came the reply, but I felt that there was power in a small synchronicity that made friends out of strangers from different worlds. I was reminded of a peace message:

"In the communicating of similarities is the finding of harmony between peoples."

We took to pushing up the steepest bits, and resting when there were clouds of steam coming from the engine. It gave us a chance to see the magnificent scenery. We were in verdant farmland. It was mostly patchwork agriculture, small fields, steep and well terraced. The black and white cattle looked fat and healthy. Young heifers and steers gazed at us through fences made from stakes that were themselves sprouting, such was the fertility of the rich volcanic soil. Sweet little black piglets snuffled around fine horses with intelligent eyes, and large-leafed plants rambled as though with picturesque intent. It was all so prolific and green, reminding me of Queensland, Australia. There were even rows of tall eucalyptus amongst spinneys of native forest, all a lovely example of nature and man working well together.

As we gained more height we could see voluminous cloud formations drifting south to the far distance, joining the alluring nebulous covers of the Avenue of the Volcanoes. Somewhere down there was Cotopaxi… and beyond that… Chimborazo.

Then came the moment that we had been expecting. Fernando declared the rabbit-warren-like track impassable and he would go down. Pushing and lifting we helped turn the car around in the narrow space mindful of the steep precipice on one side. In hugging 'hasta la vista' and negotiating the rather more than standard fare, we managed to communicate great thanks to him for his valiant efforts in getting us this far. We even managed to explain that it was Pete's birthday (a

81

difficult concept in sign language), but we were not sure if we had convinced him to try and pick us up later. It was a very remote chance anyway that he would actually want to, given the state of his beaten up little car... We watched forlornly as the yellow city taxi disappeared over the horizon leaving us alone in thousands of square kilometres of mountain, not quite the one we had planned to climb, but it appeared we had no choice.

Gradually we left the trees behind and the green gave way to the warm and lovely beige of tussock grasses blowing in the gathering wind. This was the beginning of the Andean páramo. Ahead of us a dark volcanic plug loomed, drawing us on. Could this be Pichincha after all? It must be Guagua Pichincha, but from the other side.

It took us only three hours to follow the track to 4,500 metres where there was a locked up volcanologists' refuge hut at the base of the tuffaceous cone. We saw no-one except for a man with a shovel and a muddy grey horse, which appeared to be the road maintenance crew.

I felt fine apart from a slight headache that was soon sorted out with guarana, but we were careful to go slowly and steadily and not overexert ourselves. What a breeze, we concurred, as we were scarcely out of breath. Thank goodness for our fitness. We had spent some time in the Alps a couple of months ago, skiing and ski-mountaineering, and keeping as high as possible for as long as possible. We had even dug a snow hole at 3,000 metres and slept a cold night in it, thinking it to be useful training should we be benighted. It felt like we were retaining some of the acclimatization gained then.

Suddenly the wind got up and it became really cold. In the lea of the hut we put on all the clothes we had and got moving across the brittle volcanic ash to the rim of the crater. It was only then that I realised how Pichincha had got its name, 'boiling mountain'. It is an 'active' volcano. We had been warned that in 1993 volcanic gases in the crater had overcome a group of people and everyone had died. I understood it then, standing on the edge of the cauldron in the howling wind, with an eerie swirling mist bellowing out, sulphur fumes attacking my nostrils, and peering down into a white nothing which I knew to be 700 metres deep. Momentarily the smoking spectre veered and I saw tall pyroclastic pinnacles reaching out. I shuddered not wanting to stay there too long, but caught mesmerised by the stunning scene. Then, turning, I hurried on after Pete up the crater edge to the high point, one foot in the warm blood of Mother Earth.

Above the summit rock, painted 4,781 metres, we flew the Tibetan flag and with raised hands palmed together chanted 'OM MANI PADME HUM'. This is the popular blessing generally interpreted as 'hail to the jewel in the lotus', invoking His Holiness the Dalai Lama, the embodiment of compassion. It is always spoken for the wellbeing of all sentient beings. The spirit of Tibet soared on the wild Andean winds and we were content. Though we had been further and higher than we knew we should have, our first peak had been reached with relative ease and it augured well for the whole venture.

Then down. Ash running was fun in the descent of the first bit at an angle of about 35° and we laughed at the exhilaration. Afterwards came the long slog. Down... down... two hours... three hours... four... The soles of my feet hurt intensely and my knees were heavy and crying out with shooting pains. Thank goodness for the ski sticks to take some of the downward pressure. But I was so tired. We were both so very tired (well, Pete was quite tired.) Sometimes I thought that I could go no further, and then there was a little burst of renewed energy. The eyes saw so much beauty, but the body pleaded 'Stop! Stop!' knowing that there was no choice. A night out at this altitude with no gear was not something we wanted to contemplate. Perhaps this was a test for us to try out our resolve, a practice run to keep the mind focused and to gather strength.

In spite of the pain, or just maybe because of it, I felt that there was a sense of being guided, that there was spiritual assistance available. This feeling was to remain with me. I wished that I had brought the crystal. For some reason I felt that it would be easier to access help with it. I decided always to carry it with me in future.

Night fell fast, killing a rose-quartz evening sky. It was 6.30 pm. The suddenness of it surprised us. We had not yet become used to being so close to the equator. Hobbling on, through the darkening gloom, we eventually came to a place where we could just make out the first outlying little farmstead of the village. There, next to it, like a vision of an angel, stood a small yellow taxi... and then there was Fernando rushing out to take our rucksacks. How very sweet it was.

'Someone upstairs is looking after us.' Pete grinned, but I am not sure that he thought that later back at the hotel when he was raring to go out for the birthday supper that he had been looking forward to. Feeling like I would never walk again, shivering all over and unable to eat, I refused to go. He went out, and returned after a while with a bag of chips.

I knew that my system was in a weakened state and had not yet recovered from the stress in the lead-up to coming and the lack of sleep on the flight out and

83

that I had overdone the altitude adaptation, which had caught up with me. It seemed to be a delayed reaction. I continued to shake, had a raised temperature, felt dizzy and could not sleep all night. Every two hours I took vitamin C and homeopathic belladonna. It was to this that I attributed the fact that the chills had gone in the morning and that I could climb out of bed. However, we were both unsettled and bad tempered with each other, and the tiredness meant that we were not thinking things through very clearly. There was much to discuss, research and decide which was annoying whilst we were grumpy.

We talked a lot about Chimborazo. Pete's main worries were about the practicalities of getting up it and making sure that everyone was to be safe. Being the most experienced member of the team, this responsibility lay heavily on him, particularly with Migmar being a novice. I was more concerned with making sure that we carried out properly all that we should do for it to be a pilgrimage up to the Watchtower of the Universe with the intent of helping Tibet and the Earth. We decided that the two days we had before Mig came would be put to best use by journeying down to the mountain to do a recce.

The main problem before that was to establish a suitable base in Quito, somewhere that was cheap and able to accommodate the comings and goings of our expanding team. There was also the possibility of a film crew joining us. We wearily traipsed the streets checking out various recommendations. Eventually we narrowed the options down to two, one hostel that Pete liked and one that I liked. There seemed to be no compromise to our disagreement.

'Well, there's only one way to sort out an argument' he said, taking out a coin. 'Call!'

'Heads!' I obliged, my gambling instincts coming to the fore.

'Heads it is. You win.' He conceded graciously. With our accommodation sorted out we became more at ease and tolerant with each other. By allowing the apparent wider influence of lady luck to decide, we had dived into the river of life with all its interacting forces and were going with the flow, rather than clinging to our own hanging branches. We had moved a little towards trusting that all would be well.

I was really happy with the place that the 'river' had provided for us, the Hostal Posada del Maple. It was in the centre of the new area near the main street Avenida 6 de Diciembre, so named after Quito's day of foundation. It was in a quiet little street Juan Rodriguez, which was stuffed full of pollarded but shady maple trees. There were two delightful courtyards painted in the typical burnt-pink colour, and dripping with lovely ferns and tropical plants. Interesting items of Ecuadorian art abounded and it was run by a charming lady Manuela who spoke good English. We arranged to leave some gear there whilst on the Chimborazo recce.

However, more frustrations were in store for us that thrust us back into a grumpy mood. We had a long list of people in England and the USA to get in touch with, not the least of whom were our children. Having tried unsuccessfully the South American Explorers Club and various hotels, we discovered the telecom centre a lengthy walk away. Here we queued, handed over money and were sent to little cubicles in abortive attempts to find overseas lines. It seemed that there were blockages everywhere. It was perhaps a good thing that we did not know then that communications with the outside world, essential to the running of 'Climb For Tibet', were always to be fraught with difficulties. It was as though we were being told 'focus on the 'here'… focus on the 'now'… the important thing is that you get up the mountain in the 'right spirit'.

That thought helped me find some inner peace. After all, how I felt had to come from me. I could not blame what was going on in the environment around me. If I was giving out churning, soggy, boring vibes then that is what the 'river' would be like. If I was in harmony with myself, then I would float in peaceful loving energy.

'C'mon girl, get a grip,' I told myself 'you're doing exactly what you want to do with your life. This is exactly where you need to be…'

Back at the Café Cultura for our last night we tried to celebrate the delayed birthday with a nice meal by a welcoming log fire, but with my two sips of wine, I was gone. Sleep, the great healer, took over and finished the work of restoring my equanimity.

10 - The way to Chimborazo

I couldn't wait to be near Chimborazo. We were going to see our special sacred eminence of the Earth. Our feet were actually going to touch the lower reaches of the mountain about which we had talked and dreamed for so long.

We rationalised that it was logical to go down to assess things whilst there was just the two of us. It would help the planning of the climb itself. However it felt as though we were cheating... going too soon... we weren't acclimatized... we didn't have the whole team with us... the time was not yet right. But we were being drawn there. We both knew that we could not keep away... we had to go. Yet like a premature birth, there would be no going back... there could be only one first meeting. I would savour this journey.

We rose early at 5.00 am, pumped water for all our bottles, packed up, taxied our spare bags to Posada del Maple and ourselves to Terminal Terrestre de Cumandá, Quito's main bus station.

'I wonder if they all go to taxi-rip-off night school.' I said to Pete as we were done as usual, paying far more than we should have. 'Ah well, maybe it's helping balance out the world.' It was almost comforting as it was expected. Maybe it happened because we held the expectation in our minds and that was the energy we gave out. Maybe this was the way the karma of my own greed was working its way through.

It had cost us 60,000 sucres for the short trip, whereas the whole four hour bus journey to Riobamba, a distance of nearly 200 kilometres, would only be 17,000 sucres (about £2 sterling) – though this was not the height of luxury.

We drew noisily out of the bus station emitting the predictable smelly black fumes into the early morning rush hour. We were very much part of the pollution haze that hung everywhere, adding to the low cloud. The driver drove fast, weaving in and out of the people walking in the road, the languishing broken-down vehicles and the ubiquitous cracks and other hazards. The bus stopped frequently and soon filled up with men, women and children piling on and off with varying interesting looking loads. One Quechuan Indian lady in a red shawl and typical Ecuadorian hat brought a basket of what could have been washing, and one a little wicker bird cage from which loud cheepings were coming forth. From the front of the bus emanated a strange sort of wailing. One man was wearing a smart Western-type suit. Everyone was smiling and joking and it felt like in their day-to-day business there was an air of contentment. There was a TV on board so there was nothing better than to be able to travel along watching the national pastime – the football.

We sat at the back, thinking that the elevated rear seats would offer us the best view (of Ecuador, not the football). Squashed between one that was completely full of holes and one that had collapsed, I settled down to writing my diary up to date, a job which soon became difficult and then impossible to carry out with anything but an unintelligible scribble, as the bumps grew in magnitude. I looked up to see my erstwhile imperturbable boyfriend flying through the air, hitting his head on the roof of the jolting old bus, and succumbed to a helpless fit of the giggles.

'Very funny,' he laughed, rubbing the bruise. 'I see why they all wear hats... How can we possibly film in this roller coaster?' He had at the ready our little Sony digital video camera which was capable of producing broadcast quality footage - if it could be held steady. We had been charged with filming everything interesting. I tended to press all the wrong buttons and take fantastic pictures of my feet, but Pete was very good at it. 'I was hoping to get some worthwhile stuff going along.'

'Well, we'll have to be part of the 'being' instead of 'the observers'' I commented, regaining my composure whilst hanging on tight to the bar on the seat in front.

In fact we seemed to be rather more 'the observed'. In spite of the football, we were receiving sidelong glances and downright stares. This was not in an unfriendly way, just that, as accepted in a child, it was OK to look at peculiar things. A wonderful old Indian man came and sat beside Pete in the collapsing seat. He was of the usual stocky build with a bright red striped poncho and standard brimmed hat. His face was dark brown and weather beaten, his nose aquiline and distinguished. There was a simple proudness about him that said 'my race has walked this land for generations'... He stared fascinated by the hairy beard on this tall stranger. Suddenly he could contain himself no longer. Reaching across the hessian bag of celery that he was holding, he pulled at the tawny hair on Pete's arm. His face lit up in a brilliant smile, which even his brown and broken teeth could not dull. Then he gently stroked his own hairless arm.

Was this another example of the breaking down of barriers between nations?

"In the understanding of differences is also the finding of harmony between peoples."

My mind drifted to the Tibetan situation. Maybe, I pondered, even though very many of the Chinese people themselves have been victims, their oppression of Tibetans is a reaction of fear due to not fully understanding the basic difference between the two peoples. A way of life with the top priority being given to the State and its laws is inevitably different from a way of life that gives this ultimate position to a monk and his teachings.

Better communication should help further this understanding of differences. So with the explosion of information available through computer technology, which youngsters in particular seem to thrive on, there is hope for the future.

If we, the body of humanity, like the world wide web, are one interconnected energy system, then we are partly Chinese. More to the point we are more than one fifth Chinese. That's quite a lot of body. The more we try and understand the differences of the parts of our body, the more in harmony it will be and this cuts both ways.

Education for all is therefore critical. However, for Tibetans in Tibet, particularly in rural areas with an eighty per cent illiteracy rate, there is little access to formal education. The monasteries used to be the seats of learning, but the Chinese destroyed virtually all 6,000 and banned many of the religious practices. (Today many have been rebuilt to encourage the tourist dollar). So for the Tibetan, by deliberate racial discrimination, there is little opportunity for jobs and consequently food and housing are limited. To make matters worse they are now outnumbered by Han Chinese, who have been moved in.

There must be a way forward, as there can never be a way back now to the old ways. There must be a way forward in peace and harmony and understanding. The UN charter states that everyone has the basic right to freedom.

All of a sudden there was pandemonium on the bus. The wailing became mewing and a little bundle of black and white fur darted fearfully between the doubled up legs, looking for freedom and safety. Various passengers dived to catch the runaway amidst cursings and shoutings, but to no avail. Then the mewing became louder as our smooth new friend next to Pete calmly grabbed the kitten by the scruff of the neck and delivered him to his owner who returned him to the bag from which he had escaped. She was also an Ecuadorian Indian in shawl and hat, with big beautiful earrings and a cracked-teeth smile to match. Peace was restored.

The road to Chimborazo lay due south from Quito along the Pan-American highway, following the Central Valley of the Andes, the 'Avenue of the Volcanoes'. I wished that we could see beyond the tantalising cloud cover, but all of Ecuador's mountain jewels remained hidden. A kind lady shyly took to being our tour guide. We smiled and nodded with her and thought that we picked out a few sentences such as 'This is Cotopaxi to the left of the bus'; 'That is Iliniza to the right' and 'Why have you got a pink and purple penguin attached to your rucksack?'

Once we had left the city behind, green fields and agriculture were all around us. My eyes absorbed a predominance of dairy cattle, pigs, plantations of maize, cabbages, potatoes, large glasshouses for market gardening, eucalyptus and pine windbreaks, small flat-roofed dwellings, all with TV aerials and pretty white lilies, larger and more wealthy looking haciendas and always dogs. The lush fertile farms filled the picturesque landscape until meeting the distant black lava of the volcano slopes. Villages clustering along the main highway displayed falling down mud-brick houses, light workshops, piles of old rubber tyres and young men playing volley ball. There were market stalls, fruit and vegetable stands and, for the fast food connoisseur, roast guinea pig on a spit.

Fine churches with beautiful flowerbeds carried sway over the busy towns. It was here that noisy colourful street sellers boarded the bus whilst we slowed through traffic. They carried bulging baskets and touted their wares of interesting unknown foods, sweets and fried biscuits, that we were tempted to try but decided not to risk - particularly the speciality 'allullas' that are made from flour, pork fat and unpasteurized cheese. Pete did go for a strange orange drink. Buying it was one thing, drinking it whilst jumping up and down at a great rate was quite another, as the roads were contenders for the worst-in-the-world award. They were made more interesting by the fact that the holes were holier at the sides, so there was a natural tendency for drivers from both directions to aim at the same bit of road –

the middle.

We had a welcome stop for petrol, which seemed to be more expensive than in Britain, even though oil accounts for forty per cent of Ecuador's exports. Maybe this came with the modern world grating on an ancient gentler way of life. Yet all of us, the Indian locals who were the descendants of the fabled Inca people, those of the Spanish invader, and the modern tourist come to pay homage to a mountain in the spirit of a far off culture, all melded into a happy travelling family. A young man, looking scarcely more than fourteen years old in an old pair of jeans, staggered up and down the aisle, taking money from this group come together, though he gave no tickets.

The bus gained some height and went over a pass at 3,500 metres through pine plantations just as it began to rain, dulling our view further. Then the road dropped and we rattled and bounced down into Latacunga. This town has the rather unlucky distinction of having been totally wiped out by the erupting Cotopaxi three times, in 1742, 1768 and 1877. It says something about the trust of human nature that today it is a bustling well-built centre of 40,000 people, even though Cotopaxi continues to exhibit fumarolic activity.

A swarthy young man with a cigarette boarded, happily the only human smoker that we had seen. A lady with a baby wrapped up in a bundle got off. The little one had been considerably quieter than the cat. He was probably used to long hours strapped to his mother's back as she hoed the soil like many that we passed by. Potato crops became more frequent as we moved south and the land became dryer and dustier. Cactuses abounded and gardens became less frequent. Ambato, the next main town had been wrecked by an earthquake in 1949, but had been beautifully reconstructed with impressive avenues and fine buildings – the joys of renewal.

Climbing steeply out of the town alongside a truck full of complaining chickens, and a sheep riding precariously on the roof of a car, we had a growing sense of anticipation. Somewhere to the west, beyond the terraced slopes, behind a screen of cloud, lay a volcano that had not erupted for 10,000 years – our mountain. I could sense its presence. I anxiously felt the crystal in my pocket. We were getting close.

'The guidebook says that there should be great views of Chimborazo from this pass at 3,600 metres.' Pete was eagerly searching the mist. It had started to rain again and was dull and drab. 'It's more like Scottish climbing weather than the Andes.' Our elevation now was too high for cultivation or pine forests. A scene of blustery tussock grass stretched into the murk.

'There's more wisdom in the unseen,' I quoted usefully.

The bus took us down and spewed us out at Riobamba. It was near here that in 1797 a huge landslide had smothered and killed several thousand people. There seemed to be a certain restlessness about the Earth in these parts, as though trying to shake off human habitation. Are we, the human race, just visitors on this planet? Are the forces of nature so strong that we are irrelevant? Or are we so inextricably part of the whole system that the energy which we give out, governed somewhat by our thought processes, can make a vital powerful difference to the world around us?

The Inca people, whose empire dominated the Andes for over a century, frequently made supplications to the Gods, in the form of ceremonial rituals, human and animal sacrifices and other offerings. Mountaintop venues were considered particularly sacred. Could our pilgrimage and its offering of peace messages help appease the demons of war, aggression, greed and inhumanity that blow across the Inca Earth Goddess today?

Bidding 'adiós' to the bus driver, I asked him where I could deposit our bag of rubbish. He indicated for me to dump it in the road alongside other heaps. I shook my head saying 'No, no!' He signalled for me to give it to him. I did so. He then dumped it in the road. We all live by different values, I thought, but maybe the awareness that all things are interconnected would precipitate more of a sense of caring and responsibility, for then whatever one does to the world one does to oneself, in spite of our isolation barriers.

Our developing linguistic skills were further put to the test as we approached the line of assorted yellow taxis. Eventually we were happy with the negotiated rate of 200,000 sucres to the Refugio Hermanos Carrel and a return on the next day. Chimborazo must be one of the easiest high mountains of the world to get to the base of. There can not be many places where it is possible to take a taxi to 4,800 metres... the height of Mont Blanc.

We sped off west out of Riobamba, by now accustomed to the swerving around the potholes and rocks in the road. I chatted to the friendly taxi driver in my pretend Spanish whilst Pete tried a seasick video session out of the window. We passed cement works and were approaching an area of pine forest when we were flagged down by agentes de policia at a roadblock.

'Qué pasa?' I enquired of our driver. By way of a reply he made a sharp movement with his hand as if he was cutting his throat with a knife.

'Bandidos?'

'Si, bandidos!'

I could not help laughing. Yet again I felt that sense of unreality as though playing out a part in a film. How would it be, I surmised, if I considered the whole of life to be playing out a part in a film? Maybe it would then be possible to laugh at everything upsetting or stressful. Maybe I could then find some real inner peace.

We started gaining altitude again. Leaving one little isolated village behind with clusters of whitewashed flat-roofed houses and curious donkeys, past drumlin-like hills with clinging patchwork fields, we followed a dirt track, streams of dust following in our wake. We rose above the treeline and the landscape took on a general greyness. Ash was everywhere. By the look of the cutting on the side of the road there was very little soil for the tussock grass roots to cling to in the bands of differing volcanic material, showing ancient eruptions. This was the Earth's geological map of a time before man thought that he ruled the planet.

Then, as I looked out from the dusty window of the taxi, up into grey billowing cloud hanging from the roof of the sky, something momentarily shifted. There was a vista of distant snowfields. A dazzling white light shone. My gaze held it… and then it slipped beneath the oblivion of the unseen. Now there was a presence… right upon us… Wow! We were in the aura of Chimborazo. My relationship with the mountain was about to begin. Like a sexual exchange, would the mingling of auras affect our energetic makeup for time to come? Would there be a letting go?… surrender?… in trust?… a giving?… and what trials?… what euphoria?…

The raw beauty of the wild open páramo was held on the wind as the loose volcanic plain took over. If it was not for the low shifting cloud and gathering dust, I felt sure that we would be able to see far distant horizons with a sense of the Earth's curvature.

'Veis alli. Mira!... Vicuñas!' shouted the driver suddenly, excited to be able to show his tourist guests the sights. No Buckingham Palace, though, could compete with the intrigue and fascination of viewing our first Andean representative of the animal kingdom. He pointed to a herd of about ten llama-type guys, light chocolate brown in colour, grazing close together, looking a bit like baby camels but without the humps. They raised their long necks, unperturbed, as we passed by. I wondered what they could possibly be finding to eat here in this barren desert at an elevation of 4,000 metres.

I tried to find out more about the vicuñas from the driver but the language difference was frustrating. I did know, however, that the local Indians had long found the llama useful not only for haulage, but also as a butcher's shop, as a fine wool factory, and even for racing. Quite a handy sort of a package really. These were definitely not llamas, I gathered, but presumably from the same family. I heard the words 'Inca' and 'protección'. Yes, I figured, many early people had made wise decisions not based on greed and were in harmony with their environment, knowing that they were part of it.

The way was now seriously rutted. At times it was hard to tell which was road and which desert. In the dryness we were able to negotiate the deep sand and rocky corners, but some reversing and picking our route was necessary. On looking carefully the empty windswept wilderness was home to tiny pretty yellow flowers peeping through the harsh greyness, saying 'beauty is always there for the looking'. Meanwhile, a lone bird, which our driver called an 'alcong', soared on a freedom wind negotiating the mix of flying dust.

We had been skirting around the southern perimeter of the mountain, now we turned steeply north-east towards the base. The rough track wound its way towards a solid-looking climbers' hut, the first refuge. On either side ethereal strands of white cloud drifted in an almost eerie welcome. I wondered if this, like a Tibetan white scarf of greeting and blessing, was the gates of Chimborazo about which Beverley had spoken. I tried to open my heart, to be receptive, to be humble and sensitive to the energies around.

Our driver left us there, at the end of the road, after writing down 'una de la tarde – 13.00 horas' for the next day's pick-up. Leaning against the two-tone pink-wash wall, which prettily set off the heavily barred windows, peeling tin roof and rusty oil drums, lounged four climbers, two Americans and two British. They were waiting for their pre-arranged taxi transport to come and take them down. They had huge rucksacks full of climbing equipment and wore heavy duvet jackets. Their tired but relieved expression and exhausted pose told its own story, but we all eagerly exchanged greetings and fell into conversation about each other's accounts. There was friendship from the intense common bond of the challenge of the mountain. They had all left the higher refuge in the dark hours of the night for a summit attempt. Two had been forced to turn back early on. Two had made it to the Veintimilla lower summit and then not been able to negotiate the legendary kilometre of knee-deep and sometimes waist-deep soft snow across to the true summit.

Their gift to us was peace messages:

"The greatest sadness at the end of a life would be not to have reached for the stars."

"All men are brothers on a mountain – Let the world be a mountain."

"Now is the seed of eternity."

"Life is precious. Don't waste it."

Their gift to themselves had been their struggle.

11 - WATCHTOWER MAGIC

From here on up, above the Carrel refuge at 4,800 metres, it was to be the highest that either of us had touched the Earth. We savoured the elation. The sharp cold demanded that thermal underwear be put on (Where was the girls' changing room?) also thicker trousers, jackets, hats and gloves. This had the useful effect of lightening our loads. We set off, each with a typical element of competitiveness, determined that the altitude was not going to have an adverse affect and that fitness and strength would override. I found that it took more of an effort to breathe in the rarefied air, as though something heavy was sitting on my chest, but I felt OK and set a slow and steady pace, using ski sticks to help take the strain of the heavy rucksacks.

We had only two hundred metres of elevation to gain to reach the second hut, the Refugio Edward Whymper, somewhere just above us out of sight. We picked our way steeply up a rough trail across varying sizes of rocks, some of which were a lovely warm rust colour. Suddenly a huge one loomed at us out of the mists like a lost pyramid. On close inspection it proved to be a memorial to eleven French mountaineers who had lost their lives in an avalanche in 1993. A chill went through me that dampened my excited anticipation. This was no walk down a leafy lane.

Three quarters of an hour took us to the Whymper refuge at 5,000 metres, a lofty elevation for any building. Although wrapped in a cloak of ghostly cloud, it looked substantial and welcoming. It was slightly larger than the lower hut and a few wooden shutters almost gave it a feel of the European Alps. The dusky pink of the walls toned in with the milk chocolate sienna of the surrounding volcanic material and was warm and friendly. The colour pink, to me, has always expressed universal love and gentleness. Here was a haven of shelter from some of the world's wildest winds and unpredictable storms… a little cradle rocked by Mother Earth.

A cheerful hut warden greeted us in the dark interior where half a dozen wooden tables and benches clustered around a huge sunken fireplace. There were two small cooking areas with propane gas stoves and pots, pans and utensils which looked like they had been left there when the mountain was first surveyed by the French in 1736. Upstairs in the sleeping area there were four rooms full of bunk beds with foam mattresses and space to sleep about fifty friendly sardine bodies. En-suite facilities were sadly lacking, but outside there was a little shed containing a small noisy generator that operated lights for a couple of hours a day, a bucket of ice water fed by a hose that came down from the glacier stream and two loos. Beside each, if you were lucky, was a pile of newspaper, with a space on the other side for the used variety… nearly all the comforts of home…

We paid the US$10 per night fee for each of us and as there was still a couple of hours before dusk wandered slowly across the rocks up the route ahead. Behind the swirling mists lay the south-west face of Chimborazo. We were there – at last. I tried to harmonise my energies with those of the mountain. This is an important thing to do at the start of any meeting, but I felt that now it was particularly important. I wanted to come in the right way so that our pilgrimage would be accepted, and we needed to show respect and ask permission to climb from the 'spirit' of the mountain. This was just a little sensitivity that many would laugh at, but I remembered when I had learnt about this on a climb back in 1990.

It had been the year when many groups were fighting for the moratorium to ban mining in the Antarctic. We, two companions and myself, had climbed the Old Man of Hoy, Britain's tallest sea stack in the Orkneys. We had slept on the summit from where we had hung a huge banner stating 'Save Antarctica'. Much good had come from the venture and the moratorium had been declared, proving to me that small groups can help effect important changes. However, after abseiling down I had taken a moment to quietly meditate and had sensed the disquiet of the strong masculine spirit of the stack, from whom we had not asked permission. Subsequently none of the vital photographs taken by the camera crew had come out. OK, laugh, but I knew that at a non-physical level it was because we had not been sensitive enough to harmonise and ask permission. I have endeavoured to mentally call 'permission to climb' before every climb since.

Chimborazo did not seem to me to be particularly masculine or feminine. This I felt was unusual, as I had not experienced it before. But there was something balanced about the energy. Maybe the ancient sacredness determined this. Maybe it was that this mountain spirit was well advanced and close to the Divine Source.

It was to be by way of supplication that we decided that one of the stupas should now be built. I knew that this should somehow be carried out with a pure mind, so asked for help and tried to be receptive. In my head I heard the words that had been told to me 'prepare the way sensing the light from the heart of the angel of the mountain'. There was a strong feeling of calm presence.

The site held importance, as it was to be our gateway for the ascent. We followed what appeared to be the direct route upwards for about four hundred metres until a little promontory 'felt' like the right place. Here we collected beautiful rocks of differing colours, shapes and sizes from the variety in proximity and cleared a little round base area, showing that beneath all the loose material the body of Chimborazo was a deep burnt volcanic brown. Then, in turn, we spoke from the Chinese writing of Kuan Yin, the Deity of Compassion. We read from the right hand corner:

'NÄ MÕ HÄ LÄ DÄ NÕ DÕ LÄ YÄ YÄ...'

We then scrolled the prayer tying it with the pink ribbon, protected it with clear plastic, placed it on a flat stone in the middle of the base and carefully constructed the pyramidal cairn over it. It was about a metre high and built, we hoped, to withstand the winds of time.

'Chimborazo, Watchtower of the Universe, we ask for your blessing on our climb, that it may shine a light in the world and help Tibet and Earth Peace. May we be open to all that needs to happen. May we return safely.'

A sacred mist clung to our hearts in the loud silence.

I gently balanced the crystal on the top of the stupa... it glowed softly...

'Advarr... we have brought your crystal to the mountain... in preparation...'

On saying these words I felt the now familiar cold tingly feeling go up and down my spine, only this time it was in my legs too, and the emotion of the moment fed tears to my eyes.

Pete and I hugged. It was a deep soul hug. Together we spoke out Delphine's lovely peace message:

> "I pray with all my heart for Tibet to be free. And may that day herald
> the freeing of all our hearts into the one and great truth shining down
> on a liberated world illumined with compassion.
> OM MANI PADME HUM… OM MANI PADME HUM… OM MANI
> PADME HUM…"

The wind began to rise and howl as we returned to the hut and I was
reminded of a saying which sits on my desk at home – *Every stone raised for the
Greater Good brings the mountain nearer to perfection.*

Thus was the stupa activated in the birth of a seed of compassion. Thus
was our presence on the mountain acknowledged.

Darkness was falling fast. Amongst a handful of other climbers, it was time to
organise cooking up supper during the short period of dim lighting. We had
powdered soup and horlicks, and packets of bean mix and rice, chosen for their
quick cooking time. It was not very appetising but we knew that we had to get as
much liquid as possible into us. Also, we knew that we should eat well and stuff on
carbohydrate. For we were each aware, by an unspoken agreement, that the other
was hoping to give the mountain a go in the early morning and if it were possible
we would try. We had automatically put all our climbing equipment in our rucksacks
to come down here, just in case. We were only meant to be checking out the route.
To go further was crazy and ridiculous. We were not acclimatized. Five days ago
we had been at sea level in England. Our bodies had not had time to adapt to the
thin air. But, as every climber knows, there is an irresistible lure to see how far one
can go – Mallory's maxim of 'because it's there'. The extent to which it is tempered
with the caution required is a measure of personality. Was it brave or foolhardy?
Wild or wise? Maybe it is a product too of how much an individual's soul wants
to present the opportunity of experience to gain strength.

Our guidebook said that the Normal route takes a path left out of the
refuge until gaining a prominent scree slope, then follows a huge horizontal snow
ramp (El Corredor) to reach the edge of the main Thielman glacier. From there it

angles left up a steep snowfield to a pass above a large rocky outcrop known as El Castillo and then heads north-west up the long ridge, avoiding a large crevasse just beneath the Veintimilla summit before crossing the snow basin to the main summit. Usually the ascent takes eight to ten hours. Allow two to four for the descent. It did not appear to be too desperate a route. Top climbers could even describe it as 'just a walk'. Walking, of course is a purely relative term that I, as an inexpert climber, would probably call a 'dire walk' and a non-climber would definitely call a 'death warrant'.

There was a guide in the hut who spoke some English so happily we were able to discuss the route. He told us that the Normal route was much too dangerous this year due to heavy rockfalls in the El Corredor area. Most of the climbs were being undertaken via variations of the Direct route which was considerably harder, tricky to find and after the rocky part was mostly 45° angled ice, (Pete thought it to be graded between Peu Difficile and Assez Difficile on the Alpine system). The guidebook said that initially the Direct route heads straight up the Thielman glacier and it meets the Normal route where it leaves El Corredor. We then went on to read - This route is not recommended since it is subject to avalanches and tends to be heavily crevassed.

Up until now both of us had felt surprisingly good and little affected by our altitude of 5,000 metres. Now, suddenly as we finished eating, it hit us. The Earth started moving up and down uncontrollably. Perhaps aided by an element of apprehension, I felt as though I was about to throw up. There was an intense dizziness that made me feel that I was not in charge of my body. It was annoying and slightly frightening. I found that if I sat still with my eyes shut then I could minimise the effect. Then I discovered that I could do things very, very slowly if I did not move my head. I managed to negotiate clearing away the supper and the tricky business of taking out my contact lenses, and staggered up the wooden ladder stairs to the bunks. Lying down felt better, but it was a long time before I could pluck up the courage to sit up and blow out the candle. I felt so bad that I figured I would throw up if I moved. I sucked coca pills miserably in the dark and in the cold. Even though I had all my climbing gear on including my jacket and was in my sleeping bag, my body still seemed icy and was shivering heavily. Thoughts jabbed around in my head taunting sleep. There was an unusual silence too coming from Pete's direction, so I figured he was not planning a twenty-mile run.

In spite of how we felt, we had still set the alarm for the middle of the night to view the weather and consider climbing. Conditions on the mountain appeared to vary from minute to minute and we knew that there was always risk, but somehow I trusted that we would be guided to make sound judgements. If the wind was very strong we would not go out, as it would be horrendously wild on the ridge. The alarm went off and I turned my head-torch on. It was 11.45 pm. I could hear footsteps going up and down outside - others deciding on the weather. Pete was making negative noises. Three times I asked high inside myself if we should go out. Three times the answer came back 'no'. Still not wanting not to do it, I asked for a sign to confirm this decision. Within a few seconds a fierce and violent wind had sprung up and howled through the little window rattling it noisily. Fate, it seemed, with its habit of intervening in the right places, had dictated that on this occasion our efforts were to be saved for the right time. I realised that by wanting to climb before we were acclimatized, we had not shown respect to the mountain. I felt apologetic. Our intended purpose of seeing the hut and the route would be well carried out. All was well. There was, however, a sense of being steered and guided by an external force - external yet internal, a powerful force that was all around but also within. For the rest of the night I dozed fitfully, my stomach still churning and we did not even try to get up until 8.00 am.

Staggering up, still intensely queasy, I shuffled down the ladder in the huge hut sandals provided and, bleary-eyed, went out of the door into the waiting morning. Brilliant light hit me. It was so bright that I had to shade my face with my hands from this wonderful gift of sunshine. The cloud cover had lifted and there before us lay the south-west face of Chimborazo in all its radiance and splendour. There had been a lot of snow in the night. It was as though fresh cream had been poured from the heavens, flowing through the indigo blue mountain shadows. All around the hut was white. I looked up to the stupa area where we had scrambled across the rocks yesterday, now bespangled with glistening snow. I saw the tongue of the Thielman glacier reaching down, all newly dressed. My searching gaze took me on and up over cliffs and ledges, seracs and crevasses, to the snowfields of the sloping shoulders. Here like the crowning glory of a sage's long white hair, the spindrift blew in great clouds along the ridges... on and on, up and up into the deep cobalt sky... oh, how beautifully... to a rounded summit framed in rising snow and caught in the clutches of the Inca Sun God. Even now this was not the true summit. From our foreshortened vantage spot, the highest point lay beyond... waiting...

The excitement in Pete's eyes mirrored my own as we watched this stunning picture. He at least seemed to be feeling better and was able to take some good video footage, which would be useful to study later and show the others. A couple of French climbers came and stood with us. They pointed out two dots on the mountain – two Swiss guides who had left at the midnight hour when it was slippery and fiercely gusty with poor visibility. They were now descending and we were able to follow their progress with the loan of binoculars until we could see them with the naked eye. It was good for us to be able to pick out the route, and observing them descend with relative ease made me feel happier about the climb. My worries of the previous night dissolved and my hopes soared again that all would be well. Although those ice slopes did seem horribly steep and, if they did for me, then surely they would for Mig too.

The shifting wind brought in cloud from the south and it was no longer possible to view our shining volcano. All that tantalising beauty, all that daunting, frightening, alluring being was gone from sight. It was time to turn away and move down to the lower hut for our taxi appointment, where I hoped I would feel less sick. Pete felt fine now but was upset at the loss of his head-torch, which was vital equipment that we could not climb without. It seemed to have dematerialised from the pile of gear on his bunk. I told him that misplacing things was a typical Gemini trait but that did not seem to help much.

We were slightly surprised to find our taxi driver waiting for us. He took us down, retracing our steps across the desert and grasslands to find a bus in Riobamba. This time we scored a rather more modern vehicle, the comfort advantages of which were offset by the fact that the driver seemed to have the ambition of reaching Quito in the shortest time possible, even to the extent of leaving the conductor on the roof while he was sorting luggage. Luckily we did want to get back quickly as we were looking forward to collecting Mig at the airport – and speeding away from the distant cloud-hugged slopes of Chimborazo there was only the merest glimpse…

Merest glimpses, though, can stir thought processes. Am I in control of my life? It's exciting. I want to do it. I want to move forward. I can't wait. Yet… it's scary. It's wonderful and scary at the same time. But what if I don't make it home? What about my children? I don't need to conceptualise the 'what ifs' of avalanches, crevasses, falling and disasters at a physical level as that would be allowing negative energy to take root. However, I know that there is fear, not doubt, fear, hiding somewhere. Is it fear of the unknown? Or fear of coping? Or fear of falling? Or is it only a camouflaged racing of the heart?

Maybe something will happen so I don't have to do it. Maybe if I shut my eyes and forget about it, it will go away. But if I backed out of things in life just because they were scary, then I might get to the end and say 'I nearly did this and I nearly did that', instead of 'Wow! that was really living, man! Doing that made me feel really alive – so full of purpose. I know it was where I was meant to be'. If I don't grab it now, then perhaps my soul will have to set up a similar scenario in my next life, wherever that may be, and see if I can be persuaded to go for it then. This is presumably what my soul, hopefully with the assistance of Divine Energy, has set up for me to do here. It is my part of the river of life. My position of existence has been organised around me as it is. What I do with it … well, that's up to me. Can I go through with it now?

I was facing issues that I had swept under the carpet for years and years due to their scariness. I knew that now was the time for exposure because I seemed tied to so much else that was so big and powerful which was carrying me along. There was Pete whose presence was strong beside me. There were Mig and GT. There were all my loved ones and friends at home. There were all the hundreds of 'Climb For Tibet' supporters. There was the Tibetan nation. There were 6 billion people, more than one billion of which were Chinese. There was the Earth. The crystal was throbbing in my pocket and there were spiritual powers that I did not quite understand. Somehow it was all connected. We were all part of one big team, helping each other.

I knew that the time had come to face myself. The moment of truth was approaching.

I was determined that I would be there.

12 - THE SNOW LION-HEART

How many Tibetans had previously passed through these arrival portals at Quito airport, I wondered, as we waited amongst the excited toing and froing of the evening Ecuadorian throng. Nearly everyone was wearing casual Western gear, but there was an air of high spirits and emotion just below the surface, which differed from an English crowd.

There were small dark-skinned girls, pretty against their bright coloured hats and jerseys; clamouring men in denim jeans, complaining to nobody in particular about the delayed flight; ladies chatting non-stop to friends; and young boys, noisily creating chaos with a football in and out of pushing legs.

Though undercover, the arrivals lounge appeared to be the pavement outside in the street and a large barrier marked the area where we were allowed to be. We tied the Tibetan flag onto the bars so that it was the first thing that Migmar the Snow Lion-Heart would see as he walked out. Probably no one else would recognise this flag from half a world away, but for Mig it would say 'Welcome. Your nation is special. Today the spirit of Tibet comes to Ecuador, high in the Andes. It is carrying the message of world peace from His Holiness the Dalai Lama – from Asia, via Europe to South America'. Many stared with interest at it. We just smiled knowingly, unable to express its purpose in Spanish.

A shoeshine boy pestered Pete who finally submitted. The tiny imp of about eight years old knelt on the pavement and indicated for Pete to place a foot on his small wooden box, where he vehemently polished first one and then the other with his black brush and cloth. Then his handsome little face looked up anxiously at the tall foreigner towering above him and burst into sunshine as he was paid twice the going rate. Not so his friend who was a few years older and seemed to be helping to find customers. His brown face framed by bushy Afro hair was sad and stared at us with large mournful eyes, which revealed cares far beyond his years.

Suddenly the milling around and noise intensified as passengers began pushing their way into the greeting crowd. I clung to Pete's arm excited that we were about to have Mig with us… and then there he was… looking fit and well, walking purposefully and with his usual big cheeky grin. He carried an old faded red rucksack that he had borrowed. It was stuffed to the brim, with a yellow karrimat down the side, conjuring up pictures of adventure and daring. A small bag with 'Tibet' embroidered on it hung from his neck and, typically, whilst everyone else was covered from the chilly night air with jackets and pullovers, Mig wore a sleeveless fitted shirt which showed off his broad muscular chest to perfection. His left upper arm displayed a tattoo in Tibetan writing, 'OM MANI PADME HUM'.

Grabbing the flag and waving it madly I was eventually able to thrust it around his neck with a huge hug and joyful smiles. There was a vague sense of familiarity about the occasion. It was something to do with the manner of greeting.

'I wish I had a white scarf to welcome you in the correct Tibetan manner,' I said wistfully.

He laughed. 'You know, Tess… the flag is even better.'

Our taxi from the airport this time had a meter displayed, which meant that at last we would be charged a reasonable rate without having to haggle. This could be useful if ever we worked out how to spot metered taxis, I thought. It appeared that any make, shape or size of car was allowed to be a taxi so long as it was yellow. This one was another Lada, which rattled along with the driver in similar talkative mode. I nodded and interjected 'Si' at suitable points in the conversation. Mig, it seemed, was not going to contribute much to our Spanish either, though we did learn from this driver that the word for Tibetan was 'Tibetano' …progress! He took us back into the centre of the new town via the arterial main roads with all their accompanying noise, bustle and pollution, and turning into the one way system found our narrow, tree-lined, cobbled street. All was quiet. We drew up outside the little porch of el Hostal Posada del Maple and pressed the bell for someone to open the outer door. We could see through into the interior. There was warm mid-brown wood, small sitting spots, benches and tables, young people chatting, tourist brochures and notices and a pervading aura of friendliness. It was a traveller's oasis.

'Well, Miggie, this is home,' said Pete with a paternal arm on his shoulder. 'You'll be sharing a room with GT when he arrives in a couple of days.'

'Cool! Looks great.' He smiled.

'Get lots of sleep and keep away from the girls tonight,' Pete continued with a wink at me. 'It's going to be tough adapting to the altitude.'

'Hey, I'll be just fine. You don't have to worry about me.'

With the confidence of youth and his happy demeanour Mig tended to accept and adapt to all things that came to him in an easy going way. As a representative of a refugee nation this was to his advantage, though underneath I knew he was keen to 'get going' and that a fire of determination burned knowing he could and would do something to help his people. There was so much passion and frustration in the waiting, shackled by the enormity of the task of finding a way to regain Tibet's land, culture and freedom. At a political level the situation seemed hopeless with the world kow-towing to China, a huge economic market waiting to be exploited, while human rights needs are brushed aside. Now here with 'Climb For Tibet', there was an opportunity to raise his country's profile, to produce funds for those escaped and homeless and to assist in a non-physical way.

In Britain he had already achieved so much with extraordinary maturity and energy for one so young. He had contributed to the putting together of demonstrations, rallies and events with the Free Tibet Campaign and other organisations. I had watched him at the Wednesday evening demonstrations outside the Chinese Embassy in London. He was always the one to shout the loudest - 'Stop the murder! Stop the torture! Free Tibet! Chinese out!' Surely no one expected the Chinese to just simply walk out, but by shouting 'Chinese out!' they were representing all that everyone felt in an expression of the anger, the disgust and the desperation of the Tibetan people.

I had watched him too at the rally on the 10th of March, the anniversary of the Tibetan uprising in Lhasa in 1959 when around 100,000 Tibetans had lost their lives. This is an annual occasion when Tibetans and supporters march through the centre of London, waving banners and flags, stopping traffic and turning heads of hundreds of people, tourists and British alike. I had seen Mig shout with his whole heart and soul 'Long live the Dalai Lama!' It had stirred me to the core.

I knew that many believe that there is a natural instinct to show aggression and of wanting to fight back. How would you feel if your country had been invaded and ransacked, your culture destroyed, your religion trampled on and your fellow countrymen and women oppressed? It would hurt. Can we imagine how much it would hurt? I believe that these hostile feelings are being held in check and transcended by the Tibetan Buddhist spirit of His Holiness the Dalai Lama who radiates the light of love and compassion. The high regard that He and His beliefs are held in is the panacea of aggression and fear. This is the strength of the Tibetan people, the reflection of the light that shines into the needy world today.

Now would Mig, as a totally inexperienced mountaineer, be able to manage the climb to express the Dalai Lama's message of peace, the highest ideal, symbolically from the point furthest from the centre of the Earth? For that matter, would any of us?...

We had only been able to organise one training weekend with all four of us before leaving. This had been in the mountains of North Wales. One day had been spent being interviewed on camera by Chris from Amora, and we had included some rock climbing on Little Tryfan. Pete and I had been happy that Mig and GT had clambered up the 55° rock face and abseiled down with no problems. It had been Mig's only substantial training with a harness, helmet and ropework and he had managed with tentative ease.

We did wonder at GT's harness and methods of tying-on, which looked like they had come out of the ark, but then our respect for the hard-won experience of the 'older' climber was high. With our newer, modern climbing gear, he had called us 'You young things' in an endearing tone which we would come to love.

On the second day Pete had set us a 23 kilometre 'potter', up and over seven well-nigh 1,000 metre peaks. It was along the Carneddu range approaching from the north at Aber. We had started fresh and keen in damp early morning mists, delighted in the time to chat, recount our life stories and get to know each other as a team. There was enjoyment in the freedom of the hills with rucksack on back and heavy boots on feet striding across track, bog and rock. On the first peak we had devised the 'Climb For Tibet' formation. Standing in a circle, palms of hands flat against those on either side, arms high in the air, we chanted 'OM MANI

PADME HUM'. The unbroken circle signified unity of purpose. It was team bonding at its best and we conducted the ceremony on every peak thereafter.

The sun shone warmly as the day wore on, turning into a rare gem with wonderful shimmering views into the far distance. Hoisting the Tibetan flag on a ski stick, Mig carried it aloft attracting the attention of other hill wanderers who were then accosted with sponsorship forms. Pete started singing *Onward Christian Soldiers* which prompted a distinct sense of going into battle, with the fine sight of a bare-chested, brown Tibetan bounding from high rock to high rock in the Welsh hills and the brightly coloured Tibetan flag streaming out above him.

I had hobbled, exhausted with painful feet and knees, into the Ogwen car park with the late afternoon sun, having watched Mig relish the steep descent with leaps and bounds, and GT steadily and rather more sedately scramble down. Turning to Pete (who had to be stopped from doing another seven peaks), I had said, 'Yeah, you're right. We have a great team'.

'Training tomorrow Miggie, on Pasochoa... up to 4,000 metres!'

The breakfast daily-plan-and-jobs-list took place in the main courtyard of our hostel. There was still painting going on for a café area to be opened, dusky turquoise and deep rusty pink with tropical plants, hanging ferns and lusciously filled terracotta pots. Little tables and chairs gave a sunny sheltered 'hanging out' spot. I loved it. This was our only meal of the day provided for. The Western traveller was well catered for so we could help ourselves to oats and other cereal and hot drinks and we were brought freshly blended fruit juices of guava, strawberry and papaya, also rolls and eggs. I never did quite discover the word for 'scrambled' but if you said something like 'revolting' then scrambled was what came. Mig, being a good Tibetan, always had chilli sauce on his. Breakfast was a happy sunny time. How lucky we were to have found such a good base costing very little. This day was set aside to unpack and settle into our new home, to attempt faxes and phone calls, try and find a supermarket and search for a source of wholemeal bread.

Up above the clothes washing area was a small terrace overlooking the rooftops of Quito, with the roar of traffic and horns wafting up. A frangipani-type bush crawled up the white fencing, with bright red flowers. Here I watched a beautiful little humming bird collecting nectar with its long beak. I marvelled at its amazing wing beats, too fast to see, holding its body still in mid-air. Now I knew that we were in the tropics. As if to confirm this a few minutes sitting in the sun to write my diary gave me badly burnt shoulders. We had been given some wonderful natural products by Yin Yang and thankfully the one for burns proved very effective, but the strength of the radiation at this altitude was to be remembered.

By the time the early afternoon cloud came in high above us, I was busy getting lost in the maze of little streets around the hostel. They were full of boarding houses, small businesses, tourist agencies, shops with intriguing dark interiors, stalls displaying their wares on the pavement along with sellers of sweetcorn cobs and roasting meats of indefinable origin and distasteful aroma. In spite of this I felt hugged by the area in a benign contented way, and enjoyed the anticipation of what might be round the next corner. I was trying to find the office of Native Life; a well-respected environmentally and culturally responsible tour company, run by Lincoln who was the boyfriend of Emily, the daughter of a friend in England. We had had a happy breakfast with them one day at Café Cultura and they had been very kind, offering lots of good information and advice (in English!) - Stuff like 'The tropical forests of Ecuador hold the greatest diversity of species on Earth'; 'They are being seriously threatened, especially by the oil industry'; 'Keep a look out for condors'; 'Chimborazo is no picnic'. Lincoln had once climbed to the Veintimilla summit. It had been 'Hellishly hard'.

Now here, walking along the street was the tall, beautiful Emily.

'Hey there, just who I needed to bump into'. Emily was conducting anthropological research for a postgraduate thesis and, having already spent over a year in the country, was a mine of information. We chatted in Hampshire accents for a while. She told me that Lincoln was worried about us climbing Chimborazo and recommended quite strongly that we should take a local guide with us. I promised that we would give it some thought. Then I asked her about Pasochoa.

'Make sure you go up via the Fundación Natura Forest Reserve on the northern side of the volcano. It's a national park with an educational and research centre. It contains one of the last remaining areas of native inter-Andean forest, which used to cover the whole of this region. There're trails through it, which you'll love. It's full of wonderful things. Apparently there're more than 120 different species of birds alone. They say that there are pumas and I've known friends see condors.'

Wow! I thought, to see a condor would be the crowning gift from the Andes. I remembered the excitement of meeting a wild wedgetail eagle in Australia and feeling the regal presence of a top bird of prey... 'I'd like to know more about the condor. Are there many around?' I enthused. I knew that he was a character revered in mythology and sacred to the Incas who believed that he carried the sun into the sky each morning. He was considered to be a messenger of the gods. I had also read that the Andean condor's eyes were eaten in the belief of improving human eyesight. He must be a national treasure, even his name translates as 'gold coin'.

'Well,' she replied 'they're seriously threatened, now. I've a friend who might know about the numbers that are left. I'll try and find out for you.'

I thanked Emily and went to scour the guidebooks. Condors are of the vulture order. They are the largest flying land birds on Earth, reaching wingspans of 4 metres. Ancient fossils have been found of over 5 metres. That's a lot of bird. They live mostly on carrion, but also go for other birds and small and sick mammals, including young goats and sheep, which has made them unpopular with the farmers. Of course they can do nothing about man's hunting and poisons and a pair will only lay one egg every two years. However, they're tough – they can survive for days at a time without eating.

That was more than we could do so, later in the day, with an eye on keeping our stomachs happy, we introduced Mig to the wonders of Quito fruit milkshakes at el Magic Bean. Here was the added advantage of English language newspapers from the United States. Mig was keen to track down information on Bill Clinton's state visit to China.

'Basically, Clinton is offering the hand of friendship just to be able to stimulate trade,' he said. 'The encouragement of trade will be taken as an endorsement of the horrendous human rights abuses that the Chinese government carries out on Tibetans and on its own people too, an endorsement also of the labour camps that many of the goods are made in. If he gives China 'preferred nation' status for trade it'll take away the lever that the rest of the world has to work with to try and get them to make changes, like to boycott goods made in China and not to trade.'

109

'But surely,' Pete argued 'encouraging trade is a good thing because it means that the Chinese people, brainwashed through the Communist system, will learn more about the ways of the West, democracy and the truth about the situation in Tibet. Their propaganda machine has totally misled the people, even the Chinese children are brought up to believe that the great Chinese motherland had liberated a backward and unhappy Tibet'.

'Well,' replied Mig with a sigh, 'You may be right. But the Americans have so much power. I mean, Clinton could do a lot to help. We all have high hopes that at least he will encourage Jiang Zemin to have a meeting with His Holiness.' He looked fleetingly downhearted.

'It's not always easy to see that things are unfolding as they are meant to be on a wider perspective, is it?' I consoled, remembering my vision of Tibetan spirituality being sent out across the Earth, and added 'There's an awful lot of individuals and small groups throughout the world exercising their free will and backing the Tibetan cause... Look at all the supporters of 'Climb For Tibet'. Surely there must be a collective free will in the consciousness of humanity that is being more and more influenced in this way. Think of all the positive thoughts and prayers that are being sent out.'

By then our stomachs did not want any more positive thoughts.

'C'mon, there's something we need to show you.'

I placed the crystal gently in Mig's open hand without saying anything. He instinctively treated it with great reverence and quietly stared at it for a while sensing the energy it carried. Then he said, 'You know, I feel all cold and tingly up and down my back.'

I smiled. What strange forces were at work here? I read Advarr's card to him. All three of us felt the heavy responsibility and spiritual power surrounding the whole event.

'It's so important that we get there. Are you afraid of the climbing or the mountain?' I probed of Mig.

'Me? To be honest... No.' Came the quick reply and he fingered the small picture of Guru Rinpoche (Padmasambhava) that he always wore round his neck. It had belonged to his father who had died two years previously in India.

Daily he chanted his Guru's prayer for sacred protection:

'Hung. Ogyen yulke nub chang tsam pema gyaltser dhongpo la yamste choekyi ngodup nyen pema jing ner shel su ta kor tu khan do mang po kor ge ki je su dha dup kyi chin ki cap chir she su sol guru padma sedhen hung! Om ah hung benza guru padma sedhen hung.'

This is a very powerful prayer for all things to do with the self. Mig believes that it guides, maintains health, ensures a clear path and keeps away evil spirits. Now, it gave him great inner strength and a feeling of complete safety.

Also on a chord round his neck he wore a tiny red bag that had been given to him by his mother. It held coloured wheat which had been blessed by Nechung, the Oracle, deity of His Holiness the Dalai Lama. It carried a pervading protective force. There was certainly no need for Mig to be afraid.

I knew better than to ask Pete the same question. With his long experience in the mountains and his practical feet-on-the-ground character he would not have any tinge of fear.

But I confessed to my diary that night that the nagging fear in my heart persisted, particularly now having seen Chimborazo. I read Uri's positive *Little Book of Mind-Power,* which helped. I cradled the crystal again in my hands and felt the tingly sensation. I knew that we had so much help… but I was still frightened.

13 - CONDOR BROTHER

All our Quito mornings seemed to dawn fair and warm. Pasochoa training day was no exception. We were up early, keen to build up our altitude tolerance and get our bodies moving in a sustained way. Mig was in just-give-me-a-mountain-to-climb mode. Remembering how dozy and weak I had felt on my first day, it seemed remarkable he was in such good working order. Maybe it was the call of youth, or maybe dynamic masculinity, for Pete too hadn't seemed to have suffered much from the altitude and I had trouble recalling a time when he was not in just-give-me-a-mountain-to-climb mode. Anyway, with all this male strength around me I felt safe and loved. What more could a girl ask for, I mused?

'C'mon, Tess. Surely you're ready now!' Pete harried to get me going and in his usual considerate way grabbed my rucksack to take down to the waiting taxi. Jorge who worked at the hostel had fixed us up with a friendly driver, José, for the 30 kilometres or so journey south, which took us on a route out of the city past colourful, bustling markets. We indulged in a banana stop. Huge yellow mounds of differing varieties greeted us. I was ecstatic.

As we travelled on through the verdant farmland of the Central Valley to the vibration of the jostling engine-drone, the ever-changing shades of green started to look almost unreal. My eyes were seeing but not registering. My conscious practical mind, which does appear occasionally, was saying 'make the most of this time sitting in a car… use it for meditation… active meditation… a getting in touch with self… an opening up to the help which is available...' My body became heavy and far away...

I am viewing the Earth from a position in space… There is ethereal cloud… I am focusing on Chimborazo… The summit is prominent and holds a huge six-pointed star balancing in a horizontal plate… Light from the star reaches to the base of the mountain and beyond. My personal guides are telling me that the spirit of the mountain is revering a Council of Masters. As I watch the summit decked in the star, a shard of white light comes towards me as though it is summoning us in safety and in purpose. My sense of knowing absorbs that we have been accepted by the spirit of the mountain.

The vision had barely faded and was still touching me at a heart level, when I sensed a different presence. It was condor. I felt an opening up… a connecting… a bonding... It was as though deep in the melded energies of the universe there was sympathy with us and a touching with love by an animal essence.

The bumpiness of the road increased and the jolting brought my physical awareness back. 'I think we've just had a meeting arranged,' I shakily relayed to the others. 'We're going to see condors today.'

Pete, who was still trying to understand my rather weird way of going about things, but nevertheless seemed to have faith in me, was pleased. 'Well done, Babe.'

Mig turned and, looking over the top of his smart fashion sunglasses smiled 'Cool!'

I thought I'd try and find out more from the driver with my pigeon Spanish. 'José, es condores aqui?'

'Si, si,' came the reply.

Wondering if it was just one of those polite general 'si, si's which I tended to get whatever I asked, or worse still if he thought I meant something like 'are there condoms here?' I persisted. 'Donde los condores?'

José waved his hand about. 'La sierra…'

Ah, I must have it right. 'Cuántas condores en la sierra?'

'Unos cien.'

'Solo cien en todos las sierras?'

'Si, si.'

Could he mean that he thought there were only a hundred condors left in the whole of the Ecuadorian Andes? The vulnerability of something so special worried me. How quickly in the span of Earth time had they disappeared. The famous English climber Whymper had written of them in their droves back in 1880, having seen organised condor hunts using horsemeat for bait.

We passed tough-looking horses along the cobbled track to the Pasochoa Forest Reserve, winding our way through fertile smallholdings. There was something deeply satisfying about the rich chocolate brown earth supporting all manner of vegetables and fruit. I recognised sweetcorn, avocado, pumpkin, papaya and oranges. Chickens roamed around each little hacienda with the small children and usually there was a milking cow and sometimes pigs. Blocks of eucalyptus, some with huge trunks, acted as windbreaks and provided shade, though today the weather was gentle with cloud and drizzly showers and the air was warm and sticky.

'You know, it reminds me so much of India,' said Mig excitedly. 'It all feels so familiar.'

As the track deteriorated into gravelly ruts we weren't surprised when José, not at all brave, decided to abandon us. We set off to walk the last few kilometres watched warily by a tan mongrely dog pretending to sleep on a ramshackle veranda.

Happily a pickup truck full of youngsters came by and we were crammed into the back amidst chatter and laughter and taken to the entrance of the park. As tourists we were quite rightly charged 35,000 sucres (US$ 7), which was ten times as much as the locals. It was gratifying to see that, in this country full of poverty, high priority was given to maintaining a precious natural reserve, the beauty of which was all around us. At the education centre were boards full of information about the exceptional flora and fauna. I longed to be able to understand more of the information. I presumed that the volcanic lava had given rise to all the wonderful profusion that was blossoming, but that the steepness had prevented agriculture taking over in the past. We were, I reminded myself, in one of the few places in the world that is both at a high altitude and almost on the equator. If this was one of the last remaining forests of this type then there must be a wealth of knowledge and unique species here which could be useful for medicinal and economic purposes, as well as an important larder for Mother Earth's energy balancing feeding system. *Un bosque para todos*, one of the signs said – truly 'A forest for everyone'. I felt so lucky to be here.

Initially coloured arrows guided us along the trails as we picked our way to gain as much height as quickly as possible. From 2,700 metres at the base we were hopeful of gaining the highest part of the rim of the large crater of the volcano at 4,200 metres.

A pretty bubbling stream talked to us for a while, until we turned south and found ourselves pushing through bamboo forest. The inviting trails zigzagged up with tunnels of hanging branches and as we climbed we caught glimpses of distant patchwork hills through the thick foliage. I had always thought of bamboo as panda fodder, so I wondered if this was what it was like on the other side of the world along the slopes of distant Chinese mountains.

After an hour or so Mig called a halt in a clearing carpeted by pale brown rustly bamboo leaves. 'To be honest, my boots are killing me, guys,' he grimaced. Inspection revealed raw red blisters, which Pete doctored with plasters. The plastic boots were very old. They had been kindly donated by a Cotswold Camping sales assistant after hearing of Mig's need for equipment (sadly no one had donated us new equipment). He had to get used to plastic boots for taking crampons safely when on snow and ice. But Mig's feet were not at all happy with the idea. They had always preferred wearing sandals. From now on he would always be struggling with painful feet.

Hobbling on, Mig told me how he placed his mind on other things allowing healing energy to enter and the pain retreated somewhat. He picked a stout green bamboo pole to be his companion and we clambered on to the sound of a symphony of birdcalls and fleeting darts of colour and airborne form.

Gradually inter-Andean forest species took over. There were many podocarps – the only conifer native to the Ecuadorian Andes, mountain palmtrees, laurels, ferns, white and purple orchids, and bromeliads — the beautiful staghorns, with long entwining lianas and huge lichens. Some were epiphytes, some saprophytes, but all were species that depended on one another and formed a miraculous interconnected web of life. It was not hard for my heart to feel in tune with the joy that danced all around us.

As we climbed higher, smaller trees took over and in the diffuse light Mig was intrigued by the covering of tall mosses growing on all the branches. 'Hey, look Pete… these are just like your arms!' he teased. Actually I was quite fond of Pete's strong forearms but had to laugh too, thinking that on some deep level my hairy Viking had rainforest origins and how the Earth was such a mishmash of the energy of matter thrown together in apparent random harmony.

Suddenly, as though a line had been drawn at 3,500 metres, we reached the

115

upper limit of the forest and came out into bright sunlight. A cool wind played on our faces. We were on steep tussocky grassland interspersed with low billberry and juniper-type bushes. Wonderful views stretched towards Quito. What a beautiful land this was. It wasn't hard to imagine it in the days before human habitation. Nature dominated the picture, from the lush river valleys to the far snow-capped volcanic peaks.

Now I was beginning to feel the lack of oxygen in the air. The find-your-own-way path demanded attention on the acutely angled mud and slippery vegetation. I tried to take a slow but steady pace and practised a few mind affirmations… I am strong… I am fit… I love everything… I have all the energy I need…

Gasping a little and breathing heavily I joined the others at a level grassy knoll. It appeared to be on a spur that ran up to the crater rim. Pines spread out before us to the east. They were a spidery variety, whose three needled whorls hung like little lanterns greeting us. It was a lovely spot to munch gratefully on our lunch, (though most of the drinking water supplies seemed to have already fallen victim to the thirst of the youngest member of the team). We enjoyed the wonderful integral bread that we had found. Generally I prefer to nibble most of the time on a climb, and organise my pockets to be full of yummy grazing material, but to have lunch as such means that Pete has to stop for a bit and it's an opportunity for me to rest.

Here, Pete enjoyed filming with the video camera. It was good footage against this background of sweeping mountain landscape. Mig, wearing bright purple glacier salopettes but bare-chested, showed off his stick-twirling talents as though preparing for an ancient Tibetan jousting tournament. He then borrowed my penknife and with great mindfulness carved 'OM MANI PADME HUM' into the bamboo stick, the pale inner cream of the Tibetan lettering standing out exquisitely against the fresh green.

'I shall inscribe a mantra for every mountain I climb.' He stated with a purposefulness that expressed the wisdom of generations. 'This stick will be empowered with the energy of meditations and prayer.'

We continued across the sloping ridge of brown windswept tussock grass. Pete as usual was going well and moved ahead to check out the route. Mig and I waited at the point where the ridge meets the rim of the crater with a wonderful view at least 8 kilometres across to the far side. 100,000 years ago there would have been an eruption in a cauldron of fuming magma destroying and transforming the original ancient volcanic cone. Today, from the collapsed side, spread deep green virgin forest climbing steeply to the appointed latitude like tea in a teacup. We sat on the grass soaking up the beauty and watching the clouds moving over the wide-open sky. Mist swirled in from the west into the teacup and then more mist on mist. It was like a canvas being painted, more so as to a Tibetan, cloud represents the creative power of the mind.

'Look Tess, there's a fluffy white dragon… and look, there's another that's a fire-dragon. How brilliant! It's so lucky… it's a really good auspicious sign… especially, you know, as I was born in the year of the dragon.'

'Yeah, how lovely.'

Mig turned towards me, but his eyes became transfixed. Following his gaze I caught the scene unfolding behind me. There was a rush of wind… an atmosphere of a sudden presence of power… smell of musty quicksilver. Like a huge angelic shield, two large shiny wings glided towards us, enfolding as a tail went up in one smooth landing motion… Condor was with us.

He stood awkwardly on large feet with gruesome flesh-tearing talons. His naked head jerked from one side to the other, pink crest flopping, showing off the white ruff of his wrinkled neck and a sharp curved beak. Just for a second there was eye contact. Then he spread his great wings to the sun… and was gone.

Oh… Wow! Far out!

For a while we were too stunned almost to breathe. What an appearance!

'Hey Man! That was something!' Mig was the first to speak. 'Did you say that condors were vultures?'

'Same order. His generic name is *vultur gryphus*.'

'You know, in Tibet the vultures are considered sacred. It's because of the sky burials. I've never seen one, but basically human flesh is cut up and fed to the vultures. It's a way of recycling dead bodies in a land where there's a scarcity of burning material for cremation and little soil for ground burial. The soul has already been blessed and flown, and the body is no longer of any use. It's an important service that the vultures do for man.'

'Sort of like a system of natural harmony?'

'Mm. I mean, Tess, this might sound strange, but when the condor was

117

here… it was as though he knew…'

I nodded. 'You know, the native American Indian brave always had an animal spirit to be his brother.'

'Yeah?'

'Maybe, the condor has come to watch over you and 'Climb for Tibet'.'

'You reckon?'

'Yeah, and he is very like the Tibetan in many ways…'

'Well, he certainly looked like he had a white greeting scarf round his neck.'

'He did. You know, maybe the karma of the Tibetans and the condors has a similar sort of resonance.'

'Yeah, probably.'

'That reminds me of a story, Miggie… The son of a friend of mine went to work in a small town in China. A Tai Chi teacher was very kind to him and gave him some lessons. The teacher was very poor, but when the son offered to pay him he refused asking instead 'please, when you return to the West, please resonate my name with honour.'

'Different values.'

'Yeah, different values. I wonder if he knew of the atrocities caused by his government in the name of the honour of the motherland.'

'Most people in the world don't,' replied Mig. 'I'm sure he wouldn't have known about stuff like the monks being made to shoot their own much loved teachers… or the forced sterilisations and abortions for the Tibetan women… their babies thrown into dustbins. To take life goes against everything a Tibetan believes…'

'I simply can't see how one human being can treat another like that…'

'Well, dreadful horrors continue to go on… And you know it's worse when it's close to you. My friend Ngawang Choephel is in gaol for eighteen years for the crime of studying Tibetan culture. We know of the brutal conditions there, the torture, the beatings, the interrogations… We know that he's barely alive…'

I knew it all too well… the sickening feeling hearing about it… the tears of horror.

'C'mon Miggie. At least we're trying to do something about it. Look, there's Pete waving for us to come up.'

The joy and excitement of meeting the condor mingled with the sadness of the suffering of the Tibetan people, and was stored in our hearts.

Carrying on and up the lee side of the crater across taller and taller grasses, there was the lovely sensation of the wind blowing through ripe corn. Close by, the steep drop into the teacup was guarded by a couple of lone paper bark trees whose red and yellow bark hung in tatters, standing sentinel over the winds of time.

Ahead approached a breast-shaped cliff protecting a patch of dense scrubby vegetation. It was not the summit but needed to be negotiated if we were to continue. On closer inspection we found that the cliff was very shaly and the main holds were either small loose stones jutting out of mud or unstable looking plants - not a route to inspire delight in a rock climber. Pete just happened to have a rope with him (useful load carrying training) and being the one to always take the risks on these sort of occasions left his rucksack to haul up later and gingerly led up the face, fingers clinging to loose holds, big boots balancing on pebbles.

'Well done! Impressive Viking stuff,' I called up as he belayed to a rather insubstantial bush where the gradient eased. I tied Mig into the end of the rope and he stashed his stick and slowly and carefully managed to climb up without mishap. I followed in similar vein.

'So far, so good.'

Some serious scrambling later we were pushing our way through a surprise jungle bash to arrive at the base of the 'nipple'. Peering out from the vegetation we saw ahead of us solid rock, at last. It was a smooth grey cliff reaching up to a rounded top. It looked possible to take a diagonal line across and then maybe a circular route to the final stance.

'Here goes.' Pete set off again with the rope trailing. He managed to gain the traverse with skill, but then seemed to be searching around for some time. Eventually an 'I'm coming down,' wafted back. To lead up is one thing, to reverse down with no protection is quite another. An anxious half an hour later he was back with us, shaking his head.

'It's no good. There's absolutely nothing to belay on to. It needs a longer rope. We can't do it.' There was a sense of disappointment all round, but we knew as always safety is the number one mountaineering priority.

'Never mind, let's have a look over the crater edge,' said Pete, manoeuvring

119

through the plant growth with care. There waiting for us was a perfect ledge with just enough room for a smiley Tibetan, a girl with a penguin on her rucksack and a man with a video camera at the ready. We sat in a line, legs dangling, perched in a high eyrie. The world lay beneath us. Pete put the altimeter around Mig's neck and asked him to practice taking a reading.

'We're at exactly 4,000 metres…' he came back. ' Seems a good height.'

As though on cue, the fly-past began. They came out of the sky from the east. Like a squadron of gliders mustering on a warm thermal current they circled round and round above the Pasochoa summit. There were three of them. One was larger than the others. Each was magnificent, soaring effortlessly on wingspans the size of a car.

'Wonderful!' whispered Mig.

We watched in awe as they widened their circling and flew within the crater. Looking up against the grey clouds we could clearly see their undersides, white tails and black wings silhouetted with characteristic long feathered hands. As they banked lower the show changed to a backdrop of deep forest green picking out the white ring of the head and the upper wing feathers reflecting the light. Levelling out at 4,000 metres, they took one graceful sweep in front of us. Our auras reached out and touched.

This beautiful contact and acceptance of us in their territory demanded a response.

I called out 'Oh Spirit of Condor… We greet thee and ask for blessings on our 'Climb For Tibet' … For you are brothers of Tibet… You are rare… You are special… And you have a need for freedom.

We combine our energies… And know that we will move forward in freedom… And that the Earth will survive in harmony.'

The meeting was over.

Each in our own thoughts, we started back down reversing the route. After the pitch with the rope the sun started to sink low in the sky and a cold wind chilled our aching bodies (well, mine was aching). I was grateful to reach the darkening shelter of the forest. I brought out of my rucksack my retractable ski sticks. These I do find make a big difference on a descent. People used to rather pooh-pooh their use, thinking them just for 'oldies', but they now seemed to be more widespread and accepted. They are meant to take more than ten per cent of the weight off the legs coming down, so particularly where knees are a problem they are great and on this occasion I was more than happy to move into the 'oldies' category.

I was deeply tired, but not down-and-out as I had been on Pichincha. Pete and Mig seemed disgustingly fresh and lively – as were the mosquitoes. Night fell as we reached the education centre. It was deserted. With difficulty we found someone who explained the system of buying a card to use the phone to order a pick-up truck in order to pick up us. We then sat on a step to wait, warmed by the glow of our experiences and were entertained in the darkness by the dancing lights of fireflies, to the musical accompaniment of crickets playing their harps and rhythmic froggy drums.

Mig had done well coping with the rigours of his first training day. The rigours of an extraordinary evening were in store for him.

14 - Wisdom in the unseen

Two young North American backpackers in the hostel kitchen stared at Mig in horror as he made the post-supper tea. It was no ordinary occurrence. He had decided that he would make Tibetan tea as a lovely treat for us.

'Basically it is just normal tea with milk and salt and butter.' He explained to everyone. 'It should be yak butter to be authentic, but I've only been able to find the cow stuff.'

The backpackers disappeared hurriedly.

We sat down to enjoy the universal pleasure of friends taking tea together. Mig drank his with relish and delight. Pete, as a regular tea drinker was doing well. Personally, I'm not very keen on butter or milk or salt or even tea, but struggled through the first few sips with a smile, knowing that it was special. Then I felt the time had come to make my feelings known.

'Mig, I'll do anything for Tibet... anything that is... except drink Tibetan tea.' I really hoped that I hadn't offended him, so added, 'I'm sure it tastes better with the proper yak butter.'

'Yeah, of course.' He laughed 'It's a different taste. You know, I think it's the idea of it that takes a bit of getting used to.'

'Mm... Maybe... Some things in life seem a bit weird, but I guess you've just got to try them. Let's all take our tea upstairs where it's quiet,' I urged. 'I want to play you a tape.'

Here, I would like a little aside with my reader again. Following is a record of more conversations that some find hard to swallow. You might like to jump to the end of the chapter, or you might like to try it. You may become used to the idea...

'OK, Miggie, here we go. A couple of months ago Pete, Delphine and I went to visit the man who is the medium which the spirits of Winston Churchill and Mahatma Gandhi come through… We sat with them and taped our conversations. It could be useful and interesting for you to hear what they have to say, as we specifically wanted to ask their advice on the Tibet-China state of affairs. It was an incredible experience. They spoke very clearly and characteristically using the medium's voice-box and body. It was the second time that I'd been and at no point during either time did I have any moment of doubt of the genuineness of the happening. Anyway, this is it. Are you ready?'

Mig listened to the recording, enthralled…

Churchill came through first. He was sitting back, open-chested with his arms on the chair either side, speaking in a jovial way:

> *'I'm very happy you're here. I don't get the opportunity very often to come, indeed in recent years I have been quite absent. Hmm, it is a great joy that I'm able to speak and to welcome old friends, hmm, hmm.'*

I was thrilled at the opportunity to greet him again. I explained that we were doing a special climb, to raise awareness and funds for the heavily oppressed Tibetans and were holding up Tibet as an illustration of working for harmony in the world. We would be honoured to have his opinion.

The response was quick and somewhat grandiose:

> *'I am familiar with the situation. First of all one has to be realistic and there is no way the Chinese are simply going to abandon Tibet, therefore all this anger and all the pressure makes no difference against the Chinese. What you have to do is to shame the Chinese from inside. They're a very honourable nation. They hate being shamed. If you are going to have success and Tibet is going to renew itself as a spiritual country, it has to be done with the help of the Chinese and not in opposition. So the Chinese have to realise the desecration of this spiritual country is against their honour…*
>
> *The Chinese have always in the past believed themselves to be very*

spiritual and I believe that once the church in the heart of the people of China has been given some amount of leverage, it will start to grow again. Spiritual things are not the opium of the masses, but the food, the nourishment of the masses. So if you start telling them that what they have done is to destroy thousands of years of spiritual growth, can you not see now how the shame comes in?... When the people start to realise that they have in a sense been duped.'

So I probed as to how we could help the situation with our peace messages.

'The messages of peace should not be anti-Chinese but appealing to the spirit and honour of the Chinese to consider Tibet in a totally different way. To see it all right as a protectorate of China, which is something that you will not change, but to give back the spiritual heart, which Tibet has over thousands of years evolved and held. That's the way I would do it. That I believe is the best advice.

Therefore if you are to pass your messages to the Earth, you must focus them into the consciousness of that particular Earth which at this moment is dominated by Chinese military. There must be a working towards peaceful coexistence whereby the Chinese do not lose face. They hold control of Tibet, but their military machine must be removed from the sacred ground of Tibet. That alone is the only hope there is. I believe the Dalai Lama considers the same thing, particularly after so many years and with so many nations on this planet doing nothing to assist him.

What you have in Tibet is very disagreeable, very distasteful, as a horse dropping is... a very smelly situation. The other governments won't remove it because the horse is more important, the horse is the economic opportunity of the massive continent of China.'

I interjected that surely on a worldly basis Tibet holds great importance as a spiritual centre, to which he replied:

'On a spiritual level it's very important, as an economic part of the

124

commercial system for which the world itself applies all it's rules, it is insignificant. One day it may be different. I hope so but that will be one day, not now.'

So I asked if he could see from his perspective how things would be in the future.

'It is given that all things are like the spokes in a wheel; it depends which spoke you take, to which destiny you will go. We have no control over the destiny of mankind. We can guide you along the way. We can assist you when you stumble, but you have control.'

I was startled to hear little squeaks that seemed to be suspended in the air close by. I was intrigued to find out afterwards that 'spirit noises' are quite common, but not everyone can hear them.

'I'm being told my time's up. I've been standing up too long talking. It comes to us all...' There was the sense that he wanted to laugh. Then he became serious again. *'What I would like to say to you is this. Whatever little consciousness you create, when you make it with many people it becomes multiplied thousands of times. Two people together do not make four, they make sixteen. It is an odd thing, but spiritual energy doesn't multiply as you think in arithmetic terms. It has a magnification factor far beyond and no one quite understands why it is able to do this. I believe now it is simply that God touches the essence of man's sworn endeavour thus releasing it universally into that which is magnificent.'*

Surely he referred to peace message energy coming together and expanding – how lovely. I mentally stored his stirring words as he ended with:

'I will watch with interest... join you on this great endeavour. Thank you. Good night, God bless you all.'

There was a heavy sigh... a shifting of energies. The entity that was Winston Churchill passed from the body. The atmosphere in the room was thick with spirit. The candlelight wavered and burnt low. Quite suddenly, holding a totally different feel, we were with the lighter, distinctly Indian presence of Mahatma Gandhi. He leaned forward, hands clasped in front. There was an eagerness. I would have liked to have somehow shown respect to the wisdom of the greatest of world leaders, but he went straight in, his voice lilting…mesmerising…

'If I am to come and speak to you for a moment it is to express something which I am hearing here. When the British Raj were in India we wanted them to go as friends, not as enemies. When the Chinese leave Tibet they must leave as friends not as enemies. Therefore, if you go forth and you try to rouse human anger against the Chinese you will cause the Tibetans much pain, because the only way is to create peace through friendship… understand me. So if you're going to do your work, which is most important and it is good because it is close to my own country and we want to see an opportunity for India to make a bridge back into Tibet, think of this. At the moment there is a wall. It is bad, but if we are really going to be brothers and sisters we need to remove the wall… and the wall that is created is not one politically made because there is a war condition, it is made of fear... the Chinese fear. They do not want to leave Tibet because they are frightened what other people will do with Tibet when they have gone. So what they want is to be given the opportunity not to loose face. So if you are going to read messages why not do it in this way. Praise the Chinese for the things they have done and let them know that if they leave Tibet they will leave as friends like the British Raj left India. Forget how they came, look towards how they will go.'

The question then was, what can we praise them for? What good have they done in Tibet?

The Master of Peace, whose life had so inspired His Holiness the Dalai Lama, replied:

'It is not always that what you see, it is that which happens… and what has happened to Tibet is that it has been forced into the present century. In the end no state can rely on a barbarism of spiritual

domination which has no grounding with the rest of the world. Before the Chinese went to Tibet no one was allowed in, everyone was a foreigner. If we are going to be brothers and sisters we do not stop them coming into our house. We open our arms and let them sit in our aura. So, if the Chinese have accomplished anything it is to allow the whole world to know about Tibet.'

Yes, and now we have all had the pleasure of hearing the Dalai Lama… and the teachings that have come out of Tibet that needed to be heard in the West.

'Exactly. The Chinese did go about it the wrong way but it had the right effect. The British Raj came to India to exploit us, but when they went they had shown us how to live in a modern world, because we were many small states not connected together. We were many people ploughing the fields in poverty and being warlike to each other because we did not understand our neighbours. When the British Raj left, India was one country. Now I know you are going to talk about Pakistan.… I am also aware that it was not as it should have been, but it was not the British Raj but the Indian people that caused that disaster, and the reason they caused that disaster was because they had not learnt to live with their brothers and sisters. You cannot hold two religions and fight about them. You have to accept your neighbour's religion as he accepts yours because no one has the truth, not I as a Hindu, not a Muslim, not a Christian, not even a Buddhist, but everyone has a little bit of the truth. And in the end when we can all together merge as one family, then we will understand what this wonderful spiritual experience is all about, because it is given to us in the mystery of God that each of us has a little part, but not the whole.

The spirit requires simplicity and I believe it was true when in your holy book it says you will not go into the kingdom of Heaven unless you are like a child. The child is without wealth because it is born before it can make wealth. It has a simplicity and it has a trust… And I believe the only thing in this world that is to be taught is to trust one another… Because there is enough food to feed everyone, there are enough resources in this world to sustain everyone and in the end the richest man cannot take a single penny to Heaven. In the end only the spirit lives on and the wealth is lost. We are living in a society of greed and suffering… but it is changing.'

I wanted to ask Gandhi about his words of five years ago, about the seven years before the Earth could wither and die, but was apprehensive about what he would say. Was he feeling more optimistic now about the general outlook of humanity towards caring for the Earth?

'It is not changing, but now I do not think man will destroy it. I believe that at the last minute there will be a change, but at the moment I am distressed by what I am seeing. I had hoped to speak with you all, many people on the Earth, and change their attitudes. It became clear to me that people often enjoy a conversation which has something unusual about it, but it is not my words that count, it is not me that counts, but my conscious words into your head that count. Because, like a great electrical wire, it is only when all the little atoms are joined together that the electrical circuit works in harmony. It is only when all the people on the Earth live in harmony with each other that the whole ecology of the Earth motivates itself in harmony with the universe. You cannot take the floor from beneath you without falling. But that is what you are doing at the moment. If I were to be as one negative I would say I cannot see a change, but I am not like that. I believe that God is testing us all. I do not think He would create such beauty for it to be destroyed. And, while He has given us free will, I think He will maintain some control before we are so stupid as to destroy the very essence of what He has given us. These are my thoughts. It is true to say that very little has changed for the better.'

Can we help the peace of the Earth? Can we help with the inspiration? Gandhi sat back and the higher pitch of the voice box laughed in such an Indian way:

'Are you not already doing it? Are you not going to go and make the messages powerful and therefore internationally heard? Is that

128

The crystal atop a gateway stupa

Migmar milkshaking

GT and Yannick

Pete in the pàramo

Pala and Amala

Never mind this climbing business!

South-west face of Chimborazo

Pepé

National pride

Mig in exhaustion

Tess and Mig displaying flags

Peace Messages

OM MANI PADME HUM

not the way of it?'

I smiled, embarrassed at the acknowledgement of the great man, as he continued:

'I would be most pleased if I was in a body and I would climb with you.'

Would he do us the honour of giving us a message to speak out from the mountain?

'Umm... It is only when you reach the top of the mountain that you recognise how great is the inheritance our creator has bestowed on us and then recognise that we are all part of looking after the great gift He has given us...'

'Hmm?' And he went on to advise us *'I'm telling you, when you take such a venture as yours, it is like the salt march that I did. It is not the salt part that counts, but the effort to get there, that is very important. It is the result that comes afterwards. Therefore before I went on the march I made sure that all the media knew all about it. I knew that the newspapers would report it. I knew I was going to get coverage all the way. You must do the same thing. You must give yourself ample publicity so it is not simply the climb, but the people who are watching you. And then you will get the greatest response and the greatest success for it and the success is not simply the climb but that which the climb is symbolic of.'*

Did this also apply, I asked, to the six Tibetans who he must know were currently on hunger strike in Delhi. Surely that's going too far.

'Yes... I am well aware, for they are in my own country, but I will tell you I have also been in that particular way many times. How can you change if your heart believes that you are doing the right thing? And if in the end you give up your body, if you truly believe that you will continue to exist after this body has decayed to dust, well then it

*is the spirit which is most important. Sometimes you can afford to
give up the body.'*

I let these words pass without knowing...

*'... When I died I had my loin cloth and my shoes and I was the
happiest person, not the way I went, but I was happy that I had lived
the way I had lived. And if I had been in the Raja's palace I would
have been unhappy because I would have felt that I had ruined my
own spiritual consciousness by accepting treasure on the Earth.
Those who have made themselves rich and powerful change
completely in spirit and often question that very aspect of themselves.*

*When I came into spirit I found a strange circumstance which I had
not expected and you would call it a debating club. We are all here
trying to reason why you do the things that you are doing.... It is
given to us to believe that you are all afraid to understand that you
can perfectly and harmoniously live as a spiritual being on the
Earth. You hold on to all your possessions as if you never want to
leave your physical body. Yet you are like all terms in nature by
necessity told from the very moment you have intelligence to
understand that you are only here for a short time in this physical
form, and when you are told this, is it not sensible to seek the spiritual
aspect of yourself? What do people do? They try to shut themselves
off from reality and they bathe themselves in treasure. They take
drugs, they take drink, they do all these things because they go
against their nature, their spiritual nature. That is why you have a
world which is going the way it is because people are afraid to
recognise themselves.'*

Why then does nobody seem to learn from past mistakes or past lives or
karma?

*'God never said to you I will make you grow, He simply said I will
give you the experience from which you can grow.'*

130

And is that why there is so much pain?

'No-one can be protected from the physical experience, because everyone has freedom to do and be as they wish and natural law is given that God will not in any way impose His own power. But in all things of the Earth there is one powerful energy and, if you trust it and always honour it, it will not let you down... and that is love. Nourish the whole world with love and you will receive love back. It is the currency of the spirit. Therefore, if someone is requiring to go through an Earthly experience of a painful nature, it is not simply their physical body which is healing, it is also a giving of love to stimulate the balance, because the physical and the spirit are one. Does that make understanding to you? However, I have been here for nearly fifty years and I tell you I still do not understand the mystery of creation.'

I smiled surprised but, trusting his wise perspective, wanted to ask a personal question, not quite able to voice the words.

'I can speak to you in this body. I can walk with you without a body, but I cannot talk to you when I have not got a body.'

Well, it's about my father who died a year and a half ago and we promised each other we'd keep in touch and I've done nothing as yet to... I'm searching...

'He has visited you though.' There were squeaks of spirit high in the room. Some sort of information service was taking place. *'You have had evidence of his connection with you. He left you a message. Now he has gone on to do his own thing in this world here and he is perfectly at peace. But he will not alter anything that you are doing by contacting you, because he wants you to be yourself. You must realise that love is not a selfish act of possessiveness, but that it is a desire like a bird to be free to soar in the sky.'*

Gandhi, the great soul, prepared to take his leave and allow the consciousness of the medium to return to its body:

'It has been a delight to me. When you are in spirit you are as one isolated by a dimension which is again a mystery. When you feel the love of people on the Earth and are drawn back through a body to be able to communicate, you realise that you are not simply an observer but still part of the great motion of human tide... evolution moving it to I hope wondrous positions on mountaintops.'

The click of the ending tape on the pocket player startled us into the reality of our hostel room... the wooden floor... the yellow walls... the drip of the tap in the shower...

We held with awe a sense of the continuation of the human spirit. This is a concept that Tibetans take for granted, but Mig was still excited.

'That is so brilliant!... You know I'm sure they're right about all that stuff. I must send a copy to an old lama who I know in India. He is a huge devotee of Gandhi and the power of the peaceful way he achieved so much in his lifetime... That is just so brilliant!'

I smiled at his excitement and at the honour that I felt had been bestowed upon us to be part of the meeting, but also at the normality with which I now accepted the conversations.

Yes... Mr Gandhi... Yes... We will be a voice for your message... And we most certainly are striving for the mountaintops...

15 - WONDROUSITY

Apart from Gandhi, the only other person I've ever known to use the word 'wondrous' was GT. Enthusiastic, intellectually effusive, outgoing and fun, GT expressed the joys of life just like the word he said so often and, in keeping with the edict of balance that what one gives out one attracts, his arrival at the airport was a joyous occasion.

Whilst waiting for his flight to unload, Mig and I held out the colourful Tibetan flag with affection. There was the accustomed staring and bemusement of onlookers in the busy crowd, but we took no notice, gaining confidence in our gathering group energy and in our happy time of greeting. Anyway, there were bananas to devour – to try and beat the record of nine in one go.

Pete was practising with the video camera. He filmed the arrival area where a beautiful Ecuadorian girl was preening herself in the reflective window of an information booth. She might have been upset to know that her private moment was immortalised on celluloid, unaware that all our moments are immortalised in the great scheme of things with every little thing we do making a difference and creating the blend of eternity.

In a similar expression of grandiose open-mindedness, trying to understand the huge picture of time and space, I always called GT 'Brother of the Universe'. His response to me was 'Sister of the Cosmos'. So I searched my Spanish dictionary for the correct translation to greet him with.

'Saludos!… Hermano de Universo!' I shouted, as our fellow adventurer appeared through the mingling passengers. Standing before the crowd as though at the finale of a performance was the archetypal conductor with flowing mass of grey hair, flamboyant gleam of eyes, aquiline nose and distinguished beard. He displayed an air of graciousness even with the heavy rucksack on his back and faded old climbing boots on his feet. Cheers went up. GT grinned from ear to ear. There must have been something about his presence that caught the excitement of the crowd because everyone started clapping.

'And there you all are...' he beamed. His arms went up above his head, taking the roar of applause in his stride, 'But this is really beyond the call of duty... isn't it marvellous...'

As we hugged him, Mig observed with a smile 'D'you know what, I never got that sort of a welcome.' It was the start of a friendly, instinctive kind of competitiveness that seeped through the general banter during the coming days.

GT oozed 'Well... wondrous... this is just wondrous!'

We had been joined by warmth and merriment. There was a satisfaction in his arrival, a bonding in our sense of purpose together in a strange land. Our team was complete.

The sun shone down on our courtyard breakfast evaporating the damp of the night. GT enjoyed absorbing the sights, smells and sounds of his new environment - the rawness of the rough brown pots, Spanish chatter, tropical foliage, thin sweet air, the Inca artefacts, Ecuadorian eggs and coffee, and the friendliness of our hosts.

'Buenissimo!' He expounded in his best Italian accent.

He looked in remarkably good shape after the long journey, but there was cause for concern as Pete and I were already nine days ahead of him with the altitude acclimatization programme. His body had a lot of catching up to do. Pete was particularly worried about his fitness preparation. Although he had been able to have a few days walking the hills, his time spent waving a baton rhythmically and enthusiastically about was not what Pete would call great training. Maybe a large heart was all it would take. Time would tell.

We all poured out information at him to try and bring him up to date on the last few days.

'You're going to love it here,' said Mig. 'I feel quite at home already. You know, there's something about the Ecuadorians that's almost Tibetan. They look quite similar. I even saw someone who looked quite like my mother.'

'How very interesting,' replied GT 'It could be the influence of the early American Indian peoples... with way-back Asian origins...'

'It's the girls that Mig's looking at in particular,' interjected Pete.

'Too right, Pete,' responded Mig 'but you're OK… you've got your love bird with you…' He looked wistful.

I laughed. 'You'll soon have them falling at your feet as usual, Miggie. Keep up the training with the flowers.' I was thinking of our trip to Wales when Pete and GT had been teaching Mig the nuances of English wooing techniques.

'Mm!' came in GT. 'Give flowers… raises the quality of the ambience… very important.' He smiled and then fished around in his pocket. 'But take a look at this. This is what was given to me on the way to the airport by the lovely young Debbie, who's now my girlfriend.' He held up a handsome piece of deep royal blue stone flecked with pale brown. 'It's lapis lazuli… It's to place and leave on the top of Chimborazo.' He spoke the name of the mountain with a lilting reverence as though he was introducing a piece of music that he had just written, and I caught an edge of the feeling of the importance that this climb carried for him. 'Isn't it wondrous? She also gave me a special cloth on which she's drawn a beautiful Buddhist message of transience… And my little daughter Chloe has done me a quintessential painting to take… so many precious things…'

We studied the stone.

It is said that the healing properties of lapis lazuli were much used in the ancient times of Atlantis not only to promote good communication with the Divine but also to harmonise that which exists in the inner and the symmetry of form of the outer, expanding the essence of brotherhood, co-operation and the ability to produce abundance for all mankind. This was not just any old stone.

I fingered the lapis lazuli star around my neck, and Pete and I exchanged glances.

Synchronicity!

Quite suddenly Mig moved into overtone chanting mode, producing amazing deep vibrational sounds which changed the atmosphere of the South American courtyard to a far away Himalayan monastery. We were caught up in its spell… and enchanted.

'Marvelloso! Mig.'

Now was the time to tell GT of the magic of the crystal, the stunning message from the Master Advarr and our wonderings about the six-pointed star. He listened intently, and slowly read the message out loud, not sure what to make of it:

'Souls have been chosen within your earthly world to carry the light into

many remote places. To the mountains… …The crystal will become a signal…
…many masters have gathered… …forming the energy of a star vehicle of pure
light… …Blessings to you as you journey…'

'It's very powerful stuff.' Pete pronounced.

'This just appeared, eh?' asked GT quietly, deep in thought.

I nodded.

He gently handled the crystal, noting its exceptional clarity and took time to absorb it all. It was strange, but surely… it was wondrous.

There was a rare moment of silence. Then Pete spoke softly 'Look up. What can you see above us?'

There, encompassing us over the breakfast table were four hanging baskets, dripping with green ferns. In themselves, apart from their fresh loveliness, they portrayed nothing unusual, but then I saw what he was referring to. The wire base of each basket was in the shape of a six-pointed star.

Synchronicity?

'Ah, but there's more. Have a look at the replay of the footage of Mig arriving at the airport.' He pulled out the little screen from the video camera and pressed the play button. We all crowded round and watched. There was Mig receiving my welcoming hug with the flag, and above us a bright light dominated the picture. It shone effusively as a six-pointed star.

Synchronicity.

'Wow!' I said excitedly . 'That's excellent! I'm sure these are all little pointers on the way that we're being guided along. I don't think it matters that we don't quite understand how or why. The important thing is that all around the world different groups are being guided to do wonderful work producing little blobs of light, and together they're a powerful force of change for the greater good. I see our 'Climb For Tibet' journey as a quest for one such blob of light.'

'Well, Sister… We'll leave that side of things for you to sort out,' said GT warmly.

The spirit of our coming together in aspiration was strengthening. However, if our mission was to be accomplished we had to turn to the nitty-gritty.

136

Careful planning was necessary, utilising Pete's left-brain organisation, to allocate the number of days that were available before the climb. This could not be moved from the 6th of July, the date that we had chosen months ago. It was the Dalai Lama's birthday, a sacred date in the Tibetan calendar, which is celebrated world wide as a focus on His Holiness and the Tibetan philosophy of peace.

We had to make sure that GT had the chance to acclimatize to the level of the rest of us as rapidly as possible whilst we were still advancing in our own programmes. It was also important to enable Mig to gain all the mountaineering experience possible. It was now the 23rd of June. We had to be on Chimborazo and able to cope over 6,000 metres by at least the 4th of July. That left only eleven days.

We could squeeze four summits in, with gradual ascension of height. Pasochoa and Pichincha were nearby and revisiting would save on time. Any other mountain needed time for investigation, the organisation of reaching it, a day to climb and time to return. My pleas to Pete for rest days fell on deaf ears, or met with a do-you-want-to-climb-Chimborazo-or-not stare, even with the excuse of fifty postcards to write. Energy had to be carefully rationed out. I found that even though I was fairly happy at 2,850 metres now, I went through phases of feeling really tired with the body reluctantly following dragging feet. This certainly was going to be no holiday.

Ideally we wanted to try and climb Cotopaxi, at 5,897 metres, four or five days before summiting Chimborazo so no acclimatization would be lost. But then, if we had a really tough time on Cotopaxi, and pushed our energy resources to the limit, then the chances are that we would be too tired for the big one. Gaining acclimatization and fitness were finely balanced with being in the right moment both physically and mentally. We were subject to the vagaries of the weather, notorious for upsetting the finely laid plans of the best mountaineers. Also, we were severely restricted by not knowing how things worked in this country where we couldn't speak the lingo.

We turned for advice to 'Safari', a tourist agency run by an ex-Englishman, David, who was more than happy to share his knowledge and experience with us. He specialised in mountaineering. Yes, he could run the whole thing for us, take us everywhere, feed us, provide guides, every little detail would be taken care of and it would only cost us a few million sucres or a four figure amount in $US. If we had been rich American tourists we might have been happy to hand over the responsibility of everything, but that was certainly not what we wanted. This was the 'Climb For Tibet' expedition.

It started a debate on whether we should think about employing guides on Chimborazo, as had been suggested by Lincoln. Pete and GT, as experienced mountaineers, were aghast at the thought of even contemplating guides. It was not really climbing a mountain to follow someone up, to be shown the way and not to use all one's skills of navigation, strength, bravado, technique and ingenuity. The achievement was not what a 'real' climber would call acceptable, even though they knew that decisions would finally be made on the grounds of safety.

'I say, Old Boy…What do you think?'

'It's just not proper. Good God, Man!… We're British!'

However, we had rather special circumstances. It was absolutely vital that we climb on the 6th as so many people were involved with us on that day with their own climbs or message readings, although the day before or the day after could perhaps be contemplated if necessitated by bad weather. There was little written about the possible routes up. We had scant knowledge of the area. And most importantly we had a complete novice with us and he was the one, I felt, who we wanted to make sure would reach the summit above all else.

The debate simmered. The thought of having a guide or guides did not actually bother me at all, except for the cost (I wasn't very good at non-attachment to money). At US$75 per day plus expenses, a guide was cheaper here than in Europe, though we did not know how Ecuadorian standards compared. But we were all pushing our finances to the limit. 'Climb For Tibet' had already cost us personally huge amounts and there was no way of having any of our expenses paid unless a lot of money came in on the documentary film. That was a very tenuous hope, but a hope none the less.

I felt that, although in climbing terms it would be a lesser achievement with a guide, I was not a good enough climber for it to matter. I didn't mind being 'taken'

138

up a mountain. The only reason that I had ever got up a serious mountain was because I had been lucky enough to be with good climbers. Maybe it helps sometimes having a personality of the happy-to-be-led-female variety (as long as it is in the direction that I want to go).

The important thing was the wider picture of what we were doing. If having a guide increased our chances of getting to the summit then that was good. We had to get there. We were going to get there whatever it took.

I didn't mention it to the others, even to Pete, but I certainly had no intention of going home until we had climbed it.

I knew that it would be useful to do some visualisations as the mental picture contributes to the physical actuality, so I tried envisaging the four of us on the summit. Somehow it seemed to be forced and I couldn't quite get into it. I couldn't see us there. I wondered what it was that didn't quite resonate, but had to forget about it and become busily involved in all the many things that needed doing at a practical level.

Whilst GT was coping with first day exhaustion, Mig had important things to do like buying food to cook for us all and viewing the World Cup. I passed the door of the hostel television room and watched him making friends with other football fans from around the world. I saw the 'you're cool' way they smiled at him. He seemed to have an extraordinary ability to communicate at a deep level with people even though he couldn't speak their language. Maybe football too was a bit like a language.

Pete and I found ourselves with an inordinate amount of 'office' work, for which we needed to try and sort out the communication hassles. Most were to do with the organising of the documentary film. Amora were associated with the Wisdom TV channel in the US who had commissioned a cameraman to come down and film us. Wonderful, we thought, it's all going to happen, the story of the peace climb will be told to the world and there will be huge awareness for Tibet.

Abortive attempts at fax, phone and email from all over the city accompanied by exorbitant costs, not only of money but also of our energy, finally put us in touch with Michael Tobias from Los Angeles. His credentials told us that he was rather more than a cameraman. A seriously fine climber with first ascents to his name on many continents, he had lived and wandered extensively throughout the Himalayas. He was author of some twenty or so books and had written and directed over a hundred films including documentaries about His Holiness the Dalai Lama, currently with his series on the great spiritual thinkers of the century.

His primary activities concerned animal rights, ecology and public policy. We were excited that he sounded such an extraordinarily involved human being on so many fronts. Pete spoke with him on the phone and was hit by his exuberance. 'Fantastic! Whymper's mountain! Humboldt's Ecuador! We can really help Tibet with this. Please, organise accommodation for two assistants and myself and find a local cameraman and sound guy. We need a bus to get us there and food… and a cook…'

Thus started the whirlwind that was to eat into our relatively organised plans.

'Now, I've been told to film a story about three climbers and a monk. Is that right?'

'Ah!' said Pete "well, sort of…'

We discussed the roles. The monk had to be Mig (I didn't feel strongly enough about the inkling of a previous lifetime). Tradition had it that one member of every family in Tibet took up robes and moved into a monastery. Since the Chinese invasion it had been almost impossible to uphold this way of life, but Mig had thought about the possibility. He would like to become a monk and sometimes he had yearnings. He could certainly shave his hair off as a symbol of devotion.

'Please don't, Mig.' I tried to dissuade him. 'You've got lovely hair and anyway you would get really cold up high. Maybe you could just climb in Tibetan national dress with your chuba on top of your climbing gear.'

'Well, to be honest, Tess… Yeah… It's more important to always be happy with what we've got.'

'I'll try and not forget that, Miggie… I will remember…' Even though I was so much older, I felt that our relationship was like that of long-time friends with a deep respect for each other. Although he was a typical young man, he carried an innate sense of sagacity. I was often learning from him.

However, we were already becoming influenced by the glamour and potential of a film, rather than concentrating on the business of climbing the mountain… And that included putting up with the incorrigible carry-on of Pete and GT who had risen to the challenge of portraying the ultra-English mountaineer abroad…

'I say, Archie, who's going to be the star, Old Boy?.. I'm better looking… Which do you think is my best side?'

'Redhot, Dear Boy… I'm much better looking. They're bound to choose me… but you could be my very special friend…'

140

Oh help!

At least the camaraderie relieved the stress and frustrations of trying to keep in touch with our 'Climb For Tibet' base and Amora in England and Wisdom in the US.

Pete, as the only technically literate one amongst us, was allowed to use the hostel computer, until two hours after typing long emails he was told that they were lost. There had been a power cut and they probably had not been sent. We might know tomorrow if they had gone. We might not.

The South American Explorers Club fax was still not working, though we found wonderful helpfulness and information there and directions to fax facilities at a nearby hotel. Eventually one went through. 'That will be 160,000 sucres (£20), please.'

At the Quito telephone centre I queued for half an hour and in trying to leave a message for Candy at the home base had the wonderful surprise of speaking to my son, Mark. He chatted about Paul and himself with all the usual school problems and excitements that made me long to be there to be 'Mum'. There was another life a world away that called to me. He also relayed the peace message from my middle son, Scott, who was travelling with his girlfriend, somewhere between a beach in Indonesia and a macadamia nut farm in Australia. It indicated the sense of responsibility that many young people feel today:

"Travelling around the world across three continents, we see continually the cycles and relationships between all nature and people, and we see how very crucial we are in either tipping or preserving this delicate balance. Universally we must and will take responsibility in every walk of life and stand up for the values and actions that heal our Earth - of environmental devastation and pollution, from extreme poverty, from political violence and genocide... And we must move forward with eternal and essential feelings of compassion and peace."

Scott's intelligent perception and similar thinking to myself, along with his caring-enough-to-bother attitude, enhanced my tender feeling of closeness to him. I thought of the time, two years previously when wc had visited a Tibet art exhibition in London together and viewed a team of monks constructing an exquisitely lovely Tibetan sand mandala – a sacred circular pattern used to aid concentration.

141

In the process this one had been dedicated to world peace and harmony. On completion, after many weeks of careful labour, it was to be swept up and chucked into the nearest river, the Thames. This was to symbolise the Buddhist principal of transience, that all things are impermanent. Scott and I had decided, along similar lines, to dedicate a 6,000-piece jigsaw puzzle to harmony. We had enlarged our kitchen table and set about the construction of our mandala.

To this day we await the great moment of completion when we can show that all things do indeed move on.

After the brief connection with my sons, I was able to float happily around the city excited by the touching in with my mother-child bond, always the most intense influence for me. It was as though I felt in contact with instinctive natural systems. Whatever else happened in life that was always there. There was strength in its purpose and its love. I wondered though, would I ever understand how Tibetan mothers must feel making the heartbreaking decision to send their children secretly across the Himalayas on a harsh and life-threatening journey to try and reach a strange land wherein they might find freedom, education and a future.

Back at the hostel, in keeping with the priority of bodies in good working order, Mig cooked us up a yummy meal of rice, vegetables and lentils, adding chilli and meat for himself. His carnivorous habits always surprised me, as they seem to go against Buddhist thoughts of reverence, but then Tibetans, like condors, don't usually kill animals but will eat the sustenance that life offers in a way of survival in a harsh land.

GT voted the meal the best that he'd ever tasted and showed his appreciation by conducting the washing up symphony with a couple of plates held aloft. 'Crescendo… now pianissimo…'

142

Pete, in spite of all the many things that he had been trying to sort out all day, had found time to search out a lovely bunch of flowers to give to me. It was an expression of love and partnership in our great endeavour. Yes guys, being given flowers does work. I felt cared for, feminine and special.

Curling up with Pete to go to sleep, I thought, at this moment it's not hard to be happy with what I've got.

It was a joy too to return to Pasochoa to show GT the delights. He loved the wondrous sounds of all the birds and the magic of the ancient forest and was able to feel in tune with the Earth.

Pete, in filming producer mode, asked him 'Well, Old Boy, what do you think of it?'

He replied from underneath his dark blue cowboy hat, grinning naughtily to the camera, 'Jolly good show, what! This is simply spiffing.' But by the time he reached 3,800 metres he was coming up very sluggishly to the grassy knoll near the pine trees where we waited for him.

'I'm so sorry I'm so slow,' he apologised, out of breath. 'I never used to suffer like this.'

'Don't be silly. You're not slow. You mustn't say that,' I replied a little cross that he kept letting the thought into his psyche. 'This is only your second day. You must take it very gently.'

'Oh, aren't we all lovely,' he responded, but confessed that never in his life had he bothered with training for a climb. What strength of character he must have, I thought, to simply just go and carry out a climb without preparation. Was that the old way to do it?

In spite of the focus on our altitude training we all tended to forget what height we were at, that we were nearly as high as the top fifty mountains in Europe, and that we shouldn't expect the body to respond in the normal way. Even my superman Pete was breathing heavily, though he wouldn't admit it. I knew because I could hear it on the replay of the video.

That night Mig had a dream about climbing Everest. This said to me that what we were doing was affecting us on all levels... that the anticipation and stress was seeping through our minds whilst we were trying to cope with all the day to day things that needed doing. Would we be able to keep the pressure in check and put it to good use to motivate ourselves?

It was Jorge who usually produced the breakfast for us. His sunny demeanour prompted us to smile and joke with him, behaving like life-long buddies, though none of us had any idea what the other was saying.

Jorge was delighted to bring us in an early morning visitor. It was Emily who had come to say 'cheerio'. She was going down to the lowlands for a while, but suggested we contact Lincoln's office to find help with our planning. Also she had checked out information on the condors for us. There were, according to the last census, believed to be only thirty left in Ecuador. Research had found that many condor eggs had been sterilised by insecticides in the food chain. However, as they were on the 'Cites' endangered species list, in theory they were protected and the numbers were now thought to be increasing. With a possible life span of forty years and reintroduction programmes being put into operation in parts of the Andes, there was hope. But how very lucky we had been with our exciting meeting.

'You should have seen them,' enthused Mig. 'They were just wonderful, you know.'

'What were they really like, though, in essence?' asked GT.

It was at this point (sadly) that the condor impression was born. Pete slowly took off his glasses and placed them on the table. He rose to his full 6 foot 2 inches height, puffed out his chest, stuck his large beak regally in the air and with startled staring eyes managed to ruffle his beard. His long arms stretched out horizontally with large fingers parted and he flew around the courtyard.

'Redhot!' shrieked GT. 'You are a master.'

The rest of us fell about laughing, which was not a good response as therein after condor impressions were the order of the day. Perhaps the only saving grace was the thought that the spirit of condor had appeared through Pete to keep a watching brief over Migmar.

'Bye!' said Emily. 'Good luck. I'll see you when you get back from Chimborazo.'

Funny, I puzzled, I had never considered afterwards. Everything was geared up to the climb, to the summit and to getting there. I simply had not thought about afterwards. A flash of fear went through me. Was there to be no afterwards? Was this why I had not visualised it? Don't be so stupid, I told myself. We're all going to survive this. All will be well, and I buried the thought deep inside me. No manner of doubts would stop me. I had reached this far...

It was comforting to know that Lincoln had been nearly as far as the main summit and returned safely. At his tour office I gazed wide-eyed at the walls thick with all kinds of inspiring photos. There were brightly coloured parrots and butterflies showing off the lush green of the jungle, inviting an exploration by long dugout canoe; brown, barren iguana land with giant tortoises heading down to clear Galapagos waters; ice-cream topped volcanoes floating in purple skies; the dark handsome face of an indigenous Indian, showing pride...

We were met by Lincoln's young assistant Carlos a charming Ecuadorian who spoke good English. He was warm and welcoming, shook our hands vigorously and seemed pleased to be able to help us.

'I am so glad to be of service to such important tourists,' he beamed.

'How insulting to be referred to as a tourist,' commented GT in dramatic indignation.

Pretending that he was not with us, I told Carlos of our urgent need to reach as many peaks as we could and he came up with the idea of putting us in touch with a friend who had a jeep.

'He'll be perfect. He maintains his own vehicle, loves going into the mountains, charges only 300,000 sucres per day and, yes, he is available for a few days.'

Gustavo would pick us up in the morning.

At last away from the worry of exorbitant taxi drivers, bewildering local knowledge and unfulfilled travel schemes, things were beginning to flow for us.

Pete in particular was happier that proper plans could now be made and this rubbed off on the rest of us. Pouring over the guidebook he concluded Pichincha at 4,794 metres, Iliniza Norte at 5,126 metres and Cotopaxi at 5,897 metres. We would have to come back to Quito for nights in between.

Things were looking good. As if in confirmation, little synchronicities were happening. Along the Quito cobbled streets we passed two huge wooden doors littered with six-pointed stars; Mig discovered that he knew a friend of Michael Tobias; we met a young man who was about to start university with my Scott; and I received an email via the South American Explorers Club from Uri Geller, which had come at the exact moment that I was writing one to him, for Pete to try and send. That did not surprise me as Uri had always been a master of psychic serendipity – like the time he experimented with the method of a million or so people concentrating mind power on a set of numbers… It had been my only worthwhile lottery win ever.

I found time for some yoga and a meditation, long overdue, which gave me not only some much-needed peacefulness, but also an understanding about Uri. It was explained to me in the relaxed space deep within myself why Uri was involved with 'Climb For Tibet'. He has a very special energy with which he has already done many wonderful things, but which is only now beginning to be put to the full-intended use. He is to act as a transformer for high spiritual energy that is coming into the Earth and needs to be changed to a vibration that can be used at a physical level for redistributing around the world to help peace and harmony.

This revelation advanced my thinking and explained why it was important to leave his gifts on the appointed summit spot. He could then easily tune into these things, which carried his vibration, and his energy would be available for transformation. He was a vital part of the process that was being organised somewhere.

Feeling like a pawn in a game of chess without knowing the players left me feeling insecure, but it also gave me an impetus to just let things happen and flow in the direction they seemed to want to go.

That evening we had the first serious rain since we had arrived. It came down oppressively.

I was tired, in spite of the quieter moments of the day, and both Pete and I were wound up from trying to sort out the film paraphernalia.

'Let's have a decent sleep and leave late for Pichincha,' I announced. 'After all, we have a four-wheel drive vehicle and there are no unknowns. Let's see when we wake up.'

'Oh, come on, Tess,' he retorted. 'You know we have to start early when we're going for a mountain. It's only through being disciplined that we'll get the job done. We must be disciplined.'

'Why do you always have to be so organised?' I muttered irritably under my breath. 'This is not the business management awards.'

I was annoyed. This was always a source of conflict in our relationship (and right now I didn't want to learn from it). I liked to let things float along and do what felt right in the moment. I hated the thought of my life being enclosed into boxes. He liked to have everything listed, planned and ordered. He hated leaving all the decisions to the last minute.

We compromised on not quite such an early start.

17 - JAWS OF THE VOLCANO

Gustavo met us outside in the dusky morning street before the sun had found its way through the close-knit buildings and the thick leaves of the maples. He looked to be around thirty years old and typically Ecuadorian - short and strongly built. Intelligent eyes sat in a round brown face and set off a ready smile. Whether in the city or at the top of a mountain, he always wore boots, jeans and a dark blue donkey jacket. A grey peaked cap, Chairman Mao style, lived permanently on his head. We all liked him immediately and I felt a happy sense of a guardian angel come to take care of us. Mig declared that he was 'cool'.

His white jeep looked loved. It was high off the ground with a short wheelbase and a huge roof rack onto which we spread our rucksacks to be covered and tied down with a bright blue tarpaulin. There were two back seats either side facing each other and these were prettily covered with checked cotton-green gingham. This was to be our trusty steed for the next few days.

We piled in and retraced the route through the city around to the west. Once on the dirt road we were bumped and jolted about, though the rain seemed to have settled the dust. It took us over the pass then down through the village of Lloa and this time we had no problem in finding the Guagua Pichincha track. There was a contentment in having been this way before, but I missed the excitement of the unknown and unexpected treasures of the eye. I would often rather take risks and enjoy newness, than be in the safety of sureness. This was not the ideal outlook of a mountaineer who wants to survive, but there was always so much of the world out there waiting to be seen. As a child I must have been influenced by my brother Graham who had always said 'boredom is a cardinal sin'.

Now, however, I had to try and concentrate on my Spanish, as the communication seemed to be left up to me, with Mig interjecting the odd 'yeah' and GT contributing beautiful sounding Italian words. I enjoyed trying to construct some sort of sense. Improvements happened fast out of necessity. Gustavo was very patient and gesticulated in all directions to try and help. We had to establish a working language, the dictionary ever useful. Once we had invented how to say 'far out!' - 'salida lejano!', I felt that we were well on the way to international harmony – though I couldn't understand why Gustavo said that his dog had lived in his house for one hundred years.

Suddenly… Whoa!… Whoa!… the jeep started bucking and diving over a rain-deepened rut and tipping dangerously towards a steep drop. The weight on the roof shifted to the left and contributed to the tilt. Mig, quick-thinking, leaned out of the front door and rode like an Olympic sailor, watching horrified the right-hand wheels spinning off the ground. We balanced, swaying on a knife-edge. Very quickly and deliberately Gustavo made noises that suggested he would like us to exit ever so carefully from the back door. My Spanish interpretation had never been so good. Pete was the first to creep out and GT and I followed. The jeep gently returned to all fours. Phew! Baptism of fire!

'Hey, I'll never forget that moment.' Mig's words came with a gush. 'Leaning out like that probably saved us all.'

We nodded with relief and clambered back in. GT declared he would only travel if next to the door so he could jump out rapidly when necessary. Pete told him 'Actually this is quite luxurious in a jeep. You want to try the track in a Lada.'

Gustavo set off looking quite unperturbed as though nearly tipping up was a regular occurrence. Without further mishap he drove to about 4,000 metres, spat us out and went on up to the refuge hut. It was important for us to use the leg mode of transport to try to coax the body into acclimatization. We snail-paced along. At least GT and I were ponderously slow and ploddy, Pete walked purposefully and steadily with his long strides and Mig marched up as though he was hurrying to catch the no.11 bus at Piccadilly, twirling his stick as he went.

From the hut we turned and drank in the wonderful views that stretched before us. Peeking out from the heavy cloud there were distant purple hills with clinging agriculture that looked like it had been painted on. Nearer was the olive green and pale brown of the sweeping grasslands of the páramo guarded by an icy cold wind. Around us, through the collecting mists, was a lunar landscape with dark volcanic crags, lava scree and tuffaceous rocks strewn as catapulted from the belly of the Earth.

Today the refuge was open. We were able to shelter inside. Here Gustavo tried to tell us (I think) of the legend of the three Franciscan friars, who in early colonial days, when thoughts of climbing to the mountain top were riddled with fear, came up to this place. They were caught in a storm and found a cave to shelter in. The bravest of them went out to try and find a way down and never returned. When the storm had abated, the other two searched and searched and finally, overjoyed, spotted him on the high summit, kneeling in prayer. On approaching, delight turned to dismay when they discovered that he had been turned into a rock pillar and would forever be praying to God on a peak close to Heaven.

The building was as raw and cold as any cave would be at 4,500 metres. I borrowed Mig's lovely Free Tibet designer woolly hat to snug in. The stark and bleak main room had a table and benches on which we sat to eat sandwiches of cowpat, (a special sprouted bread brought over from my local Haslemere Health Foods, its energy-giving properties outweighing its unfortunate shape and weight). There was a sleeping room alongside containing bare metal bunk beds. You would have to be very keen on rocks to want to stay here... There seemed to be very little else, apart from a poster on the damp peeling wall. It was a diagrammatic picture of a volcano erupting with the title 'Los Volcanes son Peligrosos' – volcanoes are dangerous.

Simple as it sounded, yes, I thought, it's no bad thing to remind visitors that an active volcano could blow up at any moment. Guagua Pichincha had had a major eruption in 1660 that covered Quito in 40 centimetres of ash and three smaller ones in the 1800s. It had also seen human turmoil in the form of a bloody battle fought on its lower slopes in 1822 when Ecuadorians had gained independence from Spain. Since 1981 the mountain had been rumbling.

It seems, I thought, that Mother Earth knows about the principals of impermanence... Probably she is shifting uneasily at the short-sighted human policies of 'take'. A balance upset will be corrected... I shivered, not just from the cold. Maybe part of me was sensing... it would be just three months before Pichincha blew again.

There was one nice thing in the hut. It was a large visitor's book. It held names and addresses from all round the world, to which we added ourselves as 'Citizens of the Universe'. Mig wrote 'OM MANI PADME HUM' - and drew the beautiful Tibetan mantra of compassion.

ཨོཾ་མ་ཎི་པདྨེ་ཧ྄ཱུྃ

'May all living beings lead a happy life' he prayed.

I wrote 'Harmony in Tibet is but one spoke of the wheel of Earth Peace.' My prayer was that our supplications would be one small step in the right direction to redress the balance... swaying on a knife-edge...

Outside visibility had been vastly reduced. The cloud cover was low and precipitation over a hundred per cent. We donned waterproofs, trying to cover up any bare flesh (though Yannick travelled nude as usual) and headed for the rim of the crater. The wind blew fiercely and I found I had to bend double over my ski sticks to move at all. Gustavo, seemingly wanting to fulfil expectations as a tour guide beckoned me into the crater itself. Scarcely had I clambered over the loose ash and pumice of the ridge when the heat hit me. It came with the stench of the heavy sulphurous gases. There was no wind. I felt nauseous and faint and in all my layers of clothes took on the sensation of being enclosed and trapped. I started sweating. It was not hard to understand how some did not return from the jaws of the volcano...

Focusing carefully I moved out. Rather the other side of the ridge, the wild wind, the cold and the driving sleety rain than the idea of the searing heat and unseen terrors of a boiling cauldron. OK, on this occasion I was happy to err on the side of boredom.

We all gained the murky summit pillar where Pete and I had stood before. Mig and I unfurled the Tibetan flag, taking care that it did not blow from our hands. Then the two of us sat, backs against a rock, in meditation...

With far away eyes I watch Gustavo on the summit...kneeling in prayer... Beside me I sense that Mig is sleeping. Just for a moment across the mists of time there is no time... and I am the mountain...

My concentration was broken by Pete and GT arriving. 'We've just been to another summit, down and across that ridge over there. We think it's 4,794, that's 13 metres higher than here. You haven't been to the real summit.'

Only some of me wanted to get into the competitiveness of which summit was slightly higher. Most of me knew that it was far more important to have had a meditation with the mountain... for a little while... But the egotistical part was dented. I rose to the bait of 'We got higher than you' with 'Bet you didn't. We don't know for sure about the heights, there's so much variation. You didn't take a reading with the altimeter. It was in Mig's pocket.'

151

It was only the banter that went on in fun. But hang on… Did it matter? Inside of me there was a little Egbert, with a huge head, a large mouth, arms that flailed about and spindly legs that he used to jump up and down shouting 'Me…! Me…! Me…! Of course it matters. I'm the best!'

Down, boy, down… Shut up… I want to be the best that I can be within myself… competing with myself… not at the expense of others.

But Egbert was all puffed up, ' Win…! Win…!'

Go away. It's enjoying the game that counts.

'I've got to be the one who's right, no matter what!'

Egbert… Go AWAY!

'Well, if you two have been to the highest point today, I guess you'll have to pay for supper,' I declared, smiling as we were gathered that evening at the vegetarian restaurant near the hostel. Maybe the drive for achievement could be put to good use. The main thing was that apart from slight headaches and breathlessness, everyone had managed to suffer little from the altitude. This was a good indication that all would be well for Chimborazo.

'Basically, I can't wait to get there,' sighed Mig. 'All this acclimatization takes so long…'

Pete was especially pleased that GT had gone so well. 'Archie, Old Boy… You were brilliant.'

'I say, Redhot… What a wondrous day!' he replied. 'I really managed to find the rhythm of the mountain.'

When Pete came back with 'Ah… I think I feel a condor impression coming on…' I thought of disappearing under the table, but busied myself with ordering more milkshakes. They were the Quito speciality, made purely out of yoghurt and masses of fruit, and were very cheap. We felt that it was our travellers' duty to try each of strawberry, papaya, mango, passion-fruit and banana until we had the favourite sussed. I had it narrowed down to strawberry or banana. The trick was to try them before, in the middle of, and after the meal.

Mig decided on strawberry and declared 'You know, when I fulfil my ambition of having Tibetan noodle bars all over the world, I think I'll have these milkshakes in them.'

'Excellent!' I eagerly approved, conjuring up pictures of yummy multicultural venues.

'But Mig, I thought your ambition was to repopulate Tibet,' teased Pete.

'Of course, Condor,' he replied. 'There is a lot of work to be done.' There was a twinkle in his eye, but he was deadly serious. As a direct result of the Chinese occupation, well over one million out of the six million Tibetans had been murdered or lost their lives. Never was an ambition so needed…

Gustavo was not picking us up until 8.00 am, so the morning start was gentle. I was excited that we were going up a new mountain at last. Pete gave me a long hug and I sensed his strength, which I knew no matter what our differences was always there for me. It was a gift that I treasured. A heartfelt hug harmonises vibrations and gives understanding, for tight in one another's aura there can be no pretence. We knew that we both burned with the same fire of making our 'Climb For Tibet' venture a success.

'Good acclimatization is the single most important factor,' said Pete. 'Staying high at the hut tonight should really help our systems adapt.'

'Well,' I replied, 'my blood still feels pretty slow and lethargic.' I knew that even though we had had a couple of weeks at altitude it takes five months for the new red blood corpuscles to increase by the desired fifty per cent for full acclimatization. 'How's your blood doing?'

'Oh, zipping round as usual.'

'Typical... Why did I ask? You always do everything faster.' I smiled in resignation at my Viking warrior. Even my Egbert in dracular mode couldn't keep up and didn't seem to care. 'Are you still taking the Diamox?'

'Yeah, I feel great so it must help, albeit I do get pins and needles in my fingers occasionally. I've given some to GT and he's happy with it, but Mig won't take it. Western imperialistic drugs, he says!'

'I'll give him some of my homeopathic coca. He doesn't seem to be suffering at all, though, does he?'

'No, probably because of the amazing amount of water he drinks. By the way, you should check the colour of your pee. If it's yellow you're dehydrated. It should be clear. We must keep drinking all we can. There's meant to be a stream at the Iliniza hut, but we'd better take a lot of water up in case there's a problem.'

'Mm,' I groaned knowing water was always so heavy to carry. 'Maybe there'll be snow that we can melt.' The climb to Iliniza Norte's summit high at 5,126 metres was meant to be a relatively easy scramble so at least we were not going to take all the other weighty stuff – harnesses, ice axes, crampons, climbing hardware and ropes. (Though no doubt Pete would think of a good reason to take some); but sleeping bags and food would have to come, including lots of carbohydrate which was especially important for a steady energy release. I noticed Pete sneaking a heap of chocolate bars into his rucksack. Hmm... here we differed on the type of carbohydrate.

Gustavo had soon got the measure of our eating habits so took us to the Machachi market to stock up on bananas. Mig went to buy, pushing his way between the dogs, the firewood and the cooking pots. It was a delight to feast our eyes on the tones of the yellows, oranges, browns, greens and reds of the different vegetables and fruits displayed, even though it was teaming with rain. Both stalls and people were covered in plastic sheeting, chunky ponchos and Panama hats, (which actually originated in Ecuador). This was the designated dry season but, it seemed the guidebook was right, any conditions could be expected at any time, particularly after the recent El Niño Pacific currents had caused exceptional storms and extremes of temperature. Anyway we were English and it was good to have variable weather to talk about.

How we longed to be able to see the Avenue of the Volcanoes without their clinging cloud cover as we sped south down the Pan-American highway. It was about 40 kilometres (as the condor flies) from Quito to the turnoff west where we followed a gentle river winding through fertile pastures and on into the village of El Chaupi. We stopped here to stare at its beautiful little church, which was a whitewashed adobe barn with shield-shaped holes for windows and eight pillars stuck onto one end of the roof to hold up the haystack-shaped spire. It would have been sacrilege to visit by any other means than by horseback such was its air of bygone sun-baked magic. This marked the point where we left the cobbled way that could possibly be called a road, and took a sandy volcanic-grey route that could definitely not be called a road. It soon became clear that the previous day's balancing trick had not been unusual as like a ship at sea we rolled along, creaking and groaning, over ruts and holes and rocks.

'Nerve-wracking, isn't?' yelled Mig who was excitedly riding shotgun on the back, clinging onto the roof, to try and weight the wheels back onto the ground as they rose and fell.

'More like body-wracking!' cried GT being thrown about the inside of the jeep, until inevitably we were told to get out and walk behind. He could then be seen padding along in bare feet, long red socks flapping from his trouser pockets, striking his fist in the air and shouting 'I've paid good money for this!'

I wondered whether to mention that our guidebook had said to watch out in this area for particularly wild and territorial bulls being bred for the bullring, but thought better of it. It said 'if encountered move slowly and quietly.' Well, I thought, we can probably manage the 'slowly' bit.

However, it was when GT and Pete went skipping off back down the track hand in hand that I decided that the altitude had finally got to them.

The heavy showers had stopped and a watery sun pushed between scurrying clouds that swept the hilltops as we progressed upwards. The páramo stretched before us. Shrubby vegetation collected in the sheltered valleys whilst the rest was wide open grassland interspersed with compacted plants, some hairy, some waxy, and all so beautifully adapted to the harsh conditions. Tall elegant grasses and lovely purple-petalled stars with bright cobalt bluebell-like friends clumped together decorating our way, announcing that this kingdom of the wind, this abode of the condor, held its place in the heart of our Mother Earth.

At about 4,300 metres we had lunch, though my offer of the remains of yesterday's well-travelled and battered sandwiches or those of the day before was not received very graciously. We sat on a little flat patch of grass amongst a thicket of small polylepis trees. These paperbarks with characteristically gnarled and deep red trunks have the distinction, along with the Himalayan pine, of being the world's highest altitude tree. The twisted tangle of the branches was home to fungi, mosses, lichens and other epiphytes, hanging and waving, giving an enticing enchanted effect, as though custodians of the mountain telling us 'Come, wanderers, come… but advance at your peril.'

It was here that we left the jeep. Shouldering our rucksacks we followed the now bewildering trail across a dry rocky streambed and up towards a ridge, volcanic ash crunching at our feet. Our early eager steps were soon slowed.

'We should reach the hut within three hours,' I said to GT, gasping for air as I spoke.

'It may well take me six,' he replied, puffing hard too – at last, someone whose pace I could keep up with. Many good conversations are born on walk-ins to mountains. It keeps the mind happily off the agony of what the body is trying to accomplish, putting it into autopilot once the initial muscle complaints have died down.

So I asked 'Why did you really want to join us on this expedition, GT?'

'Well sister,' he began, 'two reasons really. The first was coming to Ecuador in the footsteps of Edward Whymper who's been a great hero of mine ever since I was a kid when I read his *Scrambles Amongst the Alps*. After his controversial first ascent of the Matterhorn in the Alps in 1865, when four of his team lost their lives when the rope snapped on the descent, he came to Ecuador and in 1880 undertook what must have been the most successful mountaineering expedition ever. Along with Louis and Jean-Antoine Carrel from Italy, he made eight first ascents here including the two highest, Cotopaxi and of course Chimborazo. Iliniza Sur was one of his conquests, but Iliniza Norte fell to an Ecuadorian, Martínez, in 1912.'

'I thought that the Incas had been up to a lot of these summits to make sacrifices.'

'Yes, you're right, but the Incas didn't have a system of writing, so we can't be sure, except for the ones with bones and artefacts on of course. The mountains were certainly sacred to them. But imagine how brave the early European explorers must have been to attempt to climb to these peaks which were shrouded in so much mystery and fear.'

'Yeah, and volcanic eruptions… What about your other reason?'

'Well, that's the spiritual side. It was the connection with Tibet that appealed to me… and Tibetan Buddhism, which I've been on the periphery of for most of my working life. I was privileged to know Marco Pallis and Richard Nicholson, two dedicated musicians, who went to the Himalayas in the thirties and came back as Tibetan Buddhists. When I used to go round for music sessions with them in London it was like walking into a treasure trove of Tibetan painting and Buddhist culture. That fed my initial inspiration gathered from seminal books.'

We paused for breath where the ridge went down a little before becoming steeper upwards again. It had just been possible to talk in between puffing and panting with a real slow steady pace.

'And what about your family, GT? What do they think about you coming to climb in the Andes?'

'Oh, I don't think my two sons and their families worry too much now. I've been going off all my life and they accept it... And Chloe, now that she is eleven, is becoming keen on climbing herself... She's got the bug too, if you can call it that... But Debbie, yes, she probably worries...'

I moved on ahead, leaving GT to compose music in his head, as the trail became a two-up-one-back slog through loose volcanic scoria - pyroclastic fragments and heavy ash. The angle of incline was severe. Calf muscles cried out. It might have been easier to go up a mountain of jelly with marbles as icing. It demanded an intense focus affirming... 'I am strong... I am strong... I am strong...' though the interruptions for taking gulps of air seemed to make it impossible. Step, kick, slide, breathe... Step, kick, slide, breathe... Step, kick, slide, breathe...

Somehow I was able to pull it into a rhythm, but there was a drifting... a distancing... and now the boots on my feet passing over the ground didn't seem to belong to me... I found myself moving into my mind... wonderfully... for a meditation in motion...

I am clearly visualising the star on the summit of Chimborazo. Its six points are held by the Council of Masters. There is an empty spot in the centre waiting for the presence of the crystal, so that the beacon of light may be lit. There is a grid of other beacons and the combined light will encompass the Earth. I am being told that there is something of supreme importance that I must know. It is this. The placement of the crystal can only be carried out if there is a holding in the heart of unconditional love. I must be aware.

Oh help! How? It sounds simple, but surely is impossible... Surely?... Step, kick, slide, breathe... I can only have faith that whatever my soul has chosen to draw to itself it is ready to cope with... and that there will be help available... Step, kick, slide, breathe... Step, kick, slide, breathe...

Through swirling mists I could see Pete and Mig reaching the top of the ridge. There was a saddle that came down to it between the two mountains, Iliniza Norte to the right, our route for tomorrow and Iliniza Sur to the left, a difficult technical climb. Once, during the Holocene period, possibly 10,000 years ago (just the other day in Earth terms), they had been one mountain, a stratovolcano,

158

one beautiful, heaving cone of fire. Maybe they still carried the energy of being together as one. Maybe knowing that all life was originally forged as one was how to hold unconditional love...

The heavy cloud covered all things in the greying dusk. There was no sign of a sunset. Just... Struggle to breathe... Struggle to move... Struggle to think... Drained and exhausted, eventually I gained the base of the saddle, where a gentle bowl revealed an orange building, the Refugio Nuevos Horizontes at 4,765 metres.

Climbers used to the well-appointed huts of the European Alps would have called this a hell-hole. It consisted of four walls that were wet to the touch, six metal bunk beds and a high sleeping platform above the kitchen area, which contained a couple of gas burners and a sink. Two tables with benches sat on the concrete floor and some stools against a wall shelf. There was no water except what could be carried from the stream outside, provided it wasn't frozen, and no heating or light even though the guidebook had said that a generator would be available – at least we had head-torches. I never did find the loo, though somewhere there was meant to be a hole in the ground with three protecting walls.

All this would have been fine, for it was shelter that we needed from the night and from the cold, but arriving so tired and hungry as we were, we were shocked to find that, in spite of having seen no-one all day, the place was full of people. There were about twenty Ecuadorian teenage boys and girls noisily milling around and we soon realised that they had come up for a Saturday night party. A lot of booze had obviously already been consumed and a lot more was on the way. Even though my life was used to a diet of teenagers, things looked bleak for getting any sleep or preparation for an early start to climb in the morning.

We scrounged a few very damp plastic mattresses and some floor space and waited for the chance to use a burner to cook some hot food to put inside us. The settling gloom matched our darkening mood. I felt disjointed at not having a personal spot to place my rucksack and gear that needed drying out, and out of sorts at the peace and quiet that my gathering headache was asking for. In fact I felt completely lousy. Both GT and Mig lay down unable to move with pounding headaches, nausea and dizziness. Even Gustavo looked green around the edges. I passed around the homeopathic coca remembering how I had felt at the Chimborazo hut.

Only Pete seemed his usual self and chatted to an English couple, Martin and June, who had turned up for the climbing, but were similarly upset by the situation.

159

At last, after what seemed like four hours, but was probably nearer two, we were able to boil water for hot drinks and some meant-to-be-yummy packet supper. But by then Pete was the only one who felt like eating... pasta and Mars Bars.

The worry of taking out my contact lenses without losing them in dark dirty places with other bodies pushing around was overcome and we settled down for the worst night's sleep that any of us had ever had.

The kids talked and giggled and chucked cans, some vomited, and some peed off the sleeping platform. Martin asked them to be quiet with repeated and increasing irritation. He tried in English, in some sort of Spanish and even in French. Gustavo tried in real Ecuadorian. There was a general shemozzle.

I curled up and hid inside my sleeping bag. It was intensely cold, a deep damp cold that seemed to eat into my bones. Unfortunately, there was no space to lie next to Pete, who is usually a good hot-water bottle. My knees in particular, as the bits that stuck out the most, ached from the cold as I restlessly turned from side to side to try and get comfortable.

I remembered that in one of Shirley MacLaine's books she had described picturing a sun inside herself to create warmth and then I thought of the little humming bird, the Andean hillstar, that reduces its heartbeat and goes into a state of torpor to survive an icy night. Maybe warmth is a matter of flipping the correct mind switch somewhere.

Soon my thoughts turned to the Tibetan monks who have mastery over their bodies and meditate in the deep snow creating a heat that is emitted in steam from their thin robes. I could almost imagine that I was a monk...

I know that the body is the messenger of the soul. It carries the spiritual expression... The annoyance and problems are a test... I concentrate on unconditional love... There is no sign of Egbert. He cannot cope with a love connection to others. He only likes separation...

Just for a moment I am incredibly, beautifully happy... I touch an inner peace... And I am warm...

19 - Currency of the Spirit

I must have slept for it was suddenly light and Pete was saying 'There's been a couple of inches of snow. It's debatable whether we should climb or not as we've got no equipment.'

The atmosphere in the hut was dank and smelly – an aftermath worth forgetting. Two of the youngsters approached GT and in broken English tried to apologise for their behaviour. Gracious as ever, he replied 'Oh, it was nothing…' and proceeded to become the best of friends with them.

Martin and June decided that with so little sleep and such bad conditions they would go down.

We reluctantly gathered ourselves for the ascent. Mig was feeling groggy and less than enthusiastic. 'You know,' he said, holding his still aching head in his hands and thinking of uncomfortable feet, 'I really don't want to do this.'

'You're going to do it,' rallied Pete. 'We're all going to do it. It's a training climb. It's important that you gain some experience on snow.'

I always respected Pete's mountaineering judgement. We would go.

It didn't look good outside. Snow covered everything horizontal, it was still misty and there was a very cold wind. 8.00 am was already late in the day for a mountaineering start, but the temperature was now slightly above freezing which meant that there might not be much lethal verglass on the rocks. So Pete took a rucksack with rope, first-aid kit, water, food and camera and the rest of us travelled as light as we could. That is not forgetting essentials – the crystal was safe in my fleece and Yannick just managed to sneak into the pocket of my waterproof at the last minute. Mig was not to be separated from his sacred stick.

We crossed the frozen stream and headed up to the saddle, which was the remains of the crater rim. For a while unusual yellow and clay-like volcanic material was becoming exposed underfoot. After that it was like being in an old black and white movie – white cloud, black rock, white snow. With even poorer

161

visibility we turned right up the south-east ridge, Gustavo looking overjoyed at being able to lead the way. The rocks were stable but large as we clambered over or between. Happily the snow was not a problem, except that I suffered cold hands with swollen painful joints in spite of layers of gloves, but I gradually warmed to the climbing as we worked our way up. The ridge narrowed and there were places where the run-out was steep. We were aware of this because GT dropped one of his ski sticks and we could hear it clattering down, far below us. The loss of it was annoying, as the sticks were proving so valuable on the easier general walk-ins and particularly the descents. But however useful, it was distinctly more useful to have a body that did not need to take the risk of climbing down a steep slippery volcano side to search.

A huge vertical rock face loomed at us, barring the way, so traversing right we found a series of ledges to gingerly follow above a steep drop. It was known as Paso de Muerte or 'death pass', but the ever present cloud prevented us from seeing down into the 'death' bit. Safely across, we then moved into a gully full of loose material that had to be negotiated. Hopefully it was still early enough in the day for us not to be threatened with rock-fall. Here Pete left his rucksack to pick up on the way down. He was unusually quiet. He was not panting was he? Struggling for breath? Surely not? Even Egbert didn't believe it. It must have been an illusion.

Further gullies with loose rock led us around and up to the summit at 5,126 metres. We had made it - after a three-hour battle. There were no views… Just an iron cross, the definitive expressing of the mantra of compassion 'OM MANI PADME HUM', a couple of photo poses and the warm hugs of a team achieving together.

It was an excellent success for Mig, as his first serious climb. He appeared to have managed with ease. For both Pete and I it was the highest that we had ever been. GT told us 'I'm thrilled; in fact, when I was in the Tien Shan, I enjoyed wondrous summits like this…' And as for Gustavo, well, he was not your common or garden taxi driver, was he?

There were no takers for the great honour of being sacrificed at the top of the mountain so we headed down. By now much of the snow had melted and the rocks were no longer slippery giving us some good scrambling. But I was in a sea of tiredness… down the gullies… across the ledges… out onto the ridge… drop to the hut… and down, down, down on exhausted rubbery legs and shattered knees. Once at the jeep the agony was not over. Whilst Mig rode shot-gun again to try and counter balance the almost impossible angles of the track, the rest of us had to cross seemingly mile after mile of rough grassland. There was walking when I felt like crawling, hot tears of weariness never far away, watching the little white jeep in the distance being tossed about like a tiny boat on stormy sculptured waters.

Yes, I thought, GT is right after all. He was not joking. If being a tourist means travelling for pleasure, then at this moment we are definitely not tourists. Yet how much more satisfying is it to taste the courage of the early explorers like Whymper, to feel the winds of exploration and discovery that blew in their hair, and to travel with purpose. This way is to be participating, being inside looking out.

Now we became outsiders looking in as Gustavo took us home via the tourist route. It was through the narrow cobbled streets of the old colonial part of Quito, past squares with fine buildings, imposing churches and dilapidated history full of charm. Here, on a little bun-shaped hill, beset we were told by bandidos, we looked at an enormous statue of the Virgin of Quito. She was impressive and carried a crown of stars on her head, eagles wings, and a chained dragon on a globe at her feet. The significance was out of the book of Revelations in the Bible. What was it all about? I didn't know. As a tourist overlooking the sprawl of the city below us with people going about their day to day lives, I was just passing through. I was not involved. I wondered if I was a tourist on the Earth, just passing through. Was I a taker, or was I treading softly with awareness? Monumental thoughts have a habit of drifting through when the body is tired... Thanks but I'd really rather think of nothing. Still, the thoughts persisted...

I cannot know what is happening everywhere. I cannot help everything at a practical level, except on a tiny scale. There are such huge problems in the world, like malnutrition and starving in the midst of plenty, and drastic unsustainability of the Earth's systems.

To some extent the Earth teaches us herself, like after the Chinese took over Tibet they clearfelled more than half of the forests there to take the timber back into China. This eventually resulted in the silting up of their own rivers and the flooding of their cities downstream with many of the rivers now being so degraded that they no longer support fish life, or provide clean water. Examples of insensitivity to the Earth are all around us. At what cost to human life? What about our children's lives?

I am sure that we can help. Problems can be solved from a spiritual perspective. As the physical is a manifestation of the spiritual, we can pray, we can keep our thoughts positive and compassionate, and we can give out unconditional love. It might not be easy to do, but it is powerful.

And now… now we had been asked to hold unconditional love on the summit…

I turned to the others as we drew up outside the hostel and spoke tentatively, 'We need to be in a state of unconditional love on the top of Chimborazo. My understanding is that the vibrational energy that we as catalysts emit could in some way affect the programming of the crystal whose function is to act as an amplifier for the light coming in.'

There was silence. I sensed a blocking. I had overstepped the mark. We were all on our own personal life journeys and I could not know or judge anyone else's. Nor had I the right to suggest what another should feel. What meant something to me in my terminology might mean something totally different to another. I regretted mentioning it.

'You know,' said Mig, 'it's time we all went and had a milkshake.'

'Wondrous idea!'

'Far out!'

The thought of actually having to walk the few metres to the vegetarian restaurant was not so popular, but then for a milkshake…

'First I must try and phone my kids,' said Pete, 'before it gets too late in the UK.' He spent a lot of time trying to ring through to them, to send love down the wires. He knew that Claire and Graeme at fifteen and fourteen years of age were aware of what he was doing to help Tibet and the Earth and that they were proud of his work. They wanted to talk to him whenever possible, and Caroline and Anna at nine and four needed to regularly hear Dad's voice and support over the phone. He was worried too about the little one who was soon to have an operation.

Pete was certainly loving his children unconditionally.

It is a funny thing this love bit.

Were we unconditionally loving the children at the refugee school where our sponsor money was going? Of course we expected nothing back.

Maybe I'll think of it as simply opening wide the doors of the heart…

Was GT loving unconditionally when he paid for Mig's expenses that came to more than he had planned… and our milkshakes?

Was Mig loving unconditionally when he carved his Tibetan Buddhist mantra for the day's climb into his stick, opening up to the compassion spoken of by His Holiness the Dalai Lama?

How was it when I checked with Mig that everything that we had planned to take to the summit was OK from the Tibetan point of view? For I so wanted it to be right for Tibet.

Gandhi had said that love was the currency of the spirit, a powerful energy, and that if we trust and honour it then it would not let us down... Surely he must mean unconditional love, in the paradox that it will only come back to us if it is unconditional... around every corner, every minute... there, but for the looking...

I held the crystal in the palm of my hand... searching. Still in awe as to how focusing on it gave me the cold shivers, I felt mounting excitement. The time was becoming closer. Today we had all managed to reach over 5,000 metres. There would be no problem to 6,300 metres. We were going to make it.

I noticed that the crystal had six sides. Stupid, I told myself, why be surprised? Of course it should be so. I looked at it end-on. It was a beautiful, perfectly faceted, hexagonal star.

The White Eagle Lodge leaflet, which I had brought with me on impulse waiting to be read, suggested visualising the six-pointed star. It said that it is a powerful focus symbol through which God's healing light comes and radiates to all beings. Also that it denotes perfection and stimulates the light within every human heart, the point of harmonisation between the inner and outer worlds.

Was the Master behind the work of the White Eagle Lodge involved with our guidance? Were all the different religions, sects and ways of looking at the finer side of life that we put into separate boxes in fact all part of one brilliant cosmic, pulsating rainbow that stretched across the heavens?

That night I slept heavily and awoke still wandering in a dream.

20 - One for the road

I am lying down in the road. It is hard and rough and dirty. Cars, trucks, bicycles and all manner of traffic are rushing dangerously by, just missing my head. There is raucous shouting and jeering as crowds pass by. There are some that ignore me, some who laugh at me and some who even make a point of kicking me. All of this is incidental... The only thing that matters is that by using my body for protection I am caring for the child who is cradled in my arms...

The road becomes a river and I am floating... being drawn further and further... and further...

Suddenly I am standing aside and the river is a river of monks sweeping past me... hurrying... there is much to do... so busy... so busy... maroon and saffron flapping. It is the entourage... They are slightly higher than I am... His Holiness the Dalai Lama, in flowing robes, is turning and coming down to talk to me. He explains simply that we are part of His work.

I did not want to open my eyes, nor did I want to enter the day. There was a lingering need to stay and savour the moment.

At breakfast Mig was wildly excited. 'Wow! Fantastic! This is a great blessing on our climb. Basically, every Tibetan knows that to dream about His Holiness is the ultimate blessing on a project.' His face lit up and he positively glowed with happiness.

It was infectious. We all beamed, for this was a propitious sign to balance out all the nagging pressures, and I was thrilled that it meant so much to Mig.

So it was in buoyant mood that we set off to journey to our last training climb,

Cotopaxi, claimed frequently as the world's highest active volcano (there are contenders on the Chile-Argentina border with higher peaks but lower volcanic activity). We were now used to the vigorous bouncing and bumping of our little jeep over the Quito cobbles. It must have even had rhythm as GT was inspired to expound great pearls of poetic wisdom, 'Let us swim in the oceans of the cosmos on the tides of eternity…'

No doubt it was something to do with the latest piece of music that he was composing.

The response from Pete was not quite so inspiring… 'I think I'm going to be sick!'… and he continued to concentrate on sewing wrist tags onto his waterproof over-gloves and sort out the practicalities of the day. These included the impossibilities of the communications that we had been trying to get right for days. E-mails went to the wrong people, faxes conducted wake up calls in the middle of the night, phones were engaged and engaged, photocopying involved travelling to different offices to be selotaped… It was exasperating. I was happy at the sixth place to achieve a please-pass-on-to-Malcolm-at-Amora fax via my Paul at home with an 'I love you – press fax. – Bye!'

Sometimes it seemed the old systems here were the best. I had been delighted to receive a lovely letter by post from Lawley today, full of affection and family news. Surprisingly it had only taken a week to come. We were told that even by airmail it could take six months.

Why were we now driving past the airport when we thought that we had completed all the en-route city jobs and should be going south to the Pan-American highway? It seemed that Gustavo had a surprise for us. (Maybe if my Spanish interpretation had been better it would not have been a surprise). He took us to his home. It was in a quiet, dusty street. Large metal gates opened into a small compound enclosed by tall concrete walls. The house was a long flat-roofed bungalow and there appeared to be some sort of a workshop business going on, judging by the fridges hanging about in varying states of repair. Gustavo's mum came out to welcome us. She was small, round and smiley and wore a smart, bright pink overdress. We had an instant affinity. As mothers we were both happy to chat away about our families and guess what the other was saying in a way that was so warm and affable that I wondered at the use of language. The communication was from different cultures, but of the similar joys, hopes and tears that were involved with caring for a family. It did not come from words, but from a sharing of the essence of ourselves. This gave me an insight into why the blocked energy of our recent correspondence problems may have been created...

Gustavo, she told us, was the youngest of eight children and she had copious numbers of grandchildren. The family business was based here, indeed many hands were helping to raise the jeep onto precariously balanced planks so that welding work on the leaf-springs of the suspension could be carried out. Brave wounds from the harshness of the Iliniza track were being repaired, assisted by the yapping encouragement of a little curly-haired dog that looked like a cross between a poodle and a sheep.

Would that heart wounds could be mended so easily, I thought, watching our self-assured Tibetan in his old borrowed thermal top and purple salopettes talking elatedly about the dream.

Pete took some video footage and played it back to the wide-eyed family, enjoying the pleasure it gave. There, to the accompaniment of banging and sizzling, were the boys welding, GT looking dapper and explorer-like, Gustavo over the moon at being called our 'guido' and his mum with a knowing expression.

She served us apple juice on a tray with napkins and took us up on top of her house to see the wonderful view. Across the concrete, tin and red-tiled rooftops, we could follow a couple of planes landing and taking off into a clear blue sky and disappearing over tall distant peaks, deep purple at the other side of the valley. There was just a sense that the mother could see far...

Gustavo then drove us out of Quito and south along the by-then-familiar fertile green Central Valley. To the right stretched the Cordillera Occidental mountain range holding our recent scene of trial, the twin peaks of Iliniza. To the left lay the Cordillera Oriental range with the dark emerald crater of Pasochoa, and Cotopaxi waiting demurely behind a tantalising veil of cloud.

The sun shone down on us, as it had five hundred years ago on the Inca peoples as they had constructed roads along this very same route, roads which were part of one of the greatest systems ever built. They stretched from here nearly 2,500 kilometres to the alluring, magical-sounding Machu Picchu, Cuzco and Lake Titicaca, and on a further 2,500 kilometres to Santiago. They were straight and uniform, crossing some near impossible terrain with carefully planted trees and canals alongside. Still today there is marvel and wonder at how the dovetailed blocks of stone, perfectly joined, were made without the use of mortar or steel to fashion with. The Incas would have had much to teach us, but history relates how the Spanish conquistadors invaded and set out to destroy this ancient and beautiful culture and many of the roads were dismantled to provide stone for the houses of settlers. Perhaps in the fullness of time it will be seen that foundation rocks laid to ease the path along the road of life can be a gift of unconditional love for the next people… in spite of ruthlessness and devastation.

There was still much activity in the back of our journeying jeep. Mig covered his face and exposed arms in protection cream (in the absence of yak butter) as he had been experiencing sunburn for the first time ever, and we all filled up with as much as we could eat from the large food bag, knowing how appetite diminishes with altitude. Today we also carried extra luggage as we had all the climbing equipment with us. Even Gustavo had thrown in an old grey canvas rucksack containing a helmet and short battered ice axe. It seemed that he had high hopes, though we still had no definite idea of what his mountaineering experience was, which was a little worrying.

I was busy with the tiny tape machine, recording some of the peace messages sent in from school children, with the idea that perhaps we could play them on the way up Chimborazo. They were from youngsters, aged 8 to 12, at Dunhurst in Hampshire. I had spoken to them about the climb and Tibet and the wider issues of helping the Earth. They had each written a gem full of hope for the world and their future. So many touched our hearts, tempting tears. So many left us in no doubt of the special responsibility that we had been given to deliver these precious thoughts, pledges and prayers to the Watchtower of the Universe, that they may blow around on the winds and do their work… Children so often see things in a clearer way than adults. They seem to know that what they express from the heart will reach the heart of their Earth with love, that even just conceptualising messages can precipitate changes… and that they can make a difference:

"I will care for everything."
from Gussie Maier.

"Treat every living thing with lots of respect. We should have world peace. If the Earth provides things for us, we should help the Earth in return. Don't use all of the world resources. Love all animals whatever they look like. Treat animals nicely."

from Issy Ehrlich.

"May we have the strength to find peace in our hearts."
from Harry Gillespie.

"That we stop fighting and have world peace and we look after our planet Earth."
from Giles Prowse.

"I will not fight with my mum during the World Cup."
from Simon Jones.

"Let all the hate in the world turn into love and let there never be hurt in Tibet and let the Dalai Lama be safe."
from Ross Stewart.

"Love the world, be at harmony and peace with it. Create your own shield of peace around you so you will not be angered by your fellow countrymen. Give out rays of love to the centre of the Earth. Live in harmony together, join hands and be forever family."
from Catherine White.

I smiled at the simplicity and wisdom that poured forth from the tenderness of their years, and felt humble.

Within an hour and a half we had passed the road to Iliniza and were turning off east, near the NASA satellite tracking station and up to the entrance gates and buildings of the Parque Nacional Cotopaxi. This park was Ecuador's pride and joy. It had been established in 1975 and assisted financially and technically by the World Wide Fund For Nature in 1983. Its purpose was the setting aside for posterity of a beautiful unique piece of wild land that could be used in a protected way for education, research and recreation. It seemed to me it was the essence of what so many of the children were asking for in their messages - a part of the Earth that could be left in peace though still enjoyed by mankind in a state of harmony.

We paid our US$10 foreigners entrance fee and drove through into an unexpected show of neat-and-tidiness, even to the extent of bump-free roads, which felt very strange. To begin with we were in a well-cared-for, mature radiata pine plantation, which was part of a research programme testing climatic analogy in the northern and southern hemispheres. Considering that we were at 3,650 metres the trees looked remarkably healthy, although the growth was slow and diseased areas appeared as we started to ascend. With the depleted oxygen ruling all aspects of life, we did not expect to see many animals here but were excited to find an experimental herd of llamas, all busily grazing amongst a pretty patch of grass sticks in the trees. How my Dad will love to hear about this multi-land use project, I thought to myself, forgetting for a moment that he had passed on and would not be there on my return home to regale with exciting tales of travel. He had been a forest economist and always loved to hear about different silvicultural happenings. In five minutes he would have worked out the balance of how many trees to the acre would keep the llamas happy, and vice versa.

We stopped to talk to a tiny baby at the side of the road with Mum hovering proudly nearby making little clicking noises that presumably meant 'come along now, Dear, the dairy is open.' His rusty-brown body had a twitchy tail held horizontally on a thick oily fleece. A long chunky neck supported the pert little white face with sticky-up ears expressing interest without fear and a welcome-to-my-land. I was enchanted.

The llama like many of the cleverly adapted residents of high altitude and other oxygen deprived habitats has an exceptionally large count of red blood corpuscles. These are rugby ball shaped instead of the normal roundness of a soccer ball. Both of these factors give greater oxygen absorption through the increased surface area. Wouldn't it be good if we could emulate them, I mused. Perhaps the Tibetan lama already does... But then I wondered how long it would take my blood to develop rugby playing tendencies...

The road meandered as it gained height and took us out of the forest and up to an information centre built solidly out of stone. Here the story of Cotopaxi was told. In Palaeozoic times two shifting tectonic plates had met and resulted in the creation of the Andean mountain range, leaving dynamic volcanic activity, of which Cotopaxi is a fine example. She has had more than twenty-five eruptions in the last 400 years. The last major ones had been in 1877 which had produced terrifying catastrophic lahars, (rivers of lava, melted ice, rocks and mud,) one of which had reached the Pacific coast, nearly 250 kilometres away, travelling at some 90 kilometres per hour, destroying everything in its path. Since then there had been minor eruptions around 1904 and a warming up when the snow on the summit melted in 1975. Today there is continuous fumarolic activity, gently steaming, in the 750 metre diameter crater... She rests.

Although the German geologist, Reiss, and the Colombian, Escobar, were believed to be the first to climb to the summit in 1872, it says much for the daring of Whymper and his team who spent the night in a tent on the rim of the crater in 1880... Their rubber ground sheet was melting from the heat...

The Inca, we read, worshiped this Goddess of fire and here too the spirit of water was much revered. They also cultivated llama herds not only as beasts of burden,(the male can carry 100lb loads and can go for weeks without drinking,) but also for religious purposes. The llama with his exceptional ability to process oxygen and survive at altitude was considered sacred and could be afforded the special honour of being sacrificed. It was important to keep the good will of the Gods.

The modern day sacrifices were in stuffed pose. The animal statues, meant to be life-like, looked right through us with sad glassy eyes. There was brocket and white-tailed deer, paramo fox, skunk, llama, Andean duck, Andean gull, speckled teal and the black-chested buzzard eagle, but it was when I came to the stuffed condor, wings at the ready in mock take-off, that my stomach took a sickening heave. Even Pete talking to him in best condor could not lighten the heaviness of my heart. We had seen him in beautiful freedom. At least the puma and the spectacled bear were not represented.

Would a museum of stuffed humans bring similar interest? The Inca had, after all, put on show the sacred, mummified bodies of their former emperors. Maybe it would help the species to be identified? What about representatives from nations that are threatened with extinction... I recalled the happy picture of Mig ash-running down from the summit of Pichincha, whooping in delight... A Tibetan in beautiful freedom...

The road took us onwards and up over a little hill. Suddenly we were being presented with the set from an epic movie scene. I was quite unprepared for the beautiful freedom of the Earth that Cotopaxi portrayed. Before us lay a mountain of which dreams are made. It was a perfect cone of dazzling snow reaching up skywards like the top of a six-pointed star. Only one area of rock spoiled the total whiteness, as if to say 'yes, I have a real heart'. White tresses of snow cascaded elegantly into the pinkish-brown rock-band, which in turn supported the layers of grey volcanic material and olive green grassland.

The harsh beauty did not stop here. Sweeping widely to the horizon in all directions were unencumbered páramo plains with low shrubby vegetation intervening in the sheltered parts, and our eyes led us down to a large expanse of rippling water, glinting and gleaming in the sunlight. It went by the name of Laguna Limpiopungo.

Oh! How lovely!

We seemed to have the whole of this stunning world to ourselves. Then, right on cue, along the shores of the lake came three wild horses… galloping… driven by the wind… manes and tails flying… Yes, they always gallop in films too.

'This is exactly how I imagine Tibet to be,' sighed Mig, quite moved… and all of our hearts resonated in sympathy with his longing to see his homeland as we crossed the plateau and started to climb up the other side.

From the inside of our little jeep we knew that this was the territory of the wind as we slowly jolted inch by inch over the deeply carved ruts that had appeared across the road. Then Gustavo stopped in the lee of a mound of volcanic debris and, looking out for our best interests as always, indicated for us to put on all the clothes we had. At that moment we were not sure why, but there was a growing sense of mental preparation for a battle ahead to reach the hut. As the road twisted and turned with the increased gradient, patches of snow appeared interspersed with bands of deep red material.

'Well… this is like a lunar landscape,' gasped GT.

It was a veritable desert, with great boulders and rocks of all sizes, pyroclastic bombs and lapilli that had been strewn about, carelessly scattered like seeds, from the spewing volcano. Clouds started to swirl menacingly, giving a feel of non-reality. But it was not until we reached 4,600 metres that we found out that we still had to penetrate the armour of the mountain. It was indeed the wind. We were met by one continuous, intense, gusting fury as we disembarked from a lurching jeep. Gustavo tried a few different parking positions, but there was no let up. The vehicle was vulnerable. We rolled huge rocks and placed them around the wheels.

My immediate problem was with my eyes. The wind was picking up material and using it like sandpaper in clouds of fine dust that swept around my glasses and into my contact lenses. This was agonising. The answer was to find my goggles that were in my rucksack, which was thrown from the roof of the jeep. The wind snatched it, though it weighed at least 35 lbs, held it hovering for a

173

second and then rolled it away across the stirred up volcanic debris. In hot pursuit, I gave chase, thin air and painful eyes forgotten, and with a flying rugby tackle thwarted its escape. A greying Yannick penguin sat up disgusted at having to eat dirt.

Now there was a whole new meaning to the word windproof, but I managed to organise my gear so that there was only a nose exposed and we all set off on what should have been less than an hour's walk to the Refugio José Ribas at 4,800 metres. I had thought that there could not be a worse hut walk-in than the Iliniza one. I was wrong. This time we had the wind to contend with which was dead against us, we carried a lot more weight and I found that my exertion to catch the rucksack had taken its toll. Breathing deeply, I adopted the slowest plod that I could without actually standing still. Walking upright was an invitation to be blown over, so it was a bent over plod. I knew that it was better to try and keep going steadily rather than make the stops that the body was clamouring for, so I managed for a while to move into mind awareness.

I remembered the time on a mountain on one of the Greek Islands when the wind had been so fierce that I had lain down fearful of being blown off. I had learnt to harmonise my vibrations with the wind, so that I had felt that I was one with it, and my trembling had stilled. I had tried the same technique with the sea on a boat to calm seasickness, with some success. To work with a movement rather than fighting against it produces peace. So now I affirmed... My body is one with the wind... My mind is one with the wind... My spirit is one with the wind... I am one with the wind... I am one with God in the wind... I am one... I am... Gradually the battering became me and the struggle was together...

I sense a welcome from the mountain with open maternal arms, like wings of compassion.

21 - GATHERING STRENGTH

'Oh wonderful and blessed Cotopaxi. We greet you and humbly ask for permission to dance upon your slopes for a while...'

She smiles on us...

'We have come to prepare for Chimborazo. Show us your strength... that we may learn...'

We are enveloped in an energy that is not only strong and beautiful, but is also one of joy... All is well.

Grey, grey ash – everything on the trail up was volcanic grey ash ... except from time to time I was aware of the darker tones of deeply gouged, eroded valleys and peripheral patches of white snow... and drifting mist... until... there were the steadfast hands of Pete pulling me up the last bit. He had already carried the hardware, been back down a little way to take the food bag off Mig who had insisted on carrying the heavy weight of one of the ropes too, and accompanied GT who carried the other rope. They had been up there for a while. I was the last in. Now I was faced with the happy sight of a steep yellow roof sheltering a large hut, empty of other people, with excellent facilities. Fantastic! Far out! I might have thought differently, though, if I had known then about the drama that had unfolded at this exact spot only two years previously. An avalanche of snow, broken off from the snout of the glacier above, had buried the hut and ten people had lost their lives... Even without the restless movements of the Earth, it was thought that global warming was causing Cotopaxi's glaciers to recede at 2 metres per year. We were on the front line... yet blissfully ignorant.

The others had settled into a spacious sleeping area with two-tier sardine mattresses, next to an eating area containing an enormous wooden table, which like the wooden walls I somehow found comforting. There was a kitchen (fridge outside), a civilised outhouse loo, and the luxury of lights that actually worked. We were going to enjoy a couple of nights here and happily paid the fee of $10 per night to the only other person around, a friendly warden from whom Mig had learned important information. England was out of the World Cup.

Gustavo was worried about the jeep and after talking to the warden decided to go back down to try and find a sheltered spot for it. We lent him ski sticks, head-torch and gloves and watched him bravely setting out into the gale and the falling darkness.

Mig had brought up a wonderful vegetable stew that he had cooked in Quito, so we dined with great delight. It was the first time that all of us had had a good appetite at this altitude. Our bodies were adapting.

'How are you feeling, Condor?' asked Mig of Pete after his third helping. 'Stuffed,' came the reply.

Thankfully then we heard the outer door bang and Gustavo staggered in looking wild-eyed and dishevelled. We did not have to understand Spanish to know that things were pretty bad out there. It appeared he had moved the jeep, swaying dangerously, to the shelter of some sort of old building, but on the return he had lost one of my inner gloves, eaten in a flash by the wind. I felt that it was a severe loss not only because cold hands could have serious consequences, but also as I had been particularly fond of them. Equipment that one is used to and likes is important on a mountain. Sometimes, small things like this can make up the balance of whether one reaches a summit or not. This was attachment. Oh dear! Gustavo very sweetly kept saying how sorry he was. I felt bad that it mattered so much to me for surely it was more important to share things… and where was the unconditional love now?

As I lay in my sleeping bag, the wind howled increasingly. There was continuous loud and noisy banging. It was unimaginable to think of being outside in a feeble tent, where the power of the elements reigned supreme. Man is small… but all things are relative. In the circular light of my head-torch, I watched a little dratong mouse scampering around seemingly unafraid... Then I knew that we were being snugly held and rocked in the arms of Cotopaxi.

In the morning Gustavo told us that the winds had been gusting to 159 kilometres per hour (not far short of 100 miles per hour). That's breezy. There was a weather recording station close by on an exposed knoll.

It was time to play with the climbing equipment. There was a huge amount for Mig to learn in a short time. Using the beds for anchor points, the table as the mountain and the benches for a crevasse, we showed him the putting on of his harness, tying into the rope, belaying, moving together, pitching, abseiling, prusiking, use of ice-screws and deadman and crevasse rescue. It was the potted mountaineering-in-a-minute course. A lifetime's experience comes next week. No problemo. He concentrated and absorbed it well. It is not surprising how sharp the mind can become knowing that one's life or that of one's companion may depend on it.

We then dressed like men with skinexposurephobia and headed out into the real playground. The wind had abated somewhat, though we still had to shout to each other to be heard above the roar, and a blustery sun was doing its best to have some effect. Following the track across the brick coloured slopes behind the hut we slowly worked our way up to the first substantial patch of snow. It was soft and covered in grit but served our purpose for Mig to practice walking with crampons on and to try out the ice axe arrest. This method of rolling on top of the head of the axe so that it digs in and stops a slide is potentially life saving. He enjoyed executing it, not knowing then just how much it was to be put to the test…

Our eyes followed what we could see of the track above us. It crossed the scree slope until it reached huge hanging ice seracs that marked the edge of the glacier. Somewhere here there had to be an easy way through and up, though we knew that with the presence of many crevasses, the route could frequently change. It was reputed to be a fairly straightforward climb up to the steep ascent of the crater rim and on up to the summit at 5,897 metres, as such taking up to nine hours. This was the most climbed mountain in the Andes. Why, therefore, was there nobody else around? It could not all be because of the wind, surely. Perhaps the shifting crevasses knew something that we did not… But the exciting thought of being up there dominated… and how would it be, like Whymper, to lie on the crater lip and peer into the abyss, into the depth of the open wound of the Earth…? We decided to turn back and to save our energies for the night. We would aim to leave at 1.00 am, so that the ascent and the descent could be safely completed before the snow became soft and dangerous.

It was a relief to be back in the hut and not feel like an old door being hit

177

with a battering ram. The warden, when consulted thought that the wind might ease enough for it to be all right for climbing tomorrow and that we were now into a period of eight days of forecasted good weather. Well, if this is good weather, I'd hate to see the bad, I thought, but at least it was dry. More than anything, his comment made my pulse quicken... as, even though mountains have their own microclimatic patterns, it could mean good weather for Chimborazo...

We sat round the boardroom table, still dressed in chunky jackets, warming hands around hot mugs of tea. It was important to keep up our liquid intake. Mig had offered to make us Tibetan tea and I had decided to try and give it another go. This time I did find it a little more acceptable. Gustavo was risking it also but was unusually quiet, though GT had said 'no thank you' rather too quickly and Pete had made a face muttering something about 'yuk butter'.

However there was much work to concentrate on sorting the peace messages, the weight of which I had been proud to carry up with love. They were so precious. They represented support and hope for Tibet and the Earth. They were a large part of the reason for which we were here, struggling against the hardships, revelling in the joys... and they inspired us. Everyone chose the ones that they related to best and thought they would like to carry and speak out on Chimborazo. The high altitude boardroom resounded to the unexpected expressions of peace as the messages for the summit meeting were planned...

More climbers at varying stages of acclimatization began to appear and occupy the other rooms in the eaves. Some were wandering about dazed, some were being sick. Two young men from Israel, looking decidedly pale, stopped to talk to us and hear about Tibet. Perhaps particularly because of the violence in their land, there was a feeling of empathy with their symbol of the star of David. Although the six-pointed star is used by different peoples from around the world the commonality of its sacred geometry at a spiritual level is profound. It is even the Eastern symbol for the heart chakra, the body's centre for compassion.

Pete was particularly pleased that the Israelis took away forms to write us messages. As a young child his mother had run a guesthouse and many a night he had sat and listened to tragic tales of atrocities to Jews told by a longstanding resident. His father too had held strong views. Consequently he had felt a deep sympathy for their sad victimization and desperate cries for freedom. He felt that their struggle held many similarities with that of the Tibetans.

Gustavo, too, was trying to understand the Tibetan situation. With careful thought he wrote a peace message in Spanish and gave it to Mig. I enjoyed watching them communicate earnestly and with fun, each in their own language. Gustavo really was typical of most of the Ecuadorians that we had met in that he was friendly and helpful towards people from other lands. He spoke, drawing a map to help explain, of how Ecuador had suffered incursions from Peru taking over much of their oil-rich land in the south. The Peruvians had been strong and warlike, Ecuador, the weaker brother, could do little about it, but had not wanted to fight. Maybe in the great scheme of things it was no accident that our climb should be in a country that held dear the concept of peace...

We organised our gear for the morning and as dusk was falling around 6.30 pm prepared to get some sleep. I went outside to the outhouse without full clothing on. The cold bit into me like a thousand swords, but the wind had dropped further and an orange sunset was painting the sky with raw beauty. Cloud formations were playing beneath us. I spotted a dragon and remembered Mig's forecast of luck. In the distance I could make out the twinkling lights of Quito. It seemed fairly clear. Behind, high Cotopaxi looked ready to receive us.

Back inside I discovered a new trick. We had boiled up the melted snow water for our water bottles, including purification tablets, (which gave the delightful taste sensation of drinking from a swimming pool) but mine was still hot and so was put to good use as a sleeping bag companion. People have the inclination to think, for some unknown reason, that because you climb mountains you do not feel the cold. Well, I feel the cold. Now it would not take half the night to warm up in spite of wearing near-full mountaineering kit. I felt too excited to sleep, but realised that it was not because of the Cotopaxi climb. It was the nearness of Chimborazo... Sorry Cotopaxi, my heart has already been given away...

The rooster called us at midnight. This interesting alarm on my watch tended to cause both annoyance and amusement in climbing huts and on underground tube trains alike, but it had the desired effect of waking people up. Pete and GT headed outside to check the weather and persuaded me to go with them. The wind still roared, but the main problem was that we could no longer see the lights of Quito, for much to our surprise a sleety rain was being buffeted around. This would mean snow higher up, so we reluctantly agreed to go back for a couple of hour's sleep. At 2.00 am the situation was worse. It was snowing. At this time of night the body is at its lowest ebb, and I really could not find the motivation to head out into a climb with considerably lowered safety elements, although I would have accepted Pete and GT's experience-backed decision either way. To me, even though I try and think logically (or at least what Pete would call logically), my brain just does not seem to be made that way, and it has to feel right to go ahead. Pete and GT weighed up the situation, aware that gaining altitude was vital to our whole expedition, but knowing that the visibility would be lousy. This was critical as we did not know the route. Also the snow could have obliterated the tracks that we needed to follow. Tipping the balance towards a no-go was the fact that Mig did not have his goggles with him. They would be vital for vision in these cold, windy and snowy conditions.

So we slept until it was light and awoke frustrated that we had not been able to climb. This feeling was compounded by looking out of the window and seeing the usual clouds rushing by indicating high winds, yes… but also a clear sunny day… But we had run out of time and could not stay another night. Today was the 2nd of July. I realised that it was my father's birthday and in the whisper of an instant I was visualising myself in a corner of a pleasant English field beside his liquid amber tree which was dedicated to his memory and around which we had spread his ashes.

'Isn't the mind a beautiful thing,' I said. 'The physical state can't be that important. The body thinks it is in one place and the mind can fly to wherever you want it to be.'

'The mind is truly wondrous,' replied GT. 'But I still think that we made the right decision not to take the physical body up Cotopaxi. Twelve hours or so of that wind would have been pretty bad. We probably would have been exhausted and left ourselves without the energy to tackle Chimborazo.'

'You may be right, Archie,' came in Pete. 'But it was the correct decision for safety given the conditions. At least we've now had three nights at the huts at 4,800. Not doing Cotopaxi is disappointing… but that's mountaineering…

'Certainly, Redhot,' affirmed GT. 'There's far more to it than just a summit. Mountains have always been the source of all my values, my alternative to church.'

'Yes,' said Pete. 'For my part, I find the mountains a great source of peace and tranquillity, an escapism from the real world.'

Mig did not express any disappointment. He had seen rainbows, which were a good sign, and he was excited at having woken up with his message from the summit of Chimborazo on his mind. He just contributed 'Guys, I think we all need a seriously good shower. I mean, look at us…'

Even those of us without wings flew down the mountain. We had a following wind. Still, I was left behind. I must have a body with a particularly un-going-downhill-type motion. So I sang 'Happy Birthday' to my Dad and then, as if with a direct telephone line to my mind, I chatted with him.

'It's so beautiful that I'm doing exactly what I want to be doing with my life. I'm so excited that after all these years it's happening. I know that I'm absolutely where I need to be. I feel so lucky.'

'I'm so proud of you for that.'

'I'm so proud of you too, Dad, and you know, I'll help my Paul, Scott and Mark to do exactly what they feel they must do at a heart level too.' His quiet confirmation that this was what he too felt to be right meant a lot to me. When he had been alive it had always been important to put financial security and social acceptance high on the list of priorities, as was the ethos of his generation.

I knew he was with me, and I was mindful of Gandhi's words about the freedom of love, but still I said 'Dad, it'd be so nice to have a little sign…'

He laughed 'You don't need a sign…'

Barely two minutes further on, I was stopped dead in my tracks. There, in all this vast area of desert, there, lying in the volcanic dust right in front of me, was my sign. It was a pinecone. No single item could have represented my father more. It was a moment of awe and wonderment, a moment of humble awareness and I was filled with a peaceful joy. Who am I to question the workings of our world? Sometimes, to see the beauty… that is enough.

I found the boys changing a tyre on the jeep and, still a little shaky, shared my experience with Pete. Then, away out of the wind, the snow and the dust we recrossed the dramatic landscape and headed down into a greener world.

The road home found us in high spirits. Gustavo stopped to mend the tyre. Whilst waiting Pete practised condor impressions, much to the enjoyment of a mum hoeing a dusty flower bed and little dark-faced children walking home from school, satchels on their backs like anywhere in the world. Then he and Mig had a sparring match, accompanied by big smiles, each unwittingly using a natural 'chi' energy to push the other back without harming him. I watched, wondering if the Tibetans could yet achieve this…

Gustavo decided that we needed to relax. He took us to a beautiful old hacienda with a colonial air of days long past, tall archways and pillars, flowers and fountains, panpipes wafting through a lovely garden, a chapel with bells on and huge carved doors. The thick stone walls had been privy to many a strategy of history. Charles-Marie de La Condamine had stayed here and along with Louis Godin had led the French Geodetic expedition from 1736 to 1744. Their brief had been to determine the true shape of the Earth. They had surveyed an arc of a degree of latitude here at the equator. Another team had taken similar measurements in Lapland in the Arctic. Thus it had been proved that the Earth was indeed an oblate spheroid. In the process La Condamine had bravely surveyed on Cotopaxi during an eruption, and had reached the height of 4,745 metres on Chimborazo, which was believed to be the highest mountain (above sea level) in the world for the next seventy years. The hacienda had also been the home of the explorer and naturalist Humboldt who in 1802 had attempted to climb Chimborazo attaining 5,800 metres where he had been stopped by a huge crevasse.

We of the 1998 peace climb team sat in the restaurant and were served what we thought was going to be a typical Ecuadorian meal but was egg and chips much to Pete's delight. Then we were entertained by the jolly sounds of guitar, flute, banjo and twangy voice. We were not quite dressed for the occasion but, hey, we bought some wine and nobody seemed to mind.

We drove out along a magnificent avenue of towering eucalyptus trees and turned to look back. There was a gift for us. The skyline was clear. For the first time we could see Cotopaxi without any cloud. Because we had not stood on her summit she held a mysterious countenance and we were left with a feeling of respect for her that felt good. Perhaps it was a bit like not wanting to finish a jigsaw puzzle for fear of losing an old friend... the experience of the journey that was exciting and worthwhile...

Dear Cotopaxi, you welcomed us and held us to your bosom. You sorely tested our lungs and the ability to do anything but slowly. You cared for us by not letting us climb, that we would not squander our energy. Thank you. We have been blessed.

But, although we had all coped well, apart from some shortness of breath, we had not reached as high as we needed to go and we had not given our bodies the chance to adapt to the necessary altitude. In theory we were not yet ready for Chimborazo. We should wait and find some more time to acclimatize. That, however, was a road that we were not prepared to take.

The 3rd of July was a turmoil. The monsters of doubt and fear that needed to be slain would have to wait, as would the tuning into the greater purpose and contemplation on what we were about to tackle. It was preparation feet-on-the-ground time. We were so busy that even I had to use Pete's superior management game-plans system (list of things to do).

We rose early to greet the United States filming contingent, the JMT Production Group. Michael, his dear friends and associates Robert and the production's colleague from San Francisco, Bettina, were lively, intellectual and very aware of world issues. We all suddenly found ourselves having to talk intelligently (that is even more so than normal) as we brought them up to date on all the happenings and plans. I found it a bit of a shock after the family-type relaxed fun conversations that our team had fallen into, but we soon warmed to their kindliness and excitement at what we were doing. Then a trying-not-to-get-lost walk brought us to the Hotel Sierra Nevada where we met the rest of the crew, Mateus the local cameraman, Atura the sound guy, Oswoldo the cook and Louis the driver. There were others around who seemed to be in charge of important things. Everyone had different ideas on how it was all going to work. Oh help, I thought, what a circus! It will be hard to keep focused on climbing in the right spirit with so much else going on, but if we want to tell the world about Tibet and the peace messages then we will have to put up with it. Michael however, as his achievements had indicated, was a dynamic force to be reckoned with and before too long had us and everyone else running around caught up in his infectious enthusiasm.

'Ah, gee! This is gonna be the greatest, guys.'

He never told us then that he was extremely superstitious about bad weather and avalanches, and was nervous about Chimborazo's central rock walls, which were said to hold back huge amounts of unpredictable glacier. He had managed to climb so many peaks in the world without getting wiped out that he knew his instincts were well honed... Thankfully he reserved judgement.

We left him worrying about the hut generator and sorting out equipment details and headed for an important rendezvous with David at Safari. We had finally decided to hire two guides. Even though Pete and GT had never climbed with a guide and found it ethically abhorrent I knew that they were sacrificing personal thoughts for the safety of the team. On the positive side was the extra safety needed for the cameraman, probably Michael, who it was hoped would come with us and, most importantly, we thought that having a guide would mean that we would have a radiophone with us. Ramiro and Fernando would join us at the Whymper hut the day after tomorrow. Also it was arranged that there would be an emergency bottle of oxygen plus mask that would be borrowed from the hospital for us to pick up.

Last minute as it was, I was desperate to have a cellular phone with us. I had a long list of people that I thought would be wonderful to phone from the summit, headed by His Holiness the Dalai Lama and Uri Geller, who it was vital knew the exact moment of our arrival. Traipsing the city streets to buy, beg or borrow brought no results, only frustration and disappointment.

Meeting the others at the vegetarian restaurant and guzzling milkshakes cheered me up. The table discussion returned to the possibility of a bivouac half way up the mountain, which of course was what Whymper had done but with porters to carry up the equipment and the fuel for the fire. Both GT and I, being slower, thought that it would increase our chances of reaching the summit with everyone together. Pete was so against it that we dropped the idea. He felt that carrying all the extra equipment for a night out would be crazy (even without the dried llama dung) and that the conditions would probably be too cold and windy for any sort of comfort and thus no rest. Mig finished his sixth milkshake and went off to look at renting better fitting boots and to try and track down some Tibetan monks that he had been told were in Quito, both of which proved to be an illusion. Then he was to join Oswoldo to buy the food supplies for the thirteen people for the next four days. We felt fairly safe at sending him to represent our stomachs. You could not buy yak butter here.

'Have you got plenty of milkshakes?' I called after him. We had been reduced to using milkshakes as our currency. Confusing as it was, they seemed to be better value than the sucre, were less inflationary and anyway it was a comforting thought to think of a few thousand milkshakes in one's pocket.

My next job was to pick up a fax at the local hotel. Candy had sent the last few peace messages through including a note from Uri saying that he was praying for us. I must try and contact him I thought, and let him know the most likely tune-in time if we can't track down a phone to take with us. Also I wanted to try and get in touch with my Paul. As the final hour of leaving for the mountain was approaching, thoughts of my children were tugging at my heartstrings… I couldn't help noticing a contented-looking indigenous Indian mother with giggling youngsters huddled together under a sheet of plastic sheltering from the pouring rain as I headed for the South American Explorers Club. There I found a note from Martin who we had met on Iliniza, saying how he and a couple of friends had been to try and climb Chimborazo. The weather had been so bad that it had been impossible to make an attempt, or to even think about setting off… Hmmm… have faith, girl… faith…

A new phone had been put in at the club, for which I was able to buy international phone cards. Wonderful, here was a nearly self-controlling system at last. I tried Paul for about fifteen minutes, but he was engaged. Then I tried Uri, but he was engaged also. Oh, bother! I tried again. 'Hi,' said Uri in his characteristically intense voice. 'I've just been speaking to Paul for the last quarter of an hour.' Wow! Was that synchronicity or what? Why, I wondered, did I ever doubt that Uri would know the exact moment when we were to stand on the point furthest from the centre of the Earth and place his things in the snow. Who needs telephones?

The discussion with Michael was not quite so easy. He was intensely focused on the natural world, passionately believing that it should be left as undisturbed as possible. He was a practitioner of the Jain religion, which is deeply embedded with the conviction that all life is sacred. As such he felt that it was not right to desecrate the top of a mountain by leaving anything at all there. As he was planning to come to the summit with us to film I showed him the crystal. He dismissed it. I recoiled as though part of me had been rejected and regretted letting him touch it. It served the purpose for all of us to look well at what we were doing and to strongly reaffirm, that yes we believed that to leave the crystal and other things buried in the snow and the prayer flags by age old Tibetan tradition was indeed the right thing to do. Because it was in tune with our belief systems it was OK. Just as it was OK for him to think otherwise. We would agree to differ on this point, but I felt uneasy about it. Michael spoke about the ecology of sacred space and felt that any sort of human intervention was somehow inappropriate. But he did not dwell on it. There were more important issues to concentrate on, not least

185

of which was the job of raising awareness for Tibet and expressing non-violence to assist world peace, the very essence of the project and upon which we all concurred. 'Gee! My Gard, it's gonna be amazing!' he concluded.

By now it was evening in the city and we were treated to a lovely meal at el Magic Bean by Robert in his American generosity. We ate all the vegetables and beans our bodies could take and filled up our minds with the US news. Clinton had been saying that to make friends with the Chinese was to make the world a safer place. Then at least the human rights problem and the nuclear threat could be aired.

'There are lots of Chinese nuclear missile bases in Tibet, which is hardly publicised... as well as dumps of toxic nuclear waste,' said Mig emphatically. 'I have to believe that Tibet will be free one day and then things will change. You know, a lot of my relatives and other Tibetans back in refugee settlements wake up early every day around five to listen to the voice of America which is broadcast in Tibetan, and they have so much hope... Their first priority is survival but they're so interested to hear any new news about Tibet... and the news inside Tibet is not at all good at the moment... the situation is just getting worse.'

Hope springs eternal, a distant feeling, like a flush of greenness when all that can be seen is brown winter branches, clothes that can be changed in the unending wheel of the seasons.

'Are there a lot of tears in Tibetan people's eyes?'

'Oh, yes, the situation is so saddening... but I keep telling them whenever I go back that we have a lot of support from the West... we have a lot of great organisations who are working with us towards our main goal, you know. But I don't suppose that Clinton's visit will make that much difference...'

'What will?'

'At the end of the day, this is my feeling, I don't think that anything can set Tibet free apart from the Chinese people.'

So we returned to the hostel thinking how could we reach the Chinese people? How could we touch their hearts? The Dalai Lama says that the only way forward is in brotherhood and friendship and with compassion. His shining example is like a star in the world and, as Gandhi had pointed out, the Chinese people can be thanked for the exposing of this light. We need to show appreciation and work with them, not against them... The computer revolution means that in theory loving words can caress every human being in the twinkling of an eye. We can write our peace messages inspired by the Dalai Lama's ideals onto the world-wide-web. If we can reach the point furthest from the centre of the Earth then maybe that will draw attention to them and maybe people will read them… maybe in spite of the restrictions, some Chinese… If we can reach the point…

The stresses of the day, like bandidos of the mind, had left us tired and devoid of energy. Still, typically, it seemed to take Pete about five minutes to pack and go to sleep and me the next three hours exhausted into the night. Oh no, I thought, I am not only pathetically slow and tentative at climbing up and coming down but also so slow at getting ready. Pete was always telling me that speed is safety… My weary mind was struggling with irrational worries and bogged down on what to take. Using the plastic bag method of compartmentalisation everything had to be able to be found without having to tip up the rucksacks. Climbing gear in one… wanted on climb… wanted at hut… summit things… peace messages… personal stuff that a girl needs on a mountain such as face cream, eye makeup, hair-ties, spare underwear, notes from children, torn-in-half-to-save-weight books… emergency food had to go into pockets… Keep an eye on the fact that everything has to be hauled up to the hut… Too often I come home from a mountain and discover that I have carried up and down extraneous stuff like a pad of paper, a tube of toothpaste, old socks, old rocks, half a dozen lipsalves or the next-door neighbour's keys.

But to prepare is to set free the expectation….

23 - INDEPENDENCE

The Americans were greeted at dawn on the 4th of July, their Independence Day, with our flurry of stuffing breakfast, packing up everything to vacate our rooms and leaving luggage in the cellar. For some unknown reason I could always quote the 1776 declaration: 'We, the representatives of the United States in congress, assembled appealing to the supreme judge of the world for the rectitude of our intentions solemnly publish and declare that we are and ought of right to be free and independent states.' It was a good thought that today they were championing the freedom of the Tibetan nation in this small part of the world. Freedom from oppression would do for starters.

This morning I felt much better about having an extended team. The excitement of setting off on the adventure drove the adrenaline and I enjoyed the sense of group belonging and intent as we piled all our gear into a twenty-seater, not-falling-to-bits bus. This is it, I thought.

'Oh, guys,' called Michael, ' Please take all your heavy gear off and put it back on again so that we can film it.'

Well, I enjoyed most of it.

A handsome smartly-dressed Ecuadorian seemed to be hovering around to wish us well on our journey… Wow! It was Gustavo, without his hat on. We all felt really sorry that he was not coming with us and presented him with a 'Climb For Tibet' T-shirt with which he waved us goodbye.

Instead of being part of the hustle and bustle and bumps of the city we found ourselves now somehow set apart in our luxury vehicle with space and comfort and filming equipment. We were again outsiders looking in. Maybe that is what making a film entails, but I felt slightly uneasy. Nevertheless it was nice to be taken and not have to decipher the language and rush about any more. I could write up my diary, sort out peace messages and relax into my own mind.

I knew that there was wider input which I did not understand, that we were being spiritually guided and that we each had our own part to play. I tried to be open, knowing that it was important to be so. The crystal helped me. I clasped it tightly in my hand feeling the power and sense of purpose it held. I was going to miss it. It had been with me constantly in my pocket since the first couple of days, giving me comfort and strength, even though I knew that it was not mine. I had simply been the guardian for this period of time. It had been entrusted to me...

'Oh special crystal, thank you for coming into our lives and touching them with wonder. We honour the important potential of your work. We express love for you and what you represent...' I am shown on the screen of my mind a hole in the snow... about the depth of an ice axe handle... and in it the position of the six-sided shiny crystal end... pointing up... and out... into the universe...

'Wow! Oh gosh, what a stunning location.' I was brought back to awareness by Michael's raptures over the filming opportunities. There were lovely sights in all directions that made him want to stop at every corner – beauty in the lusciousness and patterns of the Earth, geological formations long sculptured by wind, rain and sun. He was however worried about the weather. It was distinctly grey and drizzly, conditions bad for both filming and climbing.

'You'll see. It'll be perfect for us. It's been organised.' I said, totally sure that all would indeed be well.

'Look over there! Look at that!' shouted Mig, right on cue. 'You know, that's such a good omen.' Following his gaze to the west, we saw the two peaks of Iliniza, momentarily cleared of cloud, with the sun picking out the gleaming snow on the southern summit. Reaching skywards as though directing us on our way was the arc of a double rainbow... Omens are important to a Tibetan. The Dalai Lama speaks of an earthquake and the dramatic sign of a comet crossing a blood red sky in 1949 at the time of the invasion by the Chinese army. If natural systems are viewed separately from the workings of the mind and spirit of mankind, then portant signs make no sense. If however all living things are viewed as an interconnected part of one entity then it is understandable that the weather should respond to forces given out and needs may be met or disasters unfold.

To our east passed Pasochoa. I heard Pete speak something quietly. I imagined that it was 'Hail! Condor, care to fly far with us.' But I could not be sure. It could have been 'Fail! Wonder where to buy Mars Bars.'... Behind was Cotopaxi, decked in cloud. I was quite pleased that we could not see her. Somehow, I did not want the wrong mountain to look beautiful today. Mateus, who was the only one of the crew who could speak English and Spanish being of German extract, told us that apparently this season there was a very tricky final bit to the summit. The climb of Cotopaxi carried a sting in the tail in the form of a difficult crevasse that had opened up and required a swinging ladder to hairily cross. We had been spared that trial. We also learned that there had been an accident only yesterday on Pichincha with Safari guides to hand. I really hoped that we had done the right thing by having guides. Here we were setting out on our venture that we had been planning for months and about to be joined by two guides that we knew nothing about. Please, please, may they be sensitive to what we are doing, I prayed.

We passed along the fine palmtreed avenues of the valley holding Ambato, but this time climbed out heading west to approach Chimborazo from the other side. The Andes, proud as the longest mountain range in the world, displayed full colours for us. Magenta, purple and browns blended with sky tones caught on distant horizons. Deep forest green clung to the heights. Patchwork slopes blanketed almost unbelievable steepness with pale gold, lime and jade, whilst looking down on silver mists blowing like forgotten summer gossamer. The little plots providing food for survival of a people were scattered with lone trees clinging at jaunty angles as though for the fun of it. We took in the staggering beauty of the show and the immensity of the landscape, rolling and playing with our eyes. This was special magic for we were entering the realm of the Watchtower of the Universe. Our mountain was guarded by some of the most stunning scenery on Earth. How privileged we were to be here.

We stopped to be greeted on the side of the road by a little biscuit coloured mother donkey with a suckling foal. Thick furry coats told their own tale of how conditions must often be. We were watched by a young man with a forked stick making stacks out of tall cut grasses, helped by his pretty wife, typically wearing a bowler hat over black braided hair and carrying a little pink-bonneted baby. Two more shy barefooted youngsters clung to her long skirts and peered at the frightening crowd of foreigners that we were. They were Quechuan Indians, direct descendants of the Inca. This was their land. We were trespassing, though we came in peace. Can the awful massacres by the foreigners of their history be forgotten? Can anything atone for it? We gave them a handful of money and a mass of cameras took their pictures, leaving them to the backbreaking work, the cold wind, the harsh struggle to grow the food that they all needed and the simplicity of the joy in their friendship with the Earth.

As the road climbed so did the excitement in the bus. It reverberated from seat to seat rising to a crescendo as a huge mass of cloud appeared to our left, like the cloak of a high priest waiting for the sacrament to begin. We turned south off the paved road onto dirt. Now, grey, olive grey dust blew up from the wheels of the bus in football-pitch-sized clouds, playing with our panorama. We knew that we were so close. We could feel the presence... immense... powerful. My heart beat faster, partly in fear, partly in anticipation. Closer... Closer... Keep calm... Keep calm... after all we had already made friends and prepared the way. All was as it should be. There was a job to do and...

'I see it,' shouted Mig eagerly rushing up and down the bus. 'Look! Look! Wow! It's steeper than Cotopaxi.' Across the near barren sandy plain interspersed now with only small shrubby olive green vegetation, cloud was shifting and swirling to partly reveal the imposing white-topped mountain... our Chimborazo.

'Are you sure you want to do this?' grinned Michael. 'Hey you guys there's snow up there... a lot of it. Oh! Oh my Gard! We need to stop and get a shot of the whole thing.'

Outside I smiled a secret smile, greeting the mighty Watchtower, and then glanced around. Pete, looking full of confidence and keen to get at it, was pointing out the route. 'Yeah, both huts are situated over that lump, and the line is more or less on a slant coming from that tongue of the glacier right to left and up to where you see there's a rock triangle and then a rock band. The line comes through where the snow band is and comes up on to that left-hand ridge, which you take to the lower summit at 6,260. The higher summit that we want at 6,310 is over the back by about a kilometre.'

'Welcome Chimborazo! We're here! We're here!' I couldn't contain my excitement any longer. 'We're going to be there. We're going to be there.'

GT was smiling as though he'd just conducted the best symphony of his life. 'It's wondrously impressive... It looks absolutely staggering.' He was caught up in sheer delight with everything that was happening.

Michael was dancing around, as I am sure all good film directors do, enthusiastically asking the crew to take every view in sight... the mountain, the climbers, the desert, the sky, even posing for him a group of vicuñas eating lichens and the illusion of lush meadows. 'Mig, what do you think? Are you scared at all?'

'No, to be honest, but I am sure that it's going to be tough. I can definitely see myself struggling. I mean, it's looking more and more difficult, the more we see. The biggest thing is I've got to reach the top… and complete my dreams.' I had to admire his courage. He really had little idea of what lay ahead, but he was determined to put himself in one hundred per cent and I felt sure that, because of it, all would flow well for him.

'Tess,' Michael turned to me, 'What if you don't make the summit?'

I stared at him. He's obviously a great director, yes, he wears a cap inscribed with the word 'ahimsa' (Sanskrit for non-violence), he's even sporting the obligatory pigtail… but to suggest not making it…? He probably did not believe me when I said 'I've not really considered that.'

'But you must have…'

'No,' I replied simply. 'We're going to make it.' I wondered though if he could smell the conflict in my heart of the fear attacking the excitement, as easily as I could smell the dust in the air. Having such a big team meant lots more support and less need to be frightened. There was a wonderful bond and commonality of purpose, but in a way the fear also isolated me, even from Pete. There were times when I felt that I was standing alone because of it. I did not feel that anyone else was afraid. GT was, I knew, worried about his acclimatization, but that was all. Only I could face my own fear. It was a very personal thing. I suppose if I had been able to stand there shaking I would have scored big hugs and it might have gone away, but it was stiff upper lip, keep the lid on, lots to do… I needed time to myself to sort it, but that looked unlikely, so I pushed it down somewhere… to hide.

24 - BLESSING

There was no let up to the desert. The dry plain stretched to the horizon in three directions. A few straggly grasses and sandblasted bushes hung on in the ubiquitous wilderness as we turned north-east through jostling cloud to join the zigzag route, which Pete and I had taken only two weeks before. It had been just a short moment in time, but now our bodies were better prepared and we came with our own army... The bus laboured under the strain of the steep slope, the dust and the rocks, and carried us into the great enveloping aura of the omnipotent Chimborazo.

At the Carrel hut the wind was cold but not fierce, the air was thin but not razor sharp. Turning away from the mêlée of unloading people and equipment, I looked back down the way we had come and watched with awe an amazing sight. A huge covering of mist was tumbling and turning, billowing and rolling back, revealing the bed of grey desert sand. It was like the parting of the Red Sea. It was an auspicious sign... I knew, I just knew that this was the beginning of our own perfect weather system. The random chance of four good days was very slight indeed, but then so also was the chance of a peace climb in the Andes on the Dalai Lama's birthday. All was well. A welcome had been extended to us.

The smiley warden, Antonio, greeted us with hugs, but was sadly not coming up to the top hut. However, he had arranged for a man with two skinny mules to ferry equipment. This was brilliant for all the food, the extra fuel for the generator to keep the camera batteries going, and also the gear of the unacclimatized bodies. The rest of us shouldered our heavy rucksacks and started plodding. Mig and GT slung a heavy rope apiece on top of their sacks, and Pete, with the group hardware, also carried my second sack on top of his. Yes, even though this was 1998, it was wonderful being a cared-for female in a man's world. Michael marched up alongside us, astoundingly with a huge load and running a camera. Pete answered my surprised gaze with 'He's stuffed himself full of Diamox. Let's hope he can keep it up.'

Scattered gravestones warned us of the impending memorial pyramid for the French climbers. It was a grim reminder… of power… and selectivity… I had recently read the account of a mountaineer who had reached the place where the 1993 avalanche had struck, a steep slope just below the Veintimilla summit. There had been similar conditions to those during the disaster - fifty centimetres of fresh snow and strong sunshine. He had decided to turn back and had met with a German guide who had suffered serious face injuries from a rockfall. Where was this rockfall area? Which ridge had the avalanche been on? From here we could not see the whole of the south-west face, just a large gap in the cloud from whence shone a white light so bright that it seemed like it was a peephole into Heaven… Mesmerised, I sensed a strange glow of joy and a stirring of my heart. Maybe we'll find something special up there… At this moment, though, it looked completely unattainable, an altar too sacred to approach.

The gravestones had a sobering effect on Mig. 'Whoa! This is serious, isn't it?' It was the first time that it had really hit him. He rushed on up to the Whymper hut at the elevation of 5,000 metres to the tune of scrunching heavy boots on the grey and brick-red volcanic track, clattering loose rocks as he went. I noticed from behind that he carried a second smaller stick on his sack alongside his special one. I did not have to ask what it was for… Michael was full of admiration. 'Nobody goes at that speed at this altitude. He was positively running.'

'Yeah, he likes to get there,' I said. What we did not know was that he had been told that it was important to always show respect to the spirit of the mountain, and he had wanted to reach the hut quickly to do Tibetan prostrations, face down in the dirt in deference towards the revered heights. Then he would feel protected.

We moved on conscious of the fast approaching dusk. It must have been close to 6.00 pm. We wanted to do a blessing ceremony before the daylight diminished altogether. As we approached the hut a veil of magic seemed to have been drawn across our path. The peephole enlarged and we could now see the entire Veintimilla summit shining for us, staggeringly, brilliantly, heralding the presence of the true summit hidden behind. The moment of our arrival and greeting had been timed impeccably, as though by

Divine guidance…

Mig and I set up the Tibetan flag to the west of the hut, Pete and Michael the cameras. 'Come on.' I shouted to GT. 'Drop your sack and run. We've got about ten minutes of light left.'

The warm pink-brown rocks laid out the plush presentation carpet. There was an awesome physical silence overpowered by the gathering of energies that was taking place. An eerie mist, which was not a mist but more like phosphorescent ether, assembled around the top snows of the magnificent peak that glowed just like a light in a dream. Michael said that in all his years as a film director he had never seen anything like it. It was unearthly. It was a melding of energies like an emotive haka in preparation for a rugby match. It was a touching of souls. We, as climbers, coming before this highest of mountains, arising to the furthest point of our Earth, a summit so sanctified that most of the world knew little about it.

'Oh Great Chimborazo, Watchtower of the Universe, we greet you and humbly ask for permission to climb to your sacred summit. We ask for strength. We ask for oxygen. We ask for safety in our return. We climb as an expression of the light of Tibet, that the Earth may find peace.'

'OM MANI PADME HUM,' we prayed and Pete, GT, Mig and I, a warmly close team, stood with our hands in the air, together around the flag. The light fell from the mountain… and it was done… The hearts of our own guardian angels had resonated with the heart of the angel of the mountain… We knew not what was yet to come, but no amount of foreboding could take away the fact that we had been accepted and blessed.

Turning, I glanced downwards only to be reminded of our altitude… as if there was any chance of forgetting, as if the lungs could forget. Under a paling pink-tinged sky the whole world was covered, past the cotton wool horizon, with billions of churning, buffeting, white-horse clouds on a wild, unending sea. Only we were above it, only we were privileged to fly as if on the magic carpet of this lucid dream.

It felt good to be at the hut again. I loved the salmon pink exterior and solid feeling of shelter and safety. It was like an old friend. We settled into the long bunkroom in the eves, laying out our sleeping bags and hanging up all the stuff like harnesses, helmets, ropes and penguins. There were a few other climbers around whom we chatted to and collected peace messages from and Michael generously lent his bright orange jacket to one. I felt that he might have looked better in a different colour but, hey, he would be warm for his climb in the early hours.

Eventually the mules arrived with the food, and Oswoldo was able to produce an excellent meal of soup and pasta for those of us who didn't feel like throwing it back up again. Eager and excited faces, preparing for the fray, could be seen in the flickering candle light at the old wooden tables that gave a reassuring feeling of reality to the touch. We were joined by the mule driver, an indigenous Indian with bright red poncho and battered hat covering most of his face. He stared, with a rather sad and bemused expression, at our peculiar foreign antics such as filming everything in the dark, trying to filter perfectly good glacial water and adding butter and salt to tea. Maybe he would have enjoyed the condor impression but none of us, not even Pete, wanted to waste any energy here. It was too precious. With him was his young, eleven year old son who clung to him silently.

'You'll never guess what I've discovered happened here today.' Said GT, obviously thrilled. 'The most wondrous and amazing thing. A baby was born.'

'Here?' I could think of a hundred thousand better places to have a baby.

'Yes. It was the mule driver's wife, apparently. Isn't that a beautiful symbol of renewal and rebirth to set the scene for our peace messages?'

Wow! Incredible... Maybe, I thought, that's the highest baby ever produced, but then I remembered... the Tibetan refugees...

We toasted the mule driver with lukewarm drinks in little plastic cups. He did not seem to be very happy. Such is life at 5,000 metres.

'So,' asked Michael, 'what do we reckon? Is there any avalanche danger?'

'No, I don't think so,' replied Pete. 'In the Alps we have a risk of one to five. I would put it less than two. What we could see looked very glazed tonight. So it looks pretty good. Anything in the way of snow is going to be quite hard névé.'

'Yes, I would agree,' came in GT. 'I thought it looked very unlikely and I didn't think that the lower ice looked terribly problematical. I may eat my words but it looks fairly straightforward.'

'Yeah,' went on Pete, 'the only danger would perhaps be on the way down when the snow gets soft in the afternoon.'

'Well, it's the unknowns that bother me,' I said. 'We don't know how steep it is. We don't know how we're going to react. We don't know how well acclimatized we are.'

'One of us does,' said GT.

'Two of us do,' joined in Michael. (It was amazing really that he was still vertical.) 'What about you, Mig?'

'Well, the closer we get the steeper it looks, and the more, what do you call it... risk taking.'

'Terrifying perhaps?' suggested Michael.

'Yeah, but it's all such a new experience for me. I've never climbed on deep snow before. It's gotta be a belief in myself. There's no going back... in spite of problems like painful feet.' I knew too that he was battling an intense and severe headache behind his left ear and temple that would not go away. 'But then I think of the Tibetan refugees, thousands of them, trying to escape every year across the Himalayas taking the risk with their lives... I mean, for us, we have all the equipment...' His father and heavily pregnant mother had escaped in this way in 1959. She, now, was very worried by his protesting and mountain climbing and had pleaded with him 'Please, Migmar... cling to life.' But Mig was a fighter, as even his name portrays.

Names in Tibetan, commonly given by a high lama, are nearly always significant, such as Kunga – 'loved by all', or Rangdrol – 'the self-liberated'. Sometimes they indicate character such as Tagzhim - 'ferocious at home but timid outside', or have purpose such as to ward off evil spirits – Khyikyag (useful, but unfortunately meaning 'dog-shit'). Migmar means 'Tuesday', but as each day of the week is also ascribed to a heavenly body, it is associated with Mars – the planet of the warrior.

He, Migmar, would always be the first to be there if something needed to be done for Tibet, within the constraints of the Dalai Lama's non-violence policy. I wondered how it would feel if my own land was threatened. My father used to say that fighting for your country brings out the best in people. Maybe it was a bit like mountaineering, with survival at stake, when you can't pretend to be anything that you're not and have to dig deep and find yourself… when you are pushed into action, because doing nothing is not an option.

Now we had to try and sleep. The dormitory, though, was busy in the extreme. The Americans, with so little acclimatization time, were suffering dangerous altitude sickness with vomiting, headaches, and heart and breathing problems. Bettina seemed the worst hit, though Robert, trying to help, felt so lousy he could barely move. Various remedies were produced. The one that gave Bettina the most relief was Mig's Tibetan healing herbs, rolled into tiny burgundy-coloured balls known as 'mhintro'. These are usually taken to help clear the system. Mig let me try them. They were bitter to the tongue, but gave warmth to the heart, for they were special. They had been blessed by His Holiness the Dalia Lama. However, both Bettina and Robert knew that the only safe answer for them was to go back down immediately it was daylight. Michael took still more Diamox, which helped him, and he eventually set off to walk across to the glacier in the dark. He was confronted by the prowling of a lone Andean wolf, looking for scraps. What else could there possibly be to eat – unless climbers were on the menu. This barren land was completely devoid of plant and animal life.

I lay and listened to the howl of the wind rising and falling with crashings and distant rumblings to the accompaniment of snorings, loo getups and gaspings for breath. For a time I felt as bad as I had when we had been here before, with extreme nausea, headache and the shakes. Thankfully it passed, but in spite of a hot bottle of water, Yannick to cuddle and Pete sleeping comfortingly beside me, I felt cold. It was more a cold from the inside. I tried to talk to the fear that was there. I was not really sure specifically what I was afraid of. It was a sort of Garden of Gethsemane feeling, a knowledge that there was a deep, dark, inky-black river that had to be gone through. After what seemed like hours of searching I finally found the point where I knew that all was well and I opened up with joy to the light and strength all around. The Council of Masters was there, with the star. What strength – Wow! I became really warm.

The calm, cold light of the dawn of the 5th of July found us enjoying Oswoldo's breakfast mix of apples and bananas in yoghurt. Everyone looked bleary-eyed. Nobody had had much sleep. Only the four climbers looked in any fit state at all. The others were fighting severe nausea, dizziness, headaches and breathlessness. It seemed that in the planning to make a documentary no account had been able to be taken of the time necessary to acclimatize. However the crew, of a happy temperament, manfully struggled on and came out to film us building our two stupas.

As we scrambled gently up behind the hut, our eyes were naturally drawn west, scrutinising the route that we would be taking later on. It looked bleak and inhospitable. We could see three little figures with rucksacks, one in orange, making their way down steep ice painfully slowly. Somewhere up there in the frozen dark of night they had turned back. At the moment the south-west face was clear, but the visibility was not good. It was hard to make out the boundary between mountain and sky. There was no sunshine, just a flat, grey, lifeless chill.

Then, suddenly there was noise… What was it? It approached, coming nearer and nearer. Was it music? Over the brow of the track to the lower hut, snaking along, came a procession full of beauty and colour. There was a crowd of maybe twenty-five; women dressed in bright red shawls, long skirts and hats; men playing panpipes and flutes. At the back marched the drummer, leading a dancing rhythmical beat. There was an air of celebration and gaiety. They stopped to drink from a glacial melt-water stream, and then, keeping to the chocolate-brown rocks away from the snow and ice, gradually worked their way up to the highest possible edge of the hanging glacier to sing and to pray. To our horror we realised that they were close to the place where we could just make out some huge ice seracs had fallen in the night. From here they were insignificant, but we knew that up there they could swallow the whole party in the speed of a thought. However, the Inca descendants had total trust in their Watchtower of the Universe, whom they affectionately nicknamed Tayta, (meaning 'father' in their Quechuan native tongue). This mountain was their link between Heaven and Earth, the union of the spiritual and physical forces. Amazingly this was no different from the beautiful harmony and balance of the six-pointed star. I marvelled that this pilgrimage should coincide with ours. The draw of the might and power of Chimborazo was strong indeed.

To see such casualness in ascent was disconcerting as we struggled for breath and every movement was an effort. But our sense of commitment and purpose kept us together. We set to work conducting two stupa ceremonies. The stupa that Pete and I had built on our previous trip stood sentinel at the gateway as we repeated the process twice forming a triangle, but with the soul energy input of all four of us. We read the Kuan Yin prayers of compassion, the Chinese words coming from Mig a little tentatively and from GT flamboyantly (in an Italian accent). Each was rolled into a scroll, tied with pink ribbon, placed in a plastic bag and surrounded with a mindful construction of rocks. Then, in activation, we spoke peace messages, more peace messages, and still more peace messages… powerful… moving… touching… and wondrous in their coming together in love for the Earth and Tibet. The way had been prepared. All was ready. Later our boots would pass through this gateway at the start of the climb and we would know that these lights of compassion were shining forth to seek eternal healing.

Following the much-discussed plan for the day we returned to the hut for a meal of soup and rice and the eagerly awaited arrival of the guides. Somewhere along the line there had been changes. So it was Pepé instead of Ramiro who had been given to us, and he and Fernando who had walked in to join us as part of the 'Climb For Tibet' team that afternoon. They were both in their late twenties and typically nice looking, sun-bronzed and friendly. Pepé was the spokesman, confident, intelligent and definite with easily understandable English. We all immediately felt good about him.

'We have a lot of motivation for this climb,' he told us. 'When I read your papers I know it has something for the big mountains in the world and this is the contact with the Dalai Lama. The birthday of Him is interesting and also because it's a climb for the peace of the world. This is one completely interesting for the reason.'

'How long will the climb take do you think?'

'For me the weather is completely clear so we will walk between seven until ten hours today for the summit. It's definitely not windy. The conditions are very good.'

Fernando then spoke in Spanish and Mateus translated, ' He says it's a very special thing for them to climb with all these people and they will do their best to help them get to the top. For him most of the highest mountains are in Tibet and he likes it a lot, because it's like a dream for all the climbers and it's something special to be together here climbing for the same reason.'

Happily, wonderfully understanding guides had been organised, (though I could not quite relate to the word 'walk'). However there was something about Pepé that bothered me and I could not quite put my finger on it. He spoke in a really quick way with a sort of hard, twangy, singsongy accent that reminded me of something. I was not sure what it was.

The plans were laid. We would sleep from 3.00 pm to 9.00 pm, eat breakfast and leave at 10.00 pm. We would take the Direct route up the Thielman glacier tongue, turn west up the steep ice ramp, and thread through the crevassed area, traversing to join the Normal route above the Castillo rocky outcrop. We would then follow up the south-west ridge to the Veintimilla and hence across to dawn on the summit around 6.00 am. We should arrive back at the hut well before 10.00 am safely ahead of the snow becoming soft.

Michael was not to come. It was very disappointing. He told us that he instinctively knew to forgo the ordeal and dangers, as his body was not sufficiently acclimatized, nor recovered from months of exhausting work. Also his hired crampons and axe were not up to what he would have preferred. He would shoot from low on the ice.

So the teams were split, with Pete and myself in one, and GT and Mig in the other. This would be well balanced with experience and strength in each. Pepé as the most experienced and English speaking guide would take GT and Mig, so that Mig would have the most help possible. Pete and I would go with Fernando as my Spanish was the least bad. We were to be, as Mig pointed out with a typical eye on the broader picture of life's metaphysical manifestations, six people representing the six points of the star.

Sleep was not going to come easily at three in the afternoon when the whole of life's focus was rolled into this one day.

First there was the meticulous packing of the rucksacks. Nothing important could be left out as it might mean the difference between the summit or not, or worse still life or death. My problem was usually too much stuff. I think I'll take just one more jacket... 'You haven't got any books in there, have you?' asked Pete, suspiciously looking at my sack. No, but I did agonise over whether to take Yannick or a spare ice-screw. Luckily Yannick won. Accessibility of things was also important. I knew that usually if something was not easy to get at then it was not worth taking. So packets of guarana and coca, lipsalves, penknives and nibbles such as dried apricots, nuts and seeds had to be in outside pockets. Camera with lots of spare film and water bottle had to be in the top of the sack. Searching and scrumbling around in the bottom of a large sack whilst balancing in the dark on a knife edge ridge with companions waiting for you is not to be recommended. Today, though… today was unique and special and there were things more important… the precious things-for-the-summit bag, peace messages, little tape recorder and of course the crystal. I made sure that Mig had the prayer flags, which he had especially brought from India, and I gave him the Tibetan flag and the two pictures to carry. One was of His Holiness the Dalai Lama, the other of the young Panchen Lama, the second highest lama in Tibet who had been kidnapped by the Chinese at the age of six in 1995. Then Pete checked through Mig's climbing kit and reminded him to take double water rations.

I lay trying to sleep knowing that it was impossible, worrying about what I had not packed. Anyway how could I fall asleep with the point furthest from the centre of the Earth, the Watchtower of the Universe, the Great Inca God Chimborazo waiting for our supplications… I knew that I should drink all the water that I possibly could, but this eventually meant creeping up without disturbing the others, carefully negotiating the ladder, forcing boots on, heading out into the icy cold and finding the loo. This was sharing quarters with the noisy fume-ridded generator, which was working overtime for the camera batteries, and was a sleep preventer in its own right. My headache worsened. However once outside, even without my contact lenses, I was able to take in a beautiful moonlit sky with an enigmatic glow coming from the direction of the Veintimilla. My thoughts were with the Inca Indian procession. Did they make the journey down safely?

For the six hours I waited, tossing and turning and envious of those snoring. Four times I heard the wind mount, stronger and stronger to wild gale force and then become stayed… as though by an unseen hand. The 9.00 pm alarm call heralded, in readiness, a completely still and star-struck night.

Could a day start the evening before? Well, with no sleep, I guess it had started twelve hours earlier. No, perhaps this day had started six months ago when Pete and I had launched 'Climb For Tibet' – a dream which spoke of sorrow and pain and showed a way forward in brotherhood and peace, a dream of changing the consciousness of the world. No, this day had started long before that, when I had decided to put Chimborazo and Tibet together and to say, OK, Tibet's people are too precious to lose, they are part of us, they are part of the Earth. They are like a species almost extinct. They need help, protection and love. We can learn from them. Their spirituality is so high that we can barely conceive their seed of learning… Maybe it had started at the moment my heart was touched by the Earth's cry for help… for we are destroying our own mother. Little children tell us they love the Earth. It is so simple, but we do not listen and carry on in greed… Or had it been when I felt that pain in my heart for the Tibetan people… perhaps carried through lifetimes with distant brown memories of corridors of meditation… Anyway… anyhow… this day, to express the highest ideals that there are, from the highest point that there is, had finally come…

Dreamlike, I arose lethargically, nursing a throbbing headache and sick breathlessness. I desperately wanted to have had some sleep. I would have liked to have had a hug with Pete, just a second of closeness together that said keep safe, go well… but somehow that did not happen. Michael instructed us all to go back into bed to be filmed getting up. That put me into an even blacker mood of grumpiness. I had suffered the noise and fumes of the generator for the last few hours. At least, I thought, that means we will be able to have some lighting. The crew now decided to turn it off as it upset the audio, but at the exact moment when I needed some light to put in my contact lenses. I struggled in the half-dark with my head torch, even angrier. That was when they decided to interview us and start filming.

'Tess, what's the major thought going through your mind right now?' asked Michael.

Was that before or after I had throttled him? Close to tears I managed a 'How lousy I feel'.

'It's just nerves.'

Yeah… right. I was not good company. The stress of any climb was enough, let alone this one. Being interviewed was definitely not part of my preparation game-plan. I swallowed some capsules of guarana that made me feel a little better, but feeling so sick I could not force down much breakfast, just a spoonful or two of the fruit yoghurt and a mouthful of granola. I thought that I would have preferred my organic oats but it was too much effort to try and find them. I felt like throwing up. Nerves… well maybe, but mostly it was because I was annoyed. I had no inner peace. I was annoyed with the film crew, but more than anything else I was annoyed with myself for feeling so lousy for something so important.

The others seemed to be coping rather better and sang a rousing and surprisingly harmonious round of 'Happy Birthday dear Dalai Lama'.

'Long live the Dalai Lama,' cried Mig and my spirits rose a little.

'How do you say Happy Birthday in Tibetan?'

'Good question,' laughed Mig, 'we don't celebrate other birthdays really, but we do have these blessed coloured strings, known as 'jendu', which I would like you all to wear around your necks. I've also got some for the guides.

They were given to me by my mother and have been blessed by a high lama. I've been saving them up. We usually wear them when danger threatens, but they'll give you a clear climb up and down. Their main power lasts about three days, so when they drop off you must burn them.'

'Thank you Miggie.' I was so thrilled and would treasure the blessed string that he gave me. I was beginning to find more calm. 'I'm so proud that you are climbing with us.'

He smiled. 'You know I think this is one of the happiest days of my life.'

'Thank you my friend,' beamed Pete receiving his string.

'May all your wishes come true.'

'And yours too.'

Lastly, Mig turned to GT, 'I say, Old Boy…'

'Thanks… We're doing this together we are.'

'All the way to the top.'

'Yeah,' and GT continued, ' I've set off on many nights like this, but I feel this is the most exciting thing I've ever done. It's unique in my experience.'

Pete concurred, 'I've been climbing for about thirty-seven years, which is a long while and doing the serious big stuff since about '75. But this is something different, not just climbing a mountain. This is so much more meaningful. It's being done for a super cause and it's a tremendous physical challenge as well. If we have a clear day then the old adage, you climb the mountain to get the view from the top, will be there. But I think the big thing that's going to hit me when we reach the summit is the fact we've achieved something for world peace and especially for the Tibetan cause. It'll be really great because we've come together as a team of four and we've come through a lot. We've done training climbs and gradually bonded together. It'll be the culmination of a lot of hard work, and a big success story once we reach the summit.'

'Yeah,' said Mig, 'It's going to be great for the awareness. You know there's still a lot of people who don't know about Tibet… or who have forgotten… This climb means a lot to me. I'm doing it not only for Tibet, but also for the peace of the world… It's so important.' He was a young man giving out a strong positive feeling that he could take on any challenge that the mountain would throw at him. He trusted. He was not fearful or even worried about what lay ahead, even though he had not slept either and could not release the continuous intense head pain.

'Well said. We'll be thinking of the planet as a whole, won't we?' affirmed GT. Although without the boldness of youth, he gave out a sense of the sure understanding of the ways of a mountain and the finer resources that would have to be found today. 'The other nice thing is that quite a lot of people are climbing too on this very same day for the cause, those who can't perhaps physically get very high but are going to the highest point they can, to think of our purpose and the Dalai Lama. So that in itself is very exciting.'

'The fact so many are supporting us from all over the world does make an enormous difference,' I agreed. 'We've got hundreds and hundreds who have sent us their own messages and given money for the Tibetan refugees and the Tibetan cause. We're not alone, we've got everyone behind us and that's going to give us a terrific impetus to make it and to do it all for them. We have the responsibility of all these people who've given us their thoughts and their love for the Earth and for Tibet… We will not let them down.'

'Yeah,' continued Pete. 'There's going to be this great sort of bond around the world. That's got to be really powerful…'

'Doesn't sound much like the usual the-reason-I-climb-is-to-get-to-the-top,' probed Michael.

'I think it's a lot more to do with learning about yourself,' I responded. 'You push out your limits and go through fear, and you open up to clear thinking which you don't get down below. You get a spiritual high, everything seems right and you find the answers to things. You're really living when you're climbing on a mountain. You don't get many chances in life to rely on your companions to the extent that your lives depend on each other. You learn a lot very quickly.'

Sometimes prophetic words go by unnoticed…

'C'mon, enough talk. We've got a mountain to climb,' urged Pete. 'I just want to get up there and enjoy it, 'cause it looks good, it's a clear night. I just want to go well, get to the summit and be on top of the world, with my three lovely friends… and the two guides of course.'

Pepé had joined us and was quietly listening, looking fit and ready with a comforting air of confidence. With the interviews over, he checked that we had sun-protection cream and water… and, yes, let's go. That was when it hit me. I knew what that strange feeling was that I had had earlier about him. A chill went through me. Oh, that was quite scary, for fleetingly a glance across his face and the way he spoke gave me the impression that… that he was Chinese. Don't be crazy, I told myself, but there it was again… the distinct sense of Chineseness. What awareness was I tuning into… and of which time scale? Was it just my mind playing? No, it carried a taste of truth, but not in the present state…

'C'mon Tess. Get ready.'

Find stuff in the dark… Over-trousers, inner boots, outer boots, gaiters, harness, waterproof, helmet, head-torch, goggles, gloves, over-gloves… By the time I had everything on, and everyone had waited while I went to the loo yet again, I felt so bulky and awkward that I thought that I'd even have trouble waddling across a penguin colony… Yannick bobbed about in agreement, riding shotgun at his usual stance on the back of my rucksack.

A nearly full moon dominated the clear, deep black of the sky, shedding so much light that it blotted out the spangled touch of distant stardust, distracting us from the intense cold that bit sharply into our unmoving bodies. That was OK. It meant hard safe snow. However, we were not completely without cloud for wispy diaphanous shapes danced on slithers of moonglint saying, this is all for fun…

come and play… whilst a tousled breeze caressed our faces. Where was the relentless wind now? Where were the savage skies? Flashes of lightening answered, far far beneath us, carving illumination through tumultuous storm cloud.

Mig picked up a little rock and licked it several times. 'Here, try it, Tess. My cousin, Sonam, who worked high in the Karakorum glaciers, told me that it helps you cope with altitude. It's because the stone belongs to the mountain, so is a way of connecting up at a vibrational level. It really works. It's to do with belief.' I tentatively tried whilst he carried out prostrations to the huge presence a thousand metres and more above us, which loomed fearlessly at the little ants that were about to scurry across its buttress slopes. Chimborazo… Oh great Chimborazo… We have come… We hold dear your place in history… We walk in harmony with your soul…

The silence was eerie, deep and awesome as though it echoed back the whole of space. There was no sound of a glacier wind, no rockfall, no avalanche, no confusion from the world a long way below. I just heard a throbbing heart with a crystal to guard it. Then, around 10.30 pm, the jangle of man-made metal on metal, clinking of karabiner on ice-screw, clank of descender on karabiner, the brush of nylon waterproof on waterproof and the crunch-thud of six pairs of boots…

We set off at a slow easy pace to scramble up the rocks, my mind jumping and juddering hither and thither. Why did I have to feel so rotten? Would we be able to read the messages? Where was the food that I had stuffed in? How can I best carry the over-gloves? My main problem was my eyes. I knew that even the slightest wind brought dust into my contact lenses and there was no means of taking them out to clean them safely without losing them and thus my eyesight. Sunglasses were too dark, so I needed goggles, which would not fit properly over my helmet with the head torch on as well. By holding my head down at a certain angle I was able to maintain an uncomfortable compromise, which was the start of a stiff neck which became more and more painful as time progressed.

The gateway passed us by. Three silent monuments to compassion, built to withstand the winds of time. May we always open the gateway to compassion, I quickly prayed, but my thoughts were needed in the physical to concentrate on the irregular rocks over which we clambered.

Within half an hour we had reached the edge of the glacier and the moon had disappeared behind cloud. The slope stretched steeply away before us into the unknown. I focussed on the present moment. Sit on rock, crampons out of sack, point head-torch at boot, fix on crampon, check safe and firm, test on the gravel-strewn névé ice on which we had stopped.

Then we roped up. Somehow the teams did not end up as planned. This may have been critical in deciding future events that unfolded. I thought that I heard Pepé say to Fernando in Spanish that he was going to take the señora who he had assessed as the weakest of the four. Thus it was that I found myself tied on to the rope behind Pepé with Pete behind me whilst GT was on Fernando's rope with Mig at the end.

I was in fact so grateful. I felt unsteady and unsure, shaky and full of fear as we set off onto virtually continuous steep ice at about 45°. I felt as though I had never been on crampons before. They felt ungainly and awkward. I could not stop thinking that just one little trip and it could endanger the lives of everyone. I could pull the three of us off. Every little thing needed to have one hundred per cent focus. I needed to control this fear. Pepé was wonderful. He gave me clear simple instructions, which I followed to the letter. Make sure the rope is just under tension. Keep the ten downward-facing points of the crampons on the ice. Climb up using the French method, that is side-stepping up but placing one foot over the other, which saves having to front point which is less safe and uses up calf muscles. Use one ski stick and the ice axe on the uphill side. Then as we changed from a zig to a zag he told me exactly when to change hands. Everyone had to wait as I changed over and sorted out the gloves, carefully and methodically. Every single step counted… carefully… steady… steady… I felt that I was going too slowly for Pete. He was so confident on ice… 'It's a piece of cake'… But I just had to keep focussed somehow. I tried to do affirmations… I am strong… I am safe… but it would not work. I could not afford the luxury of a mind that was not in total focus. Fleeting thoughts of alarm came. Were we below the menacing ice-serac area? Was this the avalanche prone bit? But I cast them aside to fall somewhere into the depths of oblivion. Please, Mind, do not wander... Looking up was uncomfortable and anyway I was glad that it was dark. I did not want to see the horrors of the steepness ahead. After a while I pushed up my goggles. If I kept my eyes down, the cold wind was just bearable. It improved the vision of the little pool of light in an ocean of blackness, an empty circle of cold white existence. I knew definitely that I did not want to look down whilst moving. Therein lay terror. I tried very hard not to think of the going down. I needed to block it out, to be in the moment. It was too black to conceive. Ah… the gentle tug of the harness around my waist from the rope that connected me to Pete comforted my thoughts like a warm umbilical chord.

On and on through the timeless night... extreme focus... every step for humanity. The intense concentration forced me to find a rhythm... forced me to search for calm. It was truly a meditation. From time to time Pepé stopped and then I looked down. It was so steep. I could feel the terror lurking just beneath the surface, but then I knew that I had faith, faith in Pepé, in the mountain, in Pete and in the spiritual and Divine guidance of 'Climb For Tibet'. We could see the steady head-torch movement of the other three close behind us and Mig's little chemical light on the back of his sack. He and I had both decided that we would carry the small amount of added weight to be able to shine extra light. We would get through this. We would. Because we were in front I had time to sneak some guarana capsules. I shovelled in all I could. I knew that they were helping me. And I took coca pills whenever possible, although taking off gloves, reaching pockets and getting things out safely was not easy when concentrating on staying upright. Once when we were waiting for the others GT shouted apologetically 'I'm sorry I'm so slow.' Slow? It was wonderful to have a stop for a couple of minutes. 'Of course you're not' we shouted back.

Relentlessly the steepness continued. Somewhere we turned up the snow ramp into the long traverse, somewhere we must have passed through the crevassed area. Steadily, on and on and on... It was good not to have to worry about the route finding but, I thought, probably Pete felt differently. Then, about three hours after we had started on the glacier, I detected a change in the energy coming up the rope behind me. I could feel Pete's weight gradually tugging. What's he up to? Here I was stuck in the middle with Pepé going the same pace taking the rope ahead of me, but now I was getting pulled in two. Was all not well? Careful... careful... don't trip... I tried to gently pull on the rope behind me to keep stable. Something must be wrong. I could not turn easily to shout down, but the dragging pulled me back and that caused Pepé to slow. Then just as Pete was about to shout up the rope to stop, that was what we did. We were close to the south-west ridge at about 5,500 metres. There was a stance where the gradient eased a little and we could perch and take the weight off our feet. Here the wind was gathering, but we could rest for a while.

'Are you OK?' I asked Pete, as he came up beside me.

'No.' He flopped down and sat with his head between his hands, breathing heavily. ' I feel really bad, Tess.'

I tried to comfort him. 'You'll get through it. Have a rest and by the time the others get here, you'll be fine. Keep going and all will be well. Come on, have something to eat.' I offered him apricots and nuts and Pepé offered him bread, but he just sat there shaking his head, feeling too sick to try, his breath coming in unnatural gulps. I felt happy that he drank water, but I was not too concerned for I felt sure that he would be all right soon. He always had such a positive outlook and with all his strength and expectation surely would override the battle with the altitude sickness. It would pass. Indeed, on Whymper's expedition it had also been the strongest who had suffered the most.

In a few minutes the others appeared. 'I'm too slow. I'm holding everyone up,' gasped GT.

'You're not. You're only about five minutes behind,' I insisted. Please don't be so negative I thought. But he was not feeling at all well either. The altitude was attacking him unforgivingly. He was coughing and having real trouble breathing, with dizzy spells. He had been finding the going increasingly difficult and did not think that he could give much more. 'How much further?' he asked and, hearing from Pepé that it was four hours to the Veintimilla, he knew then that he could not do it. He had never had this feeling on a mountain before. Knowing that to keep going at all would mean a very much slower pace which would seriously hold back the rest of the party, he selflessly said 'Well, I think it's right if I go down. It will give the team the best chance. Is this the most suitable place to turn around?' No… No… we were all going to get there together… Please… This could not be happening. At that moment I could not guess at the enormity of his sacrifice. The climb meant so much to him…

We were now in an awkward situation. Pepé said that if GT went down with Fernando whilst the rest of us went on as a rope of four, if subsequently someone else needed to go back, then the whole team would have to turn. I looked at Pete. I could see that he had been influenced by Pepé's comments and was considering the only other alternative… I did not want it to be a reality… Please, Pete… No… How can you let go? All that we have worked for together for so long, so much planning and drive, creation of the whole project, dedication, training, pushing everyone else… Please… No… No…

Pete was good at making decisions. GT's resolve had watered the seeds of his doubt. He did not flinch at the agony. Having been a mountain instructor for so many years he knew that the safety aspect was the most important consideration. He felt he should be in control of himself on a mountain, enjoying the climbing, not being dragged up. He knew that he was losing energy and having trouble breathing. He knew that his body was not coping with the altitude and that it

210

would become worse, a lot worse. This would put pressure on the team. He had been in the risk assessment business for thirty years and now, now he would not jeopardise everyone else's safety. Mig and I seemed to be going all right. If he went down with GT it would give us a better chance.

'Tess,' he said 'I am not prepared to die for this. There are other things in life. I have my children to support and I'm not going to chuck it all away.' In his psyche there was good reason for this understanding. Ten years ago, whilst climbing on Helvelyn, he had watched his close friend Mark, an experienced climber, slip and fall to his death.

Pete was going to have to climb the biggest mountain of his life… that of turning back. The condor would fly no higher.

Would I ever appreciate the desperate disappointment that would send them into the deep pit of despair? Should unconditional love be this painful? I did not know if I could ever give in this magnanimous way. They were each stronger than me. Maybe the Incas were right about the honour of the sacrifice on the mountain.

Pete and Mig exchanged places on the ropes and I retied the knot to Mig's harness until I was happy with it. With great presence of mind Pete thrust the video camera at us.

'I'm sorry, Tess,' he said, a haunting voice in my ear... turned.... and then they were gone.

One warm tear just escaped onto a shivery cheek.

'I love you,' I shouted down the mountain into the abyss between tomorrow and eternity, but my words had been eaten by the night and were lost forever on the cold black wind.

27 - Heaven's gateway

In just a handful of minutes, in scarcely a moment of time, all had been decided. Our fates had been sealed and the hopes and dreams of GT and Pete had crashed. Not for a split second did I consider going back too. Even if the way forward had not been calling me so strongly, to go downwards for two hours in the dark on that steep ice, when one slip would mean everyone tumbling, held for me complete abject terror and dread.

I wondered, guiltily, if I should have tried harder to convince Pete to keep going, but I could not have questioned his discernment or tried to persuade him if he had felt his decision to be right. I could never judge what he needed to learn or where he needed to be for his own soul growth. In the mountains in particular, when life is at stake, it is important to listen to the sixth sense inside. I hoped that he had done that. I thought of the time earlier this year when we had been training in the Alps, ski-mountaineering. We had been approaching the top of a near vertical slope. He had followed his intuition to come and stand below me just before I had slipped. It would in all likelihood have been a fatal fall if he hadn't been there… Now he was not with me.

Our whole team had been such a warm support system, always there for each other. To split this was a bitter blow… but now… now it was all up to us. I would have to find ways to be strong, more so than ever. Having Mig, the inexperienced one, with me meant that I had to be more responsible for him, which changed my energy within and gave me strength. Egbert came briefly breezing in with a big smile on his face, singing 'I'm going to win, I'm going to win.' Yeah, yeah Egbert, we're all in this together, but it gave me a boost of adrenaline. Also the rest time had suited my body well and I had eaten all of Pepé's bread. It had just been plain integral bread, maybe left over from his bus journey up, but it had been exactly what I had needed. I had had no conflict, no choice to make. The others would hopefully soon be safe. I had to keep going now, not only for myself, but also for Mig and Tibet and all the many others who had supported us, but particularly now for GT and Pete – desperately now for them. We carried the essence of the whole... It was vital not to falter.

Still stunned by the change in circumstances, Mig was rubbing the back of his head where the pain had moved to and was drinking water in a camel-like fashion. 'Tess, we'll do it,' he said. 'You and Pete have put so much into creating 'Climb For Tibet'. I'm not going to let it be to no avail.' I felt really happy to have Mig with me. We had a strong common bond of helping Tibet. I knew it meant everything to him. He knew it meant everything to me. There was a melding of heart energy in one huge belief of determined vision, and surprisingly things felt right. All would be well. However there was a lot of work to do first.

Pepé led on and it was good to get the chilled body moving again. It must have been about 2.30 am, although lack of sleep meant that time was irrelevant. It was more like a conscious dream through the night. There was no concept of being human with specific slumber times. Now Body, please listen, you're just a tool. I need you to carry me on and up. There seemed to be strength in my half-awareness... no, c'mon... focus... every step counts... one step after the other... take care to put the points of the crampons down flat to bite into the hard white stuff... strains the ankles... they'll recover... calf muscles work, please... shoulders move precisely... I need each stick placement and each ice axe placement to be correct... Was it my imagination or was the slope easing slightly? It was my imagination.

Mig was going well, even with the annoyance of ill-fitting boots and the added weight of the spare rope. It seemed that he had absorbed all the learning and fallen into an easy climbing technique with the vigour and fortitude of youth. However, he did tend to want to rush along with his no.11-bus-at-Piccadilly syndrome and then stop for a rest, rather than keep a steady pace. I felt sure that he was being helped by his genetic inheritance from the high altitude regions of Tibet. How fitting if this was to be the factor, which tipped the balance to keep him against all odds from going down, so that he could climb the mountain that was to help his ailing country.

Stopping was beginning to get difficult. The concentration of one foot over the other, breathe, ice axe up, breathe, stick up, breathe, back foot up, breathe, foot over the other, breathe, ice axe up... blended into a continuation of movement that seemed to be taken over by something other than me. Mig described the phenomenon as someone else driving his body. To stop meant losing the driver, to gasp, to feel intensely nauseous and heady, to drift and then to have great trouble finding the reason and purpose to start up again. Then I would remember something like speaking on camera in the hut, oh so long ago, saying 'We will not let them down.'... and that would spark the ignition. At times I would call to the driver... Please help me, please help... and I would feel wonderful assistance at a deep, high level of the spirit, lifting me up from the centre of the wheel of a spinning six-pointed star... And then I would float, in a steady movement, not quite in my body, and yet the most grounded that I had ever been, both at the same time. The seeming unreality of this sensation somehow drifted into expected normality and the edges became blurred. It reminded me of the time Mig had practised moving his mind aside to allow healing energy to enter when his boots had first hurt...

Concentrate Mind... on and on, up and up, with little awareness of the ridge or the dark night around. There was only the next step and the next. The body was starting to cry out in weariness. This was a greater test than it had been designed for. How much more could it give? This is it. This is it. I can go no further. I am tired to the core. Exhaustion is no friend here in this steep cold dread. Mind cannot hold the concentration any more. It is too much... too much... but I have no choice... c'mon... focus... the crystal.... think on the crystal... Ah, peace. I am the carrier. It will act as a beacon of light, just as the Incas before us lit beacons on the summits of their watchtowers. It vibrates at the rhythm of humanity, expanding and magnifying thought a thousand times. It will channel high frequency energy onto the physical Earth plane, via this special point that is spinning faster than anywhere else on Earth, a symbol of alignment with cosmic harmony. It will reach out into space further than anywhere else on Earth, the edge of our planet, like an arrow of light that can touch the stars. But its universal importance is truly to be part of the system to bring light to the crystal heart of humanity, to act as an amplifier for the purest highest light... Divine energy...

We are God in safety... we are one in safety... please help me ... please give me strength.... I am God in strength... I am one in strength.... concentrate on each step... Oh the effort is just too much.... how can I keep this up? Oh dear God... this is hard. The angle that Pepé takes the route is too much for me. I need to zigzag more... it seems like vertical... I can't do it... I can't... I have no breath... there is no air... But a soft wind blew by and packed my lungs to capacity. Now take it in. All the

214

oxygen you need is here…

I had no concept of time. The hours went by, or were they days? The muscles were in agony, my neck excruciatingly painful, my eyes sore and tired, so tired… climbing… climbing… climbing… My sack was part of me but heavy, though what do we carry that won't be the lightest that it can ever be up here? In truth we carry the expectations of GT and Pete. We carry hope for the Tibetan nation… the flag to unfurl as the expression of the Tibetan spirit. We carry the love and support of hundreds… a focus of dedicated energies. We are accompanied by the dreams of humanity for harmony on Earth. We are messengers for the beings of light. We shall not give up.

Pepé rarely spoke now, or if he did I was just not aware of it, but there was a moment when we were stopped, gasping for breath, and he passed us a sip of warm strange-tasting liquid, which eased the parched throat. I knew that I no longer had the energy to reach into my sack for the bottle of water. 'It's only twenty minutes 'til dawn, now,' he said. How could this eternal night end? Surely it will last forever...

That was when the cold hit us. A deep biting cold that attacked our weakened and drained bodies. Mine started to shiver uncontrollably. I knew that I had to take off my sack to find my duvet jacket, but I could not organise my thoughts into the right order to go through the motions. It was all a jumble. My teeth were chattering. Somehow I had to do it.

'Tess, have you got any water left?' asked Mig. Right... For him, yes, I could get into my sack. I found the bottle and dug out the jacket, managing at length to put it on, on top of everything else, so I was nearly as round as I was tall. The shivering subsided. Bless you Pete for buying it for me… way back in another lifetime… It was snowing now, just gentle flakes, or were they gentle because they looked so pretty, dancing and frolicking to and fro in the round head-torch light. I played with them too inside the circle… catch me if you can… Each individual flake was a friend, special and magic, for in their symmetry every one was a six-pointed star. Maybe that's why there's a higher vibration on a mountain… It's all because of the lovely snowflakes… 'Tess, c'mon… We must go.'

'Go? Go where?'

'C'mon!'

Oh, the agony of moving again… though, not quite so sick… the joy of motion… not so dizzy. But why is all so white now? There's a sort of hazy grey white everywhere. The night had gone and left us to our fate. Dawn came. When did that happen? The dawn of the 6th of July… Ah, yes… and with it the steepness eased… thank goodness. It's taken away the terror of falling, though it's still down there. I can't do it… but I can ignore things I don't like. I won't think of it now.

The rope yanked behind me and I fell to my knees in the snow. Ah, now it's soft… the hard snow had left us behind too… but I don't like this stopping again… the world spins too much… my head is in some sort of a clamp… there's something funny happening inside it… it feels like it's on fire…

'Oouhrgh!' I looked down the rope to see Mig vomiting, his face wracked in pain. I wanted to go and help him, but my body would not respond to the request. I knew that if I could find some guarana, then I would feel better, but I was too confused to remember where it was and there was too little energy to try… Maybe something to eat? No way… nausea too much… churning stomach...

There was a voice. Pepé was trying to get through the haze… 'Head-torch off… Sunglasses on.' Yeah, I can do this… I can… and I'll take my helmet off too… Ah, the freedom of being able to move my neck better and to see around. It did not gain much. The blackness had been replaced by whiteness. The slope fell away to the right. We must be somewhere on the ridge, but visibility was only a few metres across snow to an unending wall of cloud.

Mig moved up to where I was. 'C'mon, Miggie,' I encouraged. 'We've got to do this. We're going to do this.' We urged each other on, each seeing in the eyes of the other the reflection of the agony that the body was going through, the throbbing head, the confusion, the disorientation, the struggle for breath, the feeling like there was a rock sitting on the chest. Above all, though, it was the feeling in my head that bothered me. Something was trying to get out of it…

We staggered up, 'C'mon, do it for the Dalai Lama.' The mind is a weird thing. It can lead the body beyond the limits of what seems possible. One thought can stir great resources of energy. It can push and push. We knew that we both burned with the same passion. There was no way that we would give up.

For a time I became quite lucid and spoke to Pepé's quiet strong presence. He was so steadfast for us. Surely our snail's pace must be frustrating him. 'It doesn't matter how, but we have to get to the summit, the real summit. We are going to get there, whatever it takes.' Maybe he was frightened by my conviction, maybe impressed, but it must have been unusual. Was he aware of the depth of importance of it all? I believed that at some level he was. He was the one who had been especially sent to guide us and show us the way.

Now there seemed to be a rough track in the snow that we were following, though we met no one else in the whole of our white, white world. It continued snowing, but not too heavily. In fact it was useful as it kept things cold, the easier for the movement, the better for the safety, and the low visibility was perfect. I did not want to see any views. We had a job in hand to do and I trusted that every detail of the weather was just what we needed.

We continued ever upwards, plodding upwards, carried by the intense determination that was overriding all things. I could feel spiritual help all around, like a gathering of souls at a party – guides, father, grandmother… but all seemed to bow to the direction of the Council of Masters. This was their show.

Onwards, always onwards, whilst the moments of clarity were lost in a sea of confusion and pain. Inside my head was a deep high feeling which I was having trouble understanding, though I could relate to the Incas practising the ancient rites of trephining, that is cutting away part of the skull to ease the pressures of the brain. It was a bit like wanting to vomit but through the head. It was stuck in a triangle and was pushing to get out. Let it out… let it out… aiheeeee… would my head explode? There was not enough space left inside. Relax, it subsided for a while.

Then I knew.

The awareness had crept up on me, whilst something else was controlling my body, working my legs. It came somewhere between the dawn and the rest of forever. My brain, that vast computer in my head controlled by the mind, was expanding and swelling. I was into the stage of Acute Mountain Sickness that was Cerebral Oedema. OK, everyone gets it I tried to pretend, but I knew that it was not so and I knew that it was serious, deadly serious. A fear took hold and with the fear a realisation. I would have to go down. Joke! We're going to the top.

We stopped again for Mig to be sick and then again and again. He had nothing left inside him. He was hunched over and wretched. I gave him the last water that we had and he idly poked his finger through the ice that had collected around the lip of the bottle. Each time one of us was close to the impossible, to the giving up, the other would say 'C'mon, we can do it.' We fed off each other's fluctuating energy. 'Do it for the Dalai Lama.' And we would move again. One of us always had to be strong, and the mind would always rationalise something.

Mig used his prayers to his Guru, which gave him persistent strength in his safety and his heart was being lifted by the thought of condor wings… but he never wavered in his belief that he would do it. He was scared, scared of going home to his friends and saying that he had not done it. It was so much tougher than he had thought it was going to be, but there was no way he could go home without having done it. Above all, though, above everything else, he had a country to free and this climb held a stepping stone towards that goal. It was something he could do. He would not fail.

His desperate tiredness and exhaustion was taking its toll. He was beginning to hear voices in his head. They came and went in the confusion of his mind that was busy with a life review. There were images of every part of his twenty-one years, friends, good things, special times... non-stop and as continuous as the mountain slope which seemed to go on and on and on...

Surely we must be nearing the Veintimilla... that must be it ... no... that must be it... no... false summit after false summit came and went... on and on... but at least the mind could wander away from the confines of the body. Behind it all was the shining star of belief that carried him... that carried me....

Weird, weird... brain trying to get out, trying to explode... expand, expand... then suddenly I would be gone, where to, I do not know. I would miss chunks of time altogether. I felt like I was hallucinating, but could not remember what I was seeing. I would shake my head and say 'I am awake... I am awake,' whilst drifting in and out of awareness...

As my physical condition deteriorated, the angle of the slope continued to ease. This was a blessing, but lurking around was a growing fear of how we would get down later, if we kept going. We were going on long after the planned time when we should by now be going down. The snow would become soft and dangerous. Sometimes the light was so bright behind the whiteout cloud that I knew that the heat of the sun would be working on the place where Pepé had said was risky for avalanches. Trust, girl, trust... but would we get down if we kept going? Don't think of going down... it will take care of itself... but I was frightened.

I seemed to be brain-dead... there was a floating feeling... thoughts would not work properly... it was too painful to stop. I felt too sick... but I felt sick anyway and it was like I was not here... I was so tired, so very tired and my brain felt so swollen... Leg after leg after leg... Oh, please help me, please help me... I called... but this time there came a different reply, 'Not so... we will help you no more. You must give every ounce of your life... everything... so that there is nothing left, nothing of yourself, no individuality... no longer child, mother, sister, lover... In the knowledge of the giving of your life, there is a letting go, a humility. Only in this way can there be an arrival at the summit on your knees, giving out the vibrational energy that is needed... that of unconditional love.'

What? I did not understand, beyond the thought that there was no help.

But there was one thing that was completely and utterly clear from that moment. I would not make it down. I was not going to make it down. If I kept going I was going to die up here... I did have the choice. I could turn right now, but if I kept going then the fluids in my brain would expand further and then I would die. Amongst all the confusion of my mind this point was crystal clear. That was my total truth. To me it was a reality.

I knew immediately that I was not prepared to turn back. There was too much at stake... all that I had worked for and dreamed of. To continue was fulfilling my life's purpose and if I was to die in this beautiful and glorious moment then... so be it. I was doing what I had to do. What about my loved ones?... My children... my children... That is another lifetime. I am here now. There is only now. There is no other... And anyway they are with me, they are part of me, for with love there is no separation. Somewhere in the far reaches of my memory there stirred a lilting voice 'If your heart believes that you are doing the right thing... if you truly believe that you will continue to exist... it is the spirit which is most important... sometimes you can afford to give up the body'...

There was no choice to be made, for I would keep going and give everything. If this frame of mind was what was asked of me to try to reach the summit then I would give it. Four times I asked myself was this right. Four times, unfalteringly came the reply... we keep going...

I am filled with unimaginable joy. I am rising. My soul is soaring. I am held on all sides by countless wings of light that emanate from loving heart chakras. They whisper on silent winds. There is a dazzling pure golden brilliance that washes me, that enfolds me, that pours at me... and I respond, for I am one and the same. I am all things and all things are me. I am love and all things are love. I yearn to be here forever and the yearning is... for there is only now forever... and I have come home. This is perfection...

I see colours flying from the heart, colours of shimmering light... the dance of purples and silver, reds and pink... I feel it... the determination and the unconditional love... a sea of rainbows... joy and excitement... show me... show me more... Oh! I am touched by this lovely display expressed from our hearts and see the wonderment of joy from this, the abode beyond the body. I am filled with insight and thankfulness.

Mig in his joy of commitment shows much white with rainbow edges, that play and waft and whirl in tints and tinges of previously unknown hues... Oh, how beautifully... Pepé is as though not human... rather our own energy and resolution that is leading us, but as a guide of energies more than a leading. His quiet strength is pink with yellows and browns at the side... And his tones are of compassion... yes, Chinese... but it is also that of all peoples for it is reaching out to the energies and dyes of humanity, melded and mixed... blended with a brilliant white Divine viscosity... painted across the Earth... that I see... that we are... From all parts of the world colours are gushing, flowing and cascading... and I watch entranced from this highest of places.

The body is taken over by the mind, and the mind is being taken over by the spirit, touching the robes of Divineness... and with it, deep inside, comes wonderful crystal clarity and understanding of all things. There is no longer any need to ask of anything.

There is complete and utter peace.

Suddenly, I was in body awareness... Please... Oh please... let me stay in that state of ecstasy and bliss... I don't want to leave.

I wanted to lie down in the snow and die. I wanted to take all my clothes off and happily go to sleep. I knew I felt funny. I knew that I should be going down quickly. I told Pepé and Mig that I felt funny, but I knew too that it was my responsibility and I knew that I had asked Pepé to keep us going whatever. But was I lying down? Or was I moving? Or was it the snow that moved?

Then I knew that I still climbed for the eyes differentiated. We took a sharp turn left, looking down at ice-forms in a deep bergschrund of wondrous swimming blue-green beauty, and then a curving slope up softening snow to the final slopes of the Veintimilla. It opened out to a broad volcanic dome. The visibility had widened, but we could not see further than the edges of the dome. There was a sense of other people having been here before.

We staggered to the middle and fell into a heap. My body lay motionless like a rag-doll abandoned. Mig was still vomiting raw stomach fluids. We became cold and then colder still within seconds. My thoughts took so long to put together that I could not manage more than simply... we had to go on... but I was in no state to move an inch in any direction.

Pepé counselled us. We should go down. It's safest to go down. Very often climbers turn back at this summit. It is 9.00 am. This is late, for the reason the snow will become treacherously loose on the steeper lower slopes. Our own condition is becoming rapidly worse. It is completely right to go down now.

28 - CRYSTAL HEART

The Veintimilla was a prize well won. We had climbed the dizzying heights of armour to this, Chimborazo's final shield of protection.

'Let's call this the real summit,' Mig suggested, but looking up into his drawn face I could see behind the glazing of his eyes that it was not what he wanted. A fire still flickered there somewhere, waiting for a fine wind of resolution to rekindle the flames.

However, we both knew that the other was at the end of their tether, that we had reached that point physically many hours ago.

'I can't go on,' he said.

'Yes you can,' I said.

'I'm going to take all my clothes off and I'm going to die,' I said.

'No you're not,' he said. 'I'm not carrying your dead body down. Tell you what, you stay here and I'll take the crystal across to the summit for us.'

Wow! To say that when he had not one single ounce of energy left... Now I knew why I always called him the Snow Lion-Heart. His heart was so very very big. I was so close to saying, yes, all right. I was going to put my head down, never to raise it again. It was OK. I was drifting into a hallucinating dream, in a state of not caring. I teetered on the edge. Then a voice in me said, if you lie still in this cold for a minute or two longer you will die anyway. Better to find a last bit of energy that must be here somewhere and move across to the summit. At least you will have got there, though there is no way that you will get back down after that.

Somewhere from this deep state of torpor there was a way out. 'Miggie, we'll do it for the Dalai Lama.'

There was one more final incentive, 'Tess, when we get down I'll buy you a milkshake. You can have banana and I'm going to go for strawberry.'

We would go the final road.

With a superhuman effort that was born of importance to someone else rather than self, I found the energy to sit up and say 'Miggie, you must take the responsibility for your own life in deciding to keep going. It reduces the chances of getting down safely.'

However, Migmar was representing the lives of all the Tibetan people, who had given so much more than us. They had suffered so much more. This… this was nothing compared to the Himalayas, escaping with no food, no clothing, no drink. We had proper mountaineering gear, we had boots and crampons, whilst they… they had pictures of frozen dead children… He was not about to give up. Between us we would do it.

So, at Pepé's insistence, we ditched the rucksacks and every bit of weight possible. If anyone was to later doubt my sanity, they would know… for I left Yannick behind at 6,260 metres on this, the western summit of Chimborazo. Mig took the flag, the prayer flags and the sticks. I pressed play on the tape recorder and Gandiva's sounds of Tibetan gongs reverberated out for a moment of time, as I gathered the things-for-the-summit bag. The crystal stirred in my heart pocket.

We now had to go due east for one kilometre, but first… first for a little way we staggered DOWN, which was a mixed-up sensation. Then, Pepé turned anxiously to look back and halted dead in his tracks. It had stopped snowing and there seemed to be a gap in the cover behind us where there was a large black cloud, just like those painted by children, as though a testing cloud floating through Heaven. It hovered close to us and I saw real fear in Pepé's eyes. 'I'm not happy,' he confirmed. 'A friend of mine died recently right here when a similar cloud appeared and he was struck by lightening.' Wow! Pepé was learning too. The mountain tops seem to be good places for soul growth. Whiteout mercifully took over, covering the visibility of the cloud. The cloud was Pepé's and I thought no more about it, except that his arrival at the summit would indeed be in the energy of unconditional love… after all I had already seen the colour of his energy.

Our main problem now was wading through soft knee-deep snow, often thigh-deep. This was where Whymper had reported being in it up to his neck. We struggled to try and keep in the huge footprints that Pepé was making for us. He must have been really tired too, but he did not show it. He left things along the way, Hansel-and-Gretel-like, to find the way back in the whiteout. Thankfully I only had to give up one of my sticks. I needed the other so badly to hold me upright. As before, things seemed more possible when moving, in spite of the almost laughably hard conditions, and I marvelled that I was still going.

Then we had to go UP. Oh dear God, if I can only do this last 'up', I will never ask for anything again. How can this body do it? The mind is so strong, so clever, it does not care if it is in the desert or a forest or up at 6,000 metres, it carries the body to places impossible, in golden dreams. It is strong. It is king... and yet flying above the mind is more than this. The spirit is supremely powerful, with neither the confines of time or space, nor conceivable limits...

Those in spirit and more in tune with the Divine watched us coming. 'Tess, you know,' said Mig with wonder seeping from his tired voice, 'I feel energised by the blessings of Churchill and Gandhi.' How lovely... It was understandable that they would not want to miss this for the world. They would see not so much the supreme physical effort, as that which we gave out, the sacrifice which we had made. They would then know that we had given our all and that we came humbly and asking for the freedom of oppression in Tibet and for the peace of the world. This was as it should be. There was no other way to come to this sacred ground. It had to be in unconditional love... and this was what I had come to learn.

Suddenly Pepé stopped. This was it. We were almost surprised. 'Well, if you can find a higher spot,' he said, 'let me know.' Higher spot? This was the furthest point from the centre of the Earth... 6,310 metres above sea level... and we were on it... But where was the summit? The gradient was a bit like that of a football pitch... Where? My heart was beginning to fill up and overflow into tears. Pepé waved at the space in front of us. There was only untouched snow. With the eyes we could see no further than the distance to the next person on the rope, after that sky and snow, snow and sky were all one huge canvas of whiteness... But with the soul we could see round the circle of eternity. There was only this moment, no past, no future, no cause, no reason... There was total oneness of all things... and joy, such joy, such beauty and completeness. Nothing else mattered, but this. The sense was of the spirit of immortality.

Somehow Pepé had the video camera... 'Please, just press the red button and keep pressing,' I entreated of him, whilst Mig stood with his green sacred stick... the stick that was a carrier of compassion and showed us the way. 'It's just that spot there.' He said as it flew from his hands to mark the place. 'We're there... Oh, God... We've made it.' His voice quavered in the passion of the moment. It had been twelve hours... twelve lifetimes... since we had set out from the shelter of the hut. Truly the mountain we had climbed had been within ourselves.

I took six final laborious steps through the soft snow, trailing the rope that connected me to Mig, and collapsed to my knees... and then to my face. I felt neither the stinging burn of the cold, nor the rasping snatch of my lungs, for it was the facing of myself that had been the most painful. I had moved into the understanding and the certain knowledge of the greater sense of self, which no amount of thinking could explain or describe, but for the experiencing it. To be one with all things was a deep feeling of being. It was no longer belief. It was knowing. In total trust of the Universe and in the letting go of my separate existence, I had been given the prize of the knowledge of my own truth. That was liberation. That was freedom.

Humbly we come… We are indeed one spirit, Chimborazo.

On our knees, Mig and I embraced. It was a long, long embrace, born of toil and hardship, of battle and undiminished determination. As we clung to each other, I allowed the tears to fall from my long-dehydrated body, gasping for the oxygen needed, and my chest heaved in pent-up emotion and relief. Suddenly, all the pains of the fire in my brain, the exhaustion and the agony were lost in one huge surge of power and energy that entered us from we knew not where.

Mig took off his gloves to unfurl the Tibetan flag… a sweet moment of devotion… and we held it up between us to speak out our messages… blue, red and yellow, bright and vibrant against the spinning white of all colours.

'We ask for humanity to listen to His Holiness the Dalai Lama of Tibet, whose shining example…' I broke down in wracking sobs as the snow dripped from my clothes onto the flag and the brittle icicles of my exposed hair stroked my cheek… '… a way forward in peace and brotherhood… for a free Tibet and our Earth in harmony…'

The snow lions on the flag reflected the strength of their brother as he pulled his maroon balaclava away from his mouth to speak, bursting from his heart. 'I… I'm going to do everything I can, dear Tibet and its people, to free you, and to heal you, within this life… and if that doesn't become possible, I want to come back in my next life to heal and to free you… Happy Birthday, Dalai Lama…'

'Happy Birthday, Dalai Lama.' I echoed as he continued '…and may your examples set the world free… of violence.'

'OM MANI PADME HUM' we prayed and his face crumpled into a wide smile. 'Tess, we did it… I gave up, down there… I thought we couldn't do it…' And he fell onto his back, his arms punching the thin air that clasped cruelly at his lungs. Through tears of exhaustion he cried from the depths of his being 'PEACE ON EARTH! PEACE ON EARTH! PEACE ON EARTH!'

The snow lapped at his body.

'Don't get cold, Mig.'

'I don't feel the cold.'

'Here, look.' I drew from my heart pocket our crystal... the last time our crystal... and offered it up for him to touch. 'Give it a kiss, Mig.' Then I held it high. 'It will be a light to shine throughout the world... filled with Divine energy... and will bring down world peace... We deliver it.'

'Tess, this has got to be it...' Mig's excitement sharpened our focus. There was a deep almost blue hole that presented itself to us. It was about the size of an ice axe handle. I placed the crystal carefully in.

'It's upright... Fill the hole with snow so it will never blow away and will bring peace for always and always.' Our souls danced in harmony with the colours that were given off... There was an ethereal sense of the Council of Masters upholding a radiant star of light all around us... and it was done.

We were a Tibetan, an Englishwoman and an Ecuadorian, gathered, representing many by the intention of their peace messages, in the name of Universal Love.

Beside the resting place of the crystal another hole waited, and into it we laid Uri's little book of positive ways forward and the spoon bent with the power of world peace coming down. We wrapped them in snow, like gifts to the spirit of the mountain, as across the globe the turn of the Earth showed teatime in an English country house. Uri was there with his family, close in their love for each other, tuning in to the place where we were. All was unfolding...

Then Mig opened Bill's ring, so beautifully and lovingly made out of copper, vibrating with the 'OM'. The message inside was an ancient Chinese proverb... 'When you reach the top of a mountain... keep climbing...' The wisdom it held brushed past us silently as Mig filled the container with snow to fulfil the prayer of coming down safely. Oh, Wow! Oh, Wow! I was allowed to think beyond this moment for the first time. There was a chance of getting down. The magic of the ring was sustained.

The cold warned of minutes too long, as with fumbling hands I opened the birdseed packet from Lawley. The energy of love for the birds of Tibet symbolised new life after death... as the seeds scattered... And Tarka's fur represented the simple power of love as Mig read Candy's message. We knew that we had neither the time nor the stamina to read more from here, except just the special one from His Holiness. We both had copies somewhere on us, but the boost of energy was beginning to drain and neither of us could find it. We were content knowing that there is more wisdom in the unseen…

Hurriedly now, I stuffed a film cartridge with snow to take for GT and Pete, whilst Mig opened out the prayer flags. 'The whole 'Climb For Tibet' team dedicates these prayer flags to the Tibetan people, in and out of Tibet, and especially to this mountain, this beautiful mountain and to the whole world.'

'May there be peace on Earth.'

'May there be peace on Earth.' Mig's hands moved up and down to emphasise each word that he brought out. 'These prayer flags are… probably… I'm sure… I'm sure… the most highest prayer flags in the world… they must be… They will fly from the highest point on Earth… Oh, Tess… we've gotta put them up.' He tied them securely to his faithful stick, which had for so long been his friend by his side, imbued with compassion – the twin soul of unconditional love. Its life purpose was about to find fulfilment. I tied the other end to the smaller stick and he staggered back to spread out the flags. 'It doesn't matter if they touch the snow… The mantras written here, on the representations of the five elements, will always be blown by the wind on top of Chimborazo, the highest mountain in the world. Basically, the wind will whistle and will speak out the prayers and mantras on all these elements and blow them around the Earth.' We pushed the sticks deep into the snow… support for the power of the messages.

'Long may they fly from the point furthest from the centre of the Earth… and may they bring down Earth Peace.' Just as we put the prayer flags up, the incredible stillness and calm that we had been experiencing changed. A steady breeze blew… I had never doubted the weather angel…

If you had been watching our planet from space that day, you would have seen the colours flying from a bright star at her furthest point… The blues, whites, reds, greens and yellows, blowing, again and again… messages from the mountain… spinning into a whiteness and purity ablaze with light… They were carried by the wind-horse, whose job it was to encompass and embrace the Earth with blessings of peace and harmony. As she turned, they had an uninterrupted journey… for there was no place higher…

29 - A LIGHT FOR PEACE

For long years of legend it had been said that Chimborazo, Watchtower of the Universe, held treasure. At the beginning of 1880, as Whymper's party set off to climb, the local officials had said 'We understand, señors, that it is necessary for you to say you intend to climb Chimborazo, although everyone knows such a thing is impossible... But we know very well that you intend to discover the treasure that is buried there.' Yes, indeed, today we had found treasure, but we had had to look in our hearts.

I had experienced the strength of the mind, fed by belief. It had pushed the body way beyond what it was capable of, carried on wings of compassion. In the knowledge of death and the opening of the gateway to Divineness I had found supreme joy and a deep peace. I had perceived the interconnected oneness of all things. I had beheld detachment, for I had undergone the ultimate letting go, that of my life... as seen through the veil of being only in the present moment... And, this day, I understood unconditional love. My treasure was these gifts wrapped in the sense of the spirit of eternity. For years, maybe lifetimes, I had been trying to learn these things. Now, as if through a passage of initiation, I had a new direction. My purpose would be to share these understandings. For this I would survive, though part of me desperately wanted not to leave. I was thrust back into life awareness. I fell back into selfness.

This self brought with it the weight of accountability. What happened to it mattered. Up until then I was always going to do what I was going to do, come what may. I had never felt that I was in the hands of Pepé. He had been there as the route guide, for safety, to record with the camera and somehow, in a way that I did not quite understand, to bring a sense of the compassion of the Chinese. He had been a strong, gentle, angelic-like presence, a guide in the true sense of the word. Now, we had done what we had come to do and I was happy to feel that I could hand responsibility over to him with a 'Let's go. Please... somehow... get us down.' Down? The concept was strange and new as though it was an idea in the future, something I had to grasp onto before it drifted away…

It must have been around 11.00 am, though I had no sense of time, as with one brief last glance at the forever picture of the fluttering prayer flags, I turned into the white wilderness. Every movement took an unimaginable effort for the instructions from mind to body did not always make much sense. The lucidity of the summit actions had disappeared. The fire in my brain seemed to have rekindled and was burning brightly, eating me away, cell by cell. I did not dare shut my eyes. I knew that I had to stay in body awareness, though the fire was so heavy that my head felt like a ball of lead. Step by slow step we retraced our way into the white mists of the ascent, picking up the trail markers, each foot wearily lifted into the deep holes, one after the other. My totally drained body responded only to the urgency of life… life… life.

At the Veintimilla we could not risk stopping longer than to gather our rucksacks through a nauseous deadening haze. Even being reunited with Yannick, sacrificial fodder, abandoned here and cast away at this critical moment of his penguin career, failed to make an impact on my awareness. There was just one thought… down… down… for every slow drag of the boot through the soft snow would mean less pain in my head.

Mig, still doubled up vomiting, led the shuffle in a reversal of the rope positions. Never had we left the comfort of our connecting umbilical chord, but exhaustion was in control. We floundered and fell like dazed toy puppets, somehow aware that whilst the gradient was gentle it was all right to do so. Even Pepé stumbled in tiredness. Crampons started balling up creating high-heel shoe effects as the snow gathered in lumps, to be whacked off by ice axe or stick. At least that roused us, for sleep was stealing its way in. I shook my head repeatedly… 'I am awake... I am awake… I am awake… but where had those last minutes gone? The body kept moving, though consciousness was not there. Can't stop… can't stop… too much agony… too hard to get up again… but then warmth crept in, as the white cloud became brighter like an almost dazzling cloak enveloping us and we had to stop to stash our outer jackets. This allowed an awareness of the extreme pain from the neck to drift in… and the mouth almost too parched to speak. I knew that I had no desire for food, nor the energy to find it… but water… Oh, I'd sell my soul for just a sip… stuffing mouthfuls of snow only seemed to make matters worse. Dehydration competed with all out weariness, leaving no room for fear, either of thoughts of the steepness to come, or of the possibility of soft snow avalanching.

We inched slowly downwards and mercifully, as the ridge gradient increased, air richer in oxygen began to enter our lungs and the cloud cover both of mountain and of mind began to lift and drift. I felt happy that the visibility widened, though it included only more bright snow and extended whiteness. No longer did I need to be isolated on an energy level, floating in space. The world could come in if it wanted to here. I quietly prayed for our safe return and visualised us all back at the hut. Then… the picture that lit my way… I saw myself hugging Pete… Ah!.. That, now, was all I wanted. Surely we must be nearly there… Surely he would be coming up to meet us soon…

The cloud lifted further and it became hotter and brighter still as we reached even steeper ground. I tried to force every tired cell, every shattered sinew to focus... focus… place the crampon points carefully… don't trip… don't trip… can I do this without stumbling?…

'Ice axe arrest time, Miggie.' I cautioned.

Pepé belayed us as we went down, with no more than his ice axe loosely in the snow. I did not fancy anyone's chances if Mig and I were to slip at the same time, or if one was to pull the other off. There would be little that Pepé could do, unless we all rolled onto our axes and arrested. Somehow, in spite of the dangers, though, I had none of the fear that had previously built up to such a level of dread. I was simply too tired and drifted too often into a dream state… I was full of a gentle peace… anyway the soft snow was thankfully so much easier than the hard névé ice of the night. I barely noticed the steepness increasing, our way disappearing over the edge. It gave a sense at last of the Earth somewhere beneath our feet far far below, as though we could fly down there at a moment's notice, condor-like, on easy soaring wings in reckless abandon.

'It is necessary to speed up here,' Pepé's insistent voice came, so we turned inwards and front pointed backwards, using the claw of the ice axe and one hand to steady ourselves, increasing the pace. Was this the avalanche risk area of which he had warned?

Meanwhile, at 5,000 metres, outside the Whymper hut, binoculars were searching… searching... Eyes were tired of the brightness reflecting back a mountain face, desolate and void of three expected figures.

After the turn-around, GT and Pete had had a quick experience-motivated descent over the tricky terrain, soon recovering their equilibrium, arriving back before the dawn. They had slept a little and talked to Michael. Then they had waited. GT had delighted in building a special fourth stupa in which he had placed his Debbie's precious gift of lapis lazuli, her Buddhist message of transience affirming that all things move on, and his Chloe's lovely painting of the mountain of peace. It had helped him reach a truce of contentment within himself for this his mountain of peace, in spite of the frustration of not being able to continue the climb. He was more than concerned for the safety of the team, but for Pete the waiting was a nightmare. He worried deeply. He deliberated on the probable positioning on the mountain. He paced up and down. He paced up and down again and again... and then again. The weather looked OK. The sun was shining. They could see nearly half way up the ridge, before a dense topping of cloud blocked the view further. By 9 o'clock there should have been a sighting of the return... at least by 10 o'clock... definitely by 11 o'clock... but Chimborazo lay still... silent... and empty...

At 1.30 pm the day was warm and a handful of others arrived at the hut, including a couple of Norwegians looking at the possibility of climbing and a couple of Frenchmen just curious... There were friendly conversations and Oswaldo cooked a meal... but Pete had no stomach for normality. He was frustrated and angry with himself at the way things had turned out. Not withstanding the intense desire for the team to reach the summit and for all to be safe, his head was swirling in an overriding black cloud of anxiety. The woman he loved was up there somewhere... Something must have happened... The guides' radiophones did not seem to work... So what was going on? The risks of mountaineering played havoc with his mind, alive with 'what ifs'... Fear was seeping through his heart... She was hours overdue... He was not with her to protect her... He was a man of action and yet all he could do was wait... and dammit... she still seemed to be teaching him patience...

It became apparent that one thing they could do was organise a search party to go up. At length it was decided that Fernando would go and take Oswaldo with him. The sun was beginning to dip lower in the sky as they left at about 3.00 pm, carrying water and ropes. The mountain face was still completely devoid of any sign of life. The visibility was even now remarkably clear to the middle of the ridge for the sky was gentle. It was as though all was in abeyance... watching and

230

waiting… waiting and watching…

Then… the moment came. It was around 3.30 pm. Pete was clutching the binoculars, his arms weary at their demand. Suddenly injected with joy, he spotted the small dark dots that appeared, descending slowly, moving in and out of the cloud on the ridge. Had they reached the summit? He could not tell… but they were there. He could see them distinctly, lonely against the sea of white… one, two… 'There's only two!' he shouted to GT in alarm and his blood ran as cold as the ice of the earlier darkness. Why were there only two? There was no one else on the mountain. It had to be the team. The guide would have been OK. Mig was young and strong. Something must have happened to Tess… Forever turned hollow… Seconds became hours… Minutes became days…

I fell. In a daze, my dragging pointy feet on jelly legs tripped and I tumbled downwards. The falling, gathering momentum did nothing for my sleeping mind. It was in relaxation. Surely I should be turning over and forcing my ice axe in?.. Phwam! The rope went taut and my harness bit into my waist. I dug in my crampons and the claw of the ice axe, brushed the snow from my nose and glasses with a wet glove and looked upwards. The rope was tight to Mig. He was lying on his ice axe with a big smile on his face.

'Hey… It works!'

'Thanks Miggie. You're a star.' We had been descending close together whilst Pepé was far above us. He had lengthened the rope between himself and us, adding the spare rope that Mig had been carrying all the way, so that he could give us a long belay at the times when we were not moving together. Mig's quick reaction had saved us... Good training guys…

Looking around we realised that we had reached the limit of the dispersing cloud. The veil was being drawn back, revealing a sun shining brightly and a world awaiting us. We were perched just down from the ridge, taking on an extensive white smooth-looking descent, which dropped steeply away. There was a sense of trying to escape from a huge cake, tiptoeing down lashings of dripping icing. Well, yes, it had been a fitting birthday celebration for His Holiness. The 'Climb For Tibet' team had lit His candles with fire from their hearts… Long may the light of His ideals shine…

231

'There're the huts!' Mig pointed excitedly. Nestled far below amongst tiny dark chocolate rocks we could see both of them, tin roofs reflecting silver but warm to our colour-starved eyes, before gazing further and beyond to where grey and white took over again in the distant curvature of the cotton-wool horizon. Viewing the way physically now gave us a false relief. It seemed like we were nearly down. The seracs, crevasses, bumps and dips barely registered. Why aren't Pete and GT up here to meet us? My feeble mind enquired, not taking on board that it would be a strenuous climb of five hours on hard ice, considerably more in these soft risky conditions. We continued down them, our way becoming hotter, the snow stickier, the lips dryer and the skin frying. Sweat was dripping inside our heavy clothes losing precious moisture.

I tried to rid my crampons of the balling up snow and slipped again... then again and again. Each time Mig held me quickly. It would have been funny if it was not so serious. There was such a feeling of non-reality to the exhaustion state. I just felt weak all over. Then... it was Mig that was falling... Oh, no!... but before gravity and speed could take over he rolled and arrested himself. He had been practising. Pepé took no part and made no comment, but when he was close I could see the weariness in the grey of his face and read the urgency of getting us down before we cracked up completely. Three more times Mig tripped and fell, threatening to pull all of us off into oblivion and three more times he stopped himself... as though his ice axe held the magic of condor claws...

Where is the rest of the team? My mind once so steadfast now floundered and gave up. I wanted Pete to tell me what to do, to take me home. Surely, if we are nearing the end of the story, then my prince should appear and carry me off on his tall white charger... I needed his strong arms around me...

Time floated as we weaved steeply between ice-carved and wind-blown forms, now peacefully bathing in the sun. Then we came close to a tumbled area of fresh avalanche material, which floated into my awareness in a detached way allowing no apprehension. Here a shout alerted us to climbers approaching from below. There were two of them. It must be Pete and GT. Ah... thank goodness... We were now following a track of footprints that made the going easier. Nearer and nearer the figures came towards the track, but in disappointment I realised that I did not recognise them. They must be passing climbers. The fact that this was not the time of day to go climbing eluded me. Where is our team? Pepé spoke to them in Spanish, then they moved past me on the track to where Mig was pleading with them and they gave him a bottle of water. Turning, I saw what I needed so desperately, but could not reach back the arm's length that was necessary. I simply could not manage that one step back. The body would not respond to the instruction. I pleaded too but with rambling, rasping words and then liquid gold was poured down the desert of my parched throat to bring back life to withered flowers...

I gratefully allowed hands to help me down to a flatter stance, where I was surprised to recognise that they belonged to Fernando and Oswaldo. They set up a long rope for prusiking down the next steep pitch, while I asked Mig to belay me on our rope into a crevasse for some privacy to answer a call of nature. Yellow pee?.. More like orange gone off the scale, but it was the first time that I had been since leaving the hut nineteen hours ago. A record for me... We took jackets off, immediately regretting it, for we became chilled in an instant, but with no time for loitering we were rushed quickly down the protected prusik rope, falling off many times. My thoughts shouted... I can't take any more... I can't go any further... but there were still feet to move... Surely... surely... we're so close... so close...

The sky was decorated with glowing pink tinges turning the light to evening magic as we approached the meeting of the glacier tongue with the rocks. Here a muddy stew took over from the soft snow and there... there was a welcoming mêlée of people. Mig unroped and rushed ahead shouting 'We made it! We made it!' and fell over in the mud. I followed and slipped landing in the mud too. There was laughter and talking, sounds of 'well done' and cameras, but I only wanted one thing. Suddenly it was there... at last. My eyes were filling with tears. Strong arms were around me... and Pete was hugging me. It was a hug that I had waited for... for so very, very long... a hug, which said this is the end of the supreme effort needed... all is well now. I sobbed uncontrollably in an emotional, exhausted letting go... and the hug spun around and around... enfolding me in love... and the knowledge that we were now safe.

Pete carried me the rest of the way down to the hut on his back. GT carried my rucksack. We paused so that I could drink, cupping my hands, from a glacial melt-water stream. It tasted better than the finest champagne that I could ever dream of. It was instinctively an acceptance of the gift of the miracle of life from the mighty Watchtower. I did not know then that Michael had filmed the Inca descendants on their pilgrimage, fulfilling the same ritual in this exact same spot... for this was the partaking of the sacramental life-blood of Chimborazo.

The way led us out through the portals of the stupa park, now four stupas for the four hearts of the 'Climb For Tibet' team, beating with the memory of the expression of compassion. The whole park carried the energy. Just as the whole team, with the wonderful sensitive assistance of Pepé, had placed the prayer flags on the summit. For GT and especially for Pete, there was the coping with the blackest grungiest of disappointments, for they had taken a different road. They too had the battle of facing themselves. But because of them the team had made it. Every part had been essential to make the whole happen... like a jigsaw puzzle. Is this not what life on Earth is about? Many do not have opportunities to reach summits, but we each have a vital, however unsung, part to play... and every energy affects the energy of the whole.

Dusk fell suddenly as we reached the hut on this day of our primordial pilgrimage. At nearly twenty hours we thought that it must have been one of the slowest climbs to the summit and back without bivouacking ever recorded... Then I learnt that Pepé had previously guided the brave mountaineer Norman Croucher. It had taken three days... but then, he has no legs... I felt very humble. Surprisingly I found that I could not eat, though I had had nothing since the bread at 2.0 am, but it was no surprise to surrender to the blessings of sleep...

I am a pillion passenger on a magnificent grey horse. The flowing mane and tail are of the purest almost translucent white. We are galloping so fast and hard that the hooves scarcely touch the Earth and I know not if we are flying. My hands clasp around the waist of the rider to save me from falling, but I do not want to touch the sacrosanct robes... for the rider is His Holiness the Dalai Lama...

I awoke with tears on my jacket pillow and the haunting dream seeping through my being.

It was time to read out the peace messages, a performance from the mountain stage close by, to our Earth. She smiled on us, the uniquely clear fourth day, with sunshine. Mig tied a purple sash around his Tibetan national costume, a rock-coloured 'chuba', worn over purple climbing salopettes, and proudly held high the Tibetan flag which had recently seen so much service. He looked every inch the warrior for peace that he had proved himself to be. The dedication and purpose of I-have-a-country-to-free drove him on with a passion. But on the question of climbing… well… it was 'I shall NEVER do any more climbing!'… We would see… He displayed the picture of His Holiness that he had carried with such love and then passed it on to the Norwegians. They were planning to climb Everest from the Tibetan side and would take it with them. The inspiration would continue to travel the world…

We started the expression of all the messages by speaking out:

"The best solution to any problem is Love."
from Paul Burrows.

"May love, compassion and peace shine throughout the world but especially in Tibet."
from Zara Fleming.

On and on into the day we spoke out every prayer, every promise, every wish, every hope… and the mountain reverberated with the beautiful words of compassion for all life, non-violence and universal responsibility… and the peace energy came together and multiplied a thousand-fold and then incalculable times more… It arose, guided by a six-pointed star, through the crystal beacon at the furthest point of the Earth… and was sent out… shining… to the far corners of the planet…

Now, we started the long journey home to become part of that world again. Far below in tall windswept tussock grassland we stopped to say farewell to the spirit of the mountain. The four of us stood in the 'Climb For Tibet' formation, raised palms together… 'Oh Chimborazo… we leave your eminent and all-powerful sacred presence. Thank you for letting us bathe in your aura and return safely. Thank you for being the place of light shining always for Earth Peace… We shall continue to hold the vision and the focus. We shall continue to spread the messages… It is done… OM MANI PADME HUM.'… And the mantra of compassion rang out to touch the crystal heart beheld in distant summit snows…

Quito greeted us with a languid gaiety. It seemed different. No, it was probably me that had changed. Was it that in my quest for inner peace I had touched a different reality? Here, now, I was just playing a game, the purpose of which was to learn and to grow through. It was to be enjoyed and not to become bogged down in... As a representation of this a wart that had been on my finger for years had completely disappeared... For the body manifests changes in its own way. My mouth which had been badly burnt by the snow reflection, was swollen both inside and out. For four weeks talking would be uncomfortable, eating painful and kissing impossible...

As the 'Climb For Tibet' team gathered at the hostel for the last time before dispersing, with the condor impression rising once again to brighten glum faces, there was a sense of purpose of much work still to be done. Pete and I were to take all the messages and reread them from the Matterhorn in Switzerland whilst delivering a friend's ashes to that mountain which had been dedicated to world peace. Then we would present them to Jiang Zemin president of the Chinese people, on his forthcoming visit to Britain, read them gently at the vigil outside the Chinese Embassy, and display them on our web-site to be available for all. And there was the collecting in of the sponsor monies, half of which Mig was to take to the Khanyara refugee camp.

'You know...' he said, 'it was a real unbelievable struggle on the mountain... but the thing that was running through my mind over and over again was the agony of those Tibetan refugees escaping across the Himalayas...'

'Certainly...' responded GT, 'when you think of all that physical effort and pain that we've been through, in a sense it's a kind of symbol for what's happening in Tibet...'

Yes... indeed... and I knew... that the burden of the body was the pathway to release the wings of the soul...

There was, however, still unfinished business to attend to... 'C'mon, Tess...' urged Mig, 'I'm going to buy you a milkshake.'

236

Special acknowledgement

The author would like to gratefully honour the Ascended Spirit Master Advarr, whose light of Spirit soul, it is now understood, was motivation for her own soul to undertake this journey.

Master Advarr, alongside many Masters from Spirit, works ceaselessly through individuals on Earth for the world expansion of light and a higher consciousness of Divine Energy. They wish this to be known.

Master Advarr's guidance is channelled through Ivy Smith for whose loving dedication special thanks are due.

The author would like to warmly acknowledge this introduction from Dorothy Forster, the inspired reviver of 'The Big Ben Silent Minute' and Peace Prayer (website www.thesilentminute.org.uk), which is a lovely expression of this pathway of Spirit light.

> "Source of my Being, help me to live in Peace
> and save my home, the planet Earth."

PEACE MESSAGES

O Excellent Earth, our only home, so wise and beautiful and mysterious, forgive us all: and help us to deliver Tibet from oppression and the rest of the world from indifference. May freedom rule with the moon and compassion shine through even the brightest day.

I send peace and love and health to everybody around the world. May all nuclear weapons be neutralised and disarmed soon.

As I stand on the highest point of the planet, the Earth below looks pristine, idyllic. At a distance, many things look different from how they really are. So my dearest wish is that the destruction of nature, the cruelty, suffering, violence, hunger and disease which darken so many corners of the world and affect both humans and animals can be brought to an end: and that with compassion and kindness to all creatures, the world will really be a beautiful place - from far and near.

Stay loose but hang in there to help free Tibet.

Peace and tranquility are of an essence, but most of all I feel we must endeavour to seek true happiness and that is through ultimate freedom of the mind, body and spirit. Seek within yourself for the answers and the result will be startlingly good. - You are free and full of love.

I pray that the people of China peacefully and soon allow the freedom of the Tibetan people.

We are just tiny specks of dust on a mountain's side. Never must we forget the humility of life, to respect and cherish Nature – She is always consistent and will always remain steadfast. We on the other hand will come and go like the wind. Surely PEACE is the only answer in our world. Surely protecting Nature is our only answer. Why then do so many want to abuse the gifts of life? On top of the mountain, may these messages be heard, loud and clear in all corners of the world. May the Universe rise up and once and for all fight for Peace, Love in our hearts and Harmony always.

All we are saying is give peace a chance.

There is no more pressing cause to climb for today than Tibet. So climb high and with high hopes – for the courage of its people and the resilience of its environment and culture. I shall be with you in spirit on July 6th.

Love will heal the planet and bring peace to all beings.

Light to all beings, compassion to all beings, joy to all beings, love to all beings.

King David wrote "May the Lord bring down peace from the mountains and from the hills justice." I have said Mass for Peace on the summit of Chimborazo. I pray that your climb will be successful and that all your prayers, as you make that pilgrimage, will be answered.

May the whole world come together in the understanding that in diversity lies mankind's strength. Love the things that are beautiful.

May the peace of the mountains spread to the hearts of the world.

May God's Healing Angels lift you even higher than the heights you have just scaled, and may your prayers and those of His Holiness for the future of your beloved Tibet be truly fulfilled.

We're shining from our hearts, we're setting ourselves free!

We are children of the Universe. May we grow to learn the consequences of our actions and become one with the Earth. Thanks to Divine Oneness for each new day and this forgiving planet. I rejoice in the beauty of life.

On behalf of the European Parliament's Intergroup on Tibet, I send you our good wishes for a safe journey. We will continue our efforts on behalf of the people of Tibet, and your epic climb will serve as a reminder to us politicians to redouble our endeavours from the comfort of our offices! Good luck.

Man is the most dangerous animal on Earth, destroying as he does everything around him through greed and ignorance. He does not own this still beautiful world. He shares it with all living creatures and if he does not get this message very soon, not only will the tiger and rhino be extinct, but man himself will be on a suicide course and tomorrow will be too late.

May your climbing the mountain be successful in drawing attention to the mountains of inhumanity which beset the Tibetan people.

May all beings be one in universal compassion. May Tibet and His Holiness continue to be a light for this dark world. May the peace and unity and respect between the world's religions be also a fruit of the work of peaceful compassion.

Goodness and justice will prevail.

It must start with me. When a critical mass of people realise that all is ONE, and determine to live according to the human values of Truth, Right Conduct, Peace, Love and Non-Violence, only then will peace reign and Mother Earth be healed.

May all beings be at peace, now and forever.

Love the world, respect the world and the world will be a happier place.

All the people should be free to determine their own future – Free the Tibetan spirit.

Freedom for all Tibetans.

May all the good that is in Tibet live on.

I, and many others, support His Holiness the Dalai Lama, and love His people. (To them) – have courage, remain persistent in what you want. Do not despair – we will support you, and we love you. (To the mountain itself) – Take great care of your people, and of yourself. You are unique and precious. We respect you. With love and affectionate best wishes.

May all the beings throughout the world experience happiness, peace, and freedom. May all living beings be free from suffering and may they find everlasting happiness. May there be peace and happiness on this planet.

I hope and pray for religious freedom for Tibetan people both in Tibet and India and pray that all religious restrictions and bans be lifted.

Peace for all.

Om Mani Peme Hung.

Freedom for all.

Peace for the World.

The Truth of Tibet is like a child. It cannot be denied. It will always be. And, will someday be set free.

May peace and compassion overrule oppression and cruelty throughout the world.

Harmony for Tibet and our once beautiful planet.

Peace in our hearts.

A little love can cure the world's pain, so may love grow and spread.

Hello world! I love you.

At the furthest point from the centre of the world, comes the resounding message from the heart of humanity

– live with and not against
– co-operate and not compete
– love and do not hate
– turn towards and not away
– walk with and not ahead nor behind
– share and not possess
and then we may find a way towards living at one with ourselves and our Earth. There are no shadows on mountaintops.

A wish for peace, tolerance and lack of fear between all people.

If the inhabitants of planet Earth fail to grasp the fragility of humanity's moment in space and time, then we will never reach the stars. I wish you the very best of luck. Take care.

Source of my Being, help me to live in Peace
And save my home, the planet Earth.

May the world be blessed in peace.

May the deep and profound spirit of Tibetan Buddhism bathe all life on Earth with joy.

May we all have the strength to climb whatever mountain may be before us and find a clear view of the right path.

Man's spirit burns ever so brightly – Humanity's greatest endeavour is to keep it in view.

Peace must be the only way forward. Let's all try to understand, love and care for each other and work together to heal ourselves and the world and save the people of Tibet.

All disagreements can be resolved in harmony.

For the children of Tibet, love, lots of love and sport.

Let there be peace in the world.

Long live the Dalai Lama.

May all beings be at Peace – now and forever.

Heaven arms with gentleness those whom it would not see destroyed.

From the highest mountain, may the smallest voice be heard.

Love – love – love.

Free Tibet – Free the world of ignorance – Open our hearts and our minds – Value simplicity and love.

I will love the Earth whatever happens.

Let us take responsibility for the world in which we live. Its life is in our hands and we must accept this duty and bring peace to all.

I will try to communicate more with my fellow humans and bring peace to our world.

Dear Earth – I don't want war, I want peace everywhere. I don't want nuclear tests, I don't want hatred. I want love and respect for the Earth everywhere, no pain, no hatred, no killings – just love and peace.

To be friends with each other.

I go forward, you go backwards and somewhere we should meet. This meeting shall bring the world together in peace and freedom.

I hope for the Tibetans' spirits to rise as high as their mountains, and that freedom can be found by compassionate measures – no cruelty, just respect.

We should respect the Earth that we live on and the elements it gives to us.

Let there be peace between the Tibetans and Chinese. Let all the love and kindness within every being on the Earth unite to stop the destruction of the Earth and the harm caused to all mankind.

You can always climb higher within.

May God speak to all of us and show us the way forward. May He soften the hearts and minds of the Chinese leadership, both in Beijing and Lhasa.

Tibet will be free.

If enough of us think peace, then there will be peace.

May the longtime sun shine upon you and all that surround you, and the pure light within you guide your way home.

Phew, we made it! Good luck to you all and safe return.

Love one another and the Earth our mother.

I will live peacefully and pray for all the people in Tibet. I will do my best to look after my family and friends and try not to harm the environment as best I can.

Love always prevails. It is the light of everyone's soul. Protect those you cherish in non-violent ways.

I will see the good in everybody.

Peace on Earth – goodwill to all mankind.

Let peace overcome war.

May we reach out to all beings with compassionate hearts and let peace blossom.

Hedowch – Peace to Tibet and peace to the people of China.

Respect and care for all citizens of our planet Earth.

For the orchestra of life to play beautiful music everyone must work together as part of the whole.

For the children of Tibet – love and peace.

Listen in the quiet of your minds and with your hearts. There is no need to fear. All is well.

I will be less negative towards others and more forgiving to my friends and family. I will be more tolerant.

I will be kind to everyone I meet and know. I will help to send out the message of world peace as I think it is important that we all preserve our Earth.

We live in a troubled world, but strength, as in the Tibetans, will see us through.

Peace to the children of Tibet and everything on Earth.

I will always try to resolve disputes peacefully.

I will respect all living things of the Earth.

Let the world be a happier and more friendly place.

This is a peace message for hope for the Tibetan refugees – And I hope for world peace – And I send my love to the children of Tibet – Love, peace and happiness.

I will honour and respect the feelings of any other human being, no matter what walk of life they come from.

Let us be mindful of the power of a loving heart.

The children of the world want to live in peace with others and the natural beauty which we must take care of and love.

I will not fight with my brother.

Inner peace brings outer peace.

May you be free in Tibet again.

That wrongs be righted and all be free under the sky.

Love will heal the planet and bring peace to all beings.

May all beings be free from suffering and the causes of suffering.

There is no power in all creation greater than love.

Be happy and don't worry. Peace and happiness is much more important than how much land you own. Enjoy life as it comes to you.

Love, respect, peace and tranquillity always throughout the world.

Let love rule.

Love is like a rainbow. It comes in many different colours and feelings, and in all shapes and sizes. If you can find the pot of gold at the end of it, you will find peace within yourself, and will therefore be able to share that peace with others – keep looking, for what may not seem apparent at first will become obvious once you have found your inner light. Peace to all my brothers and sisters of the Earth.

The Earth is our mother. We must take care of her. Her sacred ground we tread upon with every step we take. The Earth is our mother, we must take care of her.

Of all the teachings we receive this one is the most important. Nothing belongs to you of what there is, of what you take you must share.

I hope my message can be shined down upon the Earth from its highest point, and that my thoughts will help to bring peace in not only Tibet but the other places in need of support. SMILE WORLD.

Hippy rubbish and preaching to mountain wildlife will achieve very little. What's needed is action, action that will make a difference. I pledge to make a difference.

I wish you continuing harmony with the human race and the further progression of survival for all the species that inhabit you!

Man must now nurture the Earth as it first nurtured us.

I will have love and peace. I will not be judgemental of others. I will not be selfish. I will not succumb to consumerism.

Peace will be sustained if we consider everyone as equal and not hurt anyone or anything. Once that is achieved then we can all live in peace.

I will honour and respect the feelings of any other human being, no matter what walk of life they come from. Mother Earth was once a peaceful place. I hope that we can make her happy once again by working together.

I would like to see a world containing only those who don't work for personal profit, but with their first thought for others and the environment. Tibet is just one of the many gems in our world, and should be as free as any of the birds which fly our skies. I hope for eternal peace all over the world.

Respect one's neighbours. Respect their religions and beliefs. Settle arguments through peaceful means and the world will be a happier place.

Preserve today's plants and wildlife so future generations can see the beauty we see today.

I will treat the Earth with the respect it deserves, the animals, the plants and everything and everyone in it.

You can all do what you want because you are all amazingly beautiful.

Love Mother Earth like you would your own mother and love your own mother like you should love yourself.

Think peace. Believe peace. And let's keep the peace.

Respect, love and be kind to the world and all the people in it. Stop the cruelty, oppression, greed, selfishness and inequality that presently seem to rule the Earth. Choose good leaders to carry the world into peace and away from violence and wasted and unkind actions. Carry love with you and do productive things each day. Bless my mother who holds the very spirit of a wonderful person.

I will respect my share of the Earth and the animals and plants that go with it always, so give the Earth a chance.

Calm the torrent, cease the tempest, live the life, keep the peace, restore the liberty, feed the hungry, help the sick, give the freedom, comfort the oppressed, use the gift, accept the different, nurture the young, stop the fighting not by fighting, live life in happiness.

I know that it will take us all time to realise the extent and the long-term aspects of our abuse, but please do not despair of us. Many of us are truly sorry and strive to improve our society for the Earth's sake, so please don't give up – we need you. This need to preserve you will hopefully unite us in peace and harmony, regardless of our different beliefs.

In the idea of every lie there is the seed of truth waiting to blossom.

Care for animals as you care for your good friends.

Let us take responsibility for the world in which we live. Its life is in our hands and we must accept this duty and bring peace to all.

As there is the word peace in every language, so there should be the will to make it happen, for the sake of everyone on Earth now and in the future. PEACE. Frieden (Gr.), Pokoj (Polish), Pax (Latin), Mir (Croat), Shalom (Jewish), Paix (French), Shanti (Hindi).

You have one mind – use it. You have one heart – listen to it. You have one body – respect it. You have one life – live it.

I will not judge people by class or religion and I will treat everyone as an individual. In doing this the world will be a happier more peaceful place to be.

I will not have fights with friends and family. I will love nature. I will look after and respect the countryside.

Take care people.

May all beings be at peace, now and forever.

May the roof of the world be restored and may the Dalai Lama continue to flourish towards universal awakening.

SMILE....

eye**Sight**

'Our greatest fear is not that we are inadequate, our greatest fear is that we are powerful beyond measure. By shining your light, you subconsciously give permission to others to shine theirs.'
Nelson Mandela

Travel can be a liberating experience. As it was for me in 1990, when I was just one hundred yards from Nelson Mandela as he was released from prison. I watched this monumental occasion from on top of a traffic light, amidst a sea of enthralled onlookers.

This was the 'green light' moment that inspired the creation of Eye Books. From the chaos of that day arose an appreciation of the opportunities that the world around us offers, and the desire within me to shine a light for those whose reaction to opportunity is 'can't and don't'.

Our world has been built on dreams, but the drive is often diluted by the corporate and commercial interests offering to live those dreams for us, through celebrity culture and the increasing mechanization and automation of our lives. Inspiration comes now from those who live outside our daily routines, from those who challenge the way we see things.

Eye Books was born to tell the stories of 'ordinary' people doing 'extraordinary' things. With no experience of publishing, or the constraints that the book 'industry' imposes, Eye Books created a genre of publishing to champion those who live out their dreams.

Ten years on, and sixty stories later, Eye Books has the same ethos. We believe that ethical publishing matters. It is not about just trying to make a quick hit, it is about publishing the stories that affect our lives and the lives of others positively. We publish the books we believe will shine a light on the lives of some and enlighten the lives of many for years to come.

Join us in the community of Eye Books, and share the power these stories evoke.

Dan Hiscocks
Founder and Publisher
www.eye-books.com

eye**Community**

At Eye Books we are constantly challenging the way we see things and do things. But we cannot do this alone. To that end we have created an online club, a community, where members can inspire and be inspired, share knowledge and exchange ideas.

Membership is free, and you can join by visiting www.eye-books.com, where you will be able to find:

What we publish
Books that truly inspire, by people who have given their all, triumphed over adversity, lived their lives to the full.
Visit the dedicated microsites we have for each of our books online.

Why we publish
To champion those 'ordinary' people doing extraordinary things. The real celebrities of our world who tell stories that celebrate life to the full, not just for 15 minutes.
Books where fact is more compelling than fiction.

How we publish
Eye Books is committed to ethical publishing. Many of our books feature and campaign for various good causes and charities.
We try to minimize our carbon footprint in the manufacturing and distribution of our books.

Who we publish
Many, indeed most of our authors have never written a book before. Many start as readers and club members. If you feel strongly that you have a book in you, and it is a book that is experience driven, inspirational and life affirming, visit the 'How to Become an Author' page on our website. We are always open to new authors.

www.eye-books.com

eye**Community**

Eye-Books.com Club is an ever evolving community, as it should be, and benefits from all that our members contribute.

Eye Books Club membership offers you:

eyeNews – a regular emailed newsletter of events in our community

Special offers and discounts on the books we publish

Invitations to book launches, signings and author talks

Correspond with Eye Books authors, directly. About writing, about their books, or about trips you may be planning.

Each month, we receive enquiries from people who have read our books, entered our competitions or heard of us through the media or from friends, people who have a common desire – to make a difference with their lives, however big or small, and to extend the boundaries of everyday life and to learn from others' experiences.

The Eye Books Club is here to support our members, and we want to encourage you to participate. As we all know, the more you put into life, the more you get out of it.

Eye Books membership is free, and it's easy to sign up. Visit our website. Registration takes less than a minute.

www.eye-books.com

eyeBookshelf

www.eye-books.com

THE AMERICAS / ASIA

	Blue Mountains — Alastair Humphreys	The Good Life — Dorian Amos	The Good Life Gets Better — Dorian Amos	Cry From the Highest Mountain — Tess Burrows	Riding the Outlaw Trail — Simon Casson & Richard Adamson	Trail of Visions Route 2 — Vicki Couchman	Riding with Ghosts — Gwen Maka	South of the Border — Gwen Maka	Lost Lands Forgotten Stories — Alexandra Pratt	Frigid Women — Sue & Victoria Riches	Touching Tibet — Niema Ash	First Contact — Mark Anstice	Tea for Two — Polly Benge	Baghdad Business School — Heyrick Bond Gunning
eyeThinker		•	•	•			•	•			•	•	•	
eyeAdventurer	•	•	•	•	•	•				•		•	•	•
eyeQuirky														
eyeCyclist	•											•		
eyeRambler														
eyeGift	•							•						
eyeSpiritual														

| THE AMERICAS | | | | | | | | | | ASIA | | | | |

AFRICA / EUROPE

	Moods of Future Joys — Alastair Humphreys	Green Oranges on Lion Mountain — Emily Joy	Zohra's Ladder — Pamela Windo	Walking Away — Charlotte Metcalf	Changing the World One Step at a Time — Michael Meegan	All Will Be Well — Michael Meegan	Seeking Sanctuary — Hilda Reilly	Crap Cycle Lanes — Captain Yellowjersey	50 Quirky Bike Rides...in England and Wales — Rob Ainsley	On the Wall with Hadrian — Bob Bibby	Special Offa — Bob Bibby	The European Job — Jonathan Booth	Fateful Beauty — Natalie Hodgson	Slow Winter — Alex Hickman
eyeThinker		•	•	•	•	•	•							•
eyeAdventurer	•						•					•	•	
eyeQuirky								•	•			•	•	
eyeCyclist	•							•	•					
eyeRambler										•	•			
eyeGift	•							•	•					
eyeSpiritual					•	•								

| AFRICA | | | | | | | EUROPE | | | | | | |

www.eye-books.com — eyeBookshelf

ASIA / AUS

Title	Author	eyeThinker	eyeAdventurer	eyeQuirky	eyeCyclist	eyeRambler	eyeGift	eyeSpiritual
Jungle Janes	Peter Burden		●				●	
Trail of Visions	Vicki Couchman	●	●					
Desert Governess	Phyllis Ellis	●	●	●				
Fever Tress of Borneo	Mark Eveleigh		●					
My Journey with a Remarkable Tree	Ken Finn	●	●					
The Jungle Beat	Roy Follows		●					
Siberian Dreams	Andy Home	●	●					
Behind the Veil	Lydia Laube	●	●					
Good Morning Afghanistan	Waseem Mahmood	●						
Jasmine and Arnica	Nicola Naylor	●	●					
Pricky Pears of Palestine	Hilda Reilly	●	●					
Last of the Nomads	W J Peasley	●	●					
Travels in Outback Australia	Andrew Stevenson	●	●					

EUROPE / CROSS CONTINENT

Title	Author	eyeThinker	eyeAdventurer	eyeQuirky	eyeCyclist	eyeRambler	eyeGift	eyeSpiritual
The Accidental Optimist's Guide to Life	Emily Joy	●		●				
Con Artist Handbook	Joel Levy	●		●			●	
Forensics Handbook	Pete Moore	●		●				
Travels with my Daughter	Niema Ash	●	●					
Around the World with 1000 Birds	Russell Boyman		●	●	●			
Death	Herbie Brennan						●	●
Discovery Road	Tim Garratt & Andy Brown	●	●					
Great Sects	Adam Hume Kelly	●						●
Triumph Around the World	Robbie Marshall		●					
Blood Sweat and Charity	Nick Stanhope		●				●	
Traveller's Tales from Heaven and Hell	Various			●			●	
Further Traveller's Tales from Heaven and Hell	Various			●			●	
More Traveller's Tales from Heaven and Hell	Various			●			●	

eye**Bookshelf**

Touching Tibet
Niema Ash
Price: £9.99 / $14.95

Niema Ash was one of the first people to enter Tibet when its borders were briefly opened to Westerners. Niema relates with wit, compassion and sensitivity her encounters with people whose humour, spirituality and sheer enthusiasm have carried them through years of oppression and suffering. *Touching Tibet* is a unique journey into the heart of this intriguing forbidden kingdom. Niema unveils the truth behind the mystery and paints a picture of places which few of us will ever see.

'A marriage of the bizarre and the beautiful that chills the spine as often as it warms the heart.'
The Times

'Mesmerising.'
The Sunday Times

Tea for Two
Polly Benge
Price: £7.99 / $14.95

Packing away her tutu and pointy shoes, and donning cycling shorts and yellow lycra, Polly followed her heart. She soon found herself following the increasingly distant backside of her beloved, pedalling up foreign mountains, and chanting to herself that she could do this, even though she was a woman.

Starting in Katmandu this was far more than a journey to find the perfect cuppa. Unsmiling Border Officials, extreme poverty, the inadequacy of the maps, and the danger of travelling through Assam, this was not the India of Raj palaces or holy Ghats but a dangerous region of the isolated north-east. The journey was a test of stamina, self-belief and most of all her love for Tim.

'A romantic and intimate story.'
The Daily Telegraph

CLIMB FOR TIBET

A CRY FROM THE HIGHEST MOUNTAIN

Patrons:- His Holiness the Dalai Lama - Doug Scott C.B.E.
Princess Helena Moutafian M.B.E. - Joanna Lumley O.B.E. - Uri Geller

We invite you to tune in with us to assist Earth Peace. It is an important focus which takes place for six minutes at 6.00 pm (British time) on the sixth day of every month. It does not matter where you physically are, but a quiet mind concentrating for a few minutes contributes in a powerful way. It helps to think of the symbol of a six-pointed star at the furthest point of the Earth sending out rays of light and peace to all beings.

Uri Geller always tunes in too. His website is: www.urigeller.com

Do join us.

With love and respect

The 'Climb For Tibet' team

You can also send us a peace message for our next event or contact us via our website: www.climbfortibet.org

'In order to cause a shadow to disappear you must shine a light on it'

About the Author

Tess Burrows was born in Southern England in 1948, educated at Bedales School, she gained a degree in Ecological Science from Edinburgh University and moved to Australia to grow trees.

In 1984 she returned as the mother of three young boys.

It was not until 1987 that she started climbing and after a number of unusual events raising funds for charity, knew that she could help the Earth – and make a difference.
By 1998 it was time to help Tibet and world peace.

In mountaineering terms she was not an experienced or even a good climber, nor did she have the strength of youth... but it was the dream whose time had come....

Stand Tall.... Run Free
Tess is currently working on her next book 'Stand Tall... Run Free', which follows the 'Climb For Tibet' team on their mission to run up the world's tallest mountain. This is set on the Big Island of Hawai'I where the volcano Mauna Kea has its base some 5,000 metres below sea level and rises 4,205 metres above.

Dreams beget dreams....